Comprehension
and Learning

Comprehension and Learning

A Conceptual Framework for Teachers

FRANK SMITH
Ontario Institute for Studies in Education

HOLT, RINEHART AND WINSTON
New York   Chicago   San Francisco   Atlanta
Dallas   Montreal   Toronto   London   Sydney

Library of Congress Cataloging in Publication Data

Smith, Frank, 1928-
    Comprehension and learning.

    Includes bibliographical references and indexes.
    1.   Learning, Psychology of.   2.   Comprehension.
I.   Title.
LB1051.S6218   370.15'2   75-2041

ISBN: 0-03-011011-4

Printed in the United States of America
5 6 7 8 9   090   9 8 7 6 5 4 3 2 1

Preface

The aim of this book is to provide a comprehensive but coherent account of comprehension and learning for students enrolled in educational psychology courses. It could be used as a supplement when a general educational psychology text is employed to cover the conventional range of educational psychology topics, although instructors looking for a more integrated and contemporary approach might consider using this book as the main text. The book should also have utility in general courses on cognitive psychology, psycholinguistics and applied linguistics, since it attempts to provide a plain-language theoretical integration not otherwise available.

The book reflects the current change of emphasis from learning to comprehension in both psychology and education. Psychologists have become deeply interested in how knowledge and beliefs are represented in the brain, since the manner in which we comprehend the world is the foundation of all our interaction with the environment—perceptually, intellectually and emotionally. Educators are becoming aware that many instructional problems concern a child's learning ability far less than his comprehension of what he is doing in school in the first place, and of what school is trying to do to him. In theory as well as in practice, comprehension is seen as the basis of learning.

This is not a methods book. The intention is to provoke and to help teachers think, rather than depend on being told specifically what to do. Prior knowledge of psychology or linguistics is not required, although the contents will lead readers into many areas that can be further explored. The Notes contain suggestions for more detailed readings.

An outline of this book, and a little more detail about its aims and underlying philosophy, will be found in the brief Introduction.

Toronto, Canada   Frank Smith
February 1975

Contents

Comprehension
and Learning

Introduction

This is primarily a book about children. It is addressed to teachers and written from the point of view of a cognitive psychologist. In this book I attempt to analyze those mysterious and complex facets of human thought that are labelled "comprehension" and "learning", by drawing on insights from a number of specialized disciplines while endeavoring to maintain a coherence that will be both comprehensible and useful to practising or prospective teachers.

My particular concern is with the mental processes of children confronted by learning situations in school, although the nature of these processes cannot be isolated from the manner in which any individual instinctively sets about acquiring and organizing skills and knowledge of the world. Children at school are not a special race of animal, nor do their capacities change the moment they cross the threshold of the classroom. To understand a child in school, it is necessary to reflect upon the child who comes to school. It is also necessary to examine fundamental aspects of comprehension and learning that are applicable to all ages of student, from kindergarten to college, and indeed to teachers themselves.

The basic assertion is that the only effective and meaningful way in which anyone can learn is by attempting to relate new experiences to what he knows (or believes) already. In other words, comprehension and learning are inseparable. I shall refer to this continual process of relating the unfamiliar to what is already known as "making sense of the world". Most of this book is an effort to explain and illustrate what this phrase means, particularly in the context of education.

Two themes will be counterpointed. The first is that all children know how to learn. The brain of a child is a superbly efficient and instinctive learning device, so much a part of any normal living creature that it functions automatically. The task of education is not to create or even develop the ability to learn, but to understand and respect its nature, thereby facilitating its operation. Children are not empty vessels into which teachers pour selected skills and nuggets of knowledge. Rather, it is in the child's nature to express and develop innate intellectual capacities, integrating all experience into an intricate view of life that includes hopes and fears, loves and hates, beliefs and expectations, and attitudes towards other people and towards himself.

The second theme is that there are severe restrictions within which this basic propensity for learning must operate. Natural skills can be confounded.

The brain of a child may be infinite in its potentiality, but there are bounds to how much it can achieve on any particular occasion. There are overriding limitations on how much new information—uncertainty—can be handled at any one time, and also on how much new information can be assimilated into memory and subsequently retrieved. And the extent to which any individual can overcome these limitations in order to assimilate new skills or knowledge is further limited by the extent to which old skills and knowledge can be brought to bear. A fundamental problem for any instructor is to avoid interfering with natural processes of comprehension and learning.

Orientations

The approach that I take in this book reflects two distinctive theoretical orientations within cognitive psychology: "information-processing theory" and psycholinguistics. The underlying theoretical perspective of information-processing psychology is that the primary function and activity of the human brain—at least with respect to its commerce with the outside world—is actively to seek, select, acquire, organize, store and, at appropriate times, retrieve and utilize information about the world. Human learning is rarely passive or accidental; rather, it is always directed towards the purpose of increasing understanding. Learning is seldom incidental. Human beings are hardly ever content just to let events happen; not even the youngest infant is content to be an unresisting victim of the world's whims. Intentions, not habits, determine our most crucial interactions with the world. It is the nature of the human individual to be *rational*, to base decisions on the best available information, and to this end we strive to understand and predict as much as we can about the world around us. The information-processing

anti-behaviorist

bias engenders a metaphor that pervades this book, the image of "the child as a scientist". Children are conceptualized as "constructing theories" in order to make sense of the world, and "conducting experiments" to test their theories, just as the theories and experiments of scientists are designed to impose order and predictability on their particular fields of study.

The information-processing perspective in psychology does not assert that such a rational, active approach to comprehension and learning is a characteristic of just a few individuals, or that human information-processing has to be learned. Rather, the approach presents a way of conceptualizing the manner in which all humans think and learn. There is no intention to draw a distinction between "rational"—objective, logical, or intellectual—ways of dealing with the world, for example, as compared with more "emotional" or subjective ways of responding to events. The underlying assertion is much broader: individuals perceive the world and respond to events in the manner that makes the most sense to them personally at the particular time, in terms of their past experiences and current predilections. Even when there is an emotional response to an event, it is because the event has been perceived (intellectually) in a particular way. To the individual concerned, even "irrational" perceptions or behavior will appear rational. The view asserts that children who do not seem willing or even able to learn, at least in certain circumstances, may have reached what to them is a rational decision that learning is inappropriate, that it does not pay off or that it is in some other way undesirable. One aim of this book is to make clear the kind of circumstances that might in fact lead a child to decide not to learn, or that it may be smart to play stupid.

Psycholinguistics, as its name may suggest, is an interdisciplinary field of study where psychology and linguistics intersect. It is concerned with how individuals learn, use and comprehend language. Psycholinguistics has been a particularly lively and productive area of psychology during the past dozen years, partly because a number of linguists have argued that some of their descriptions of language in effect represent knowledge that every individual user of language must carry in his head. Some psycholinguists have gone so far as to suggest that part of this knowledge of language is innate: it was in our brains when we were born. Certainly our ability *to learn* language is innate.

In any case, language is vital. The mind of modern man—and of the contemporary schoolchild—to a very large extent functions as it does because of his knowledge and experiences of language. It surprises me—though it also reflects my own bias—how often language is relegated to a single chapter, and sometimes to just a few paragraphs, in many texts on human learning and educational psychology. The nature of language can be considered a reflection of the way human beings develop and organize their thought, and the way language is learned tells us a good deal about learning in general. This book is primarily about comprehension and learning in the context of schools, but I find it impossible to separate these topics from a consideration of language.

Though I have drawn widely from information-processing theory, psycholinguistics and a range of other disciplines, I am in no way trying to represent anyone else's point of view or to interpret a standard theory of any kind. This book is my own quite idiosyncratic way of trying to make sense of the phenomena of human comprehension and learning, and also to make sense of current thinking on these topics in cognitive and educational psychology, and I offer it for the same purpose to teachers and prospective teachers. I would not want to claim that these chapters are in any sense "finished", even in terms of my own thought. Each time I have embarked upon a new chapter I have found it necessary to modify the one before, and each of the three revisions of the entire book has required a radical reorganization and rewriting of what I had written before. And I do not doubt that this process would have continued; the more anyone reflects upon the complexities of the human brain, and the more brain researchers actually probe and analyze its mechanisms, the more our new knowledge seems to come in the form of better questions rather than definitive answers.

A cornerstone of the point of view that I develop is that all human beings endeavor to make sense of the world, to comprehend and to learn, in the same fundamental manner, from birth through adulthood. My themes are relevant to individuals of all ages. Of course, the *content* of a person's mind varies with his age; no one has the same kinds of thoughts or attitudes at five, fifteen and twenty-five years of age. However, this variation cannot be attributed to any constitutional differences: we do not have different brains at different ages. Rather all our individual knowledge, interests and aspirations develop as our experience of the world accumulates. Obviously there are "developmental differences" in children, but I am primarily concerned with the underlying thought processes that bring about these differences. As a consequence I have little to say about how children change as they grow older, a topic that would require a different and much larger book.

Similarly I am not primarily concerned with how two individuals of the same age might differ, even though no two individuals, not even identical twins, can be completely alike in the totality of their beliefs and knowledge of the world. In fact, different individuals might adopt quite distinctive strategies for making sense of the world, a possibility about which I shall have something to say. Nevertheless there are basic underlying processes that all brains have in common, even though they manifest themselves in a variety of ways, just as each person has two hands, which serve a common purpose for everyone, but which may come to look and behave differently, depending upon whether the individual uses them primarily in farming, football or watch-making. This book is about those aspects of human mental functioning that all individuals have in common, old and young, male and female, bright and dull, rich and "disadvantaged". It is just as much a book about the mind of a schoolteacher as it is about that of a schoolchild.

However, I have tried to write the book from the perspective of a teacher trying to understand the mental processes of a schoolchild. In other words, I try to talk about comprehension and learning primarily as they relate to children and to their experiences in classrooms throughout their school careers. Teachers are not always aware of the quite natural limitations that the minds of all children (and all adults) are heir to, and acquaintance with these limitations can help them to understand better some of the difficulties that confront children. Teachers often have a strong "intuitive" understanding of children's natural capacities and limitations, but they cannot formally articulate this knowledge, or else, perhaps they are unaware that there is a "scientific" foundation for the insights their experience has given them. The training of many teachers seems either to neglect important and relevant areas of psychology and linguistics, or else it fails to provide bridges between the abstractions of the professional literature on these specialized topics and the behavior of the real children with which the teacher will be confronted.

Furthermore, I have for some half dozen years worked closely with many teachers—and through them with many schoolchildren—and the insights with which they (teachers and children) have provided me have contributed to the way I have tried to make sense of comprehension and learning generally. It might be that I could write a fairly similar book concerning the minds of infants, or of young adults, or of senior citizens, but schools and children happen to be a particular concern to me at present, and so I address myself to teachers.

Demarcations

My particular aim has been to provide a book that will be of general utility in courses in educational psychology, although I hope my approach will also interest students and instructors in cognitive psychology, psycholinguistics and applied linguistics, all areas over which I have cast my net. I have also tried to achieve a style that would be accessible to individuals without benefit of formal instruction in these areas, for example practising teachers seeking a new perspective on their everyday experiences and problems. I have tried to avoid a ponderous academic tone, and strive to promote comprehension rather than coagulation.

Despite my focus on educational psychology, this book is not *about* educational psychology nor is it an educational psychology text in any conventional sense. For a start, it does not attempt to cover the conventional range of topics. "Learning theory" in the formal sense of the term gets short shrift; there is little about psychology's "laws" or "conditions" of learning. Rather I am concerned with *why* individuals learn, and *how* they must set about doing it. Topics such as "intelligence" or "attitudes" often emphasized in standard educational psychology texts, have little prominence in this volume, while topics such as motivation, personality and testing are scarcely mentioned, not because I think they are unimportant, but because they would make this into a different kind of book. Besides, I would like to think that the topics I do cover have some obvious if implicit bearing on these issues that I have left aside.

Furthermore, I have not tried to be exhaustive. I have refrained from double-documentation of every single assertion that I make. This is a book about ideas, not about research. In general I have tried to integrate the findings from a multitude of research studies unobstrusively, although I provide specific references in the Notes at the back of the book to the occasional classic or critical experiment, or to the significant authority who should not be ignored. Otherwise I have preferred to cite more general references—books rather than articles, surveys rather than monographs— guides to enable the reader to pursue the topics in which he is most interested to the depths at which he feels most comfortable.

But perhaps the greatest difference between this and a more conventional educational psychology text is the almost complete absence of "implications and applications". This is not a book of helpful hints. I feel quite strongly that teachers should not be given general prescriptions about what they ought to do; rather they should be given the information that they need—about children and the nature of learning tasks—so that they can make their own decisions about what to do on a particular occasion with respect to a particular child. I am not saying that teachers should not learn all they can about alternative instructional procedures and materials, the tools of their trade, but this knowledge is useless, even dangerous, unless the teacher can make a sound decision about what the methodology is trying to achieve, the demands it will make on a child, and the particular requirements, capacities and limitations of a child at a particular time. If one expert says use Method A, and a second prefers Method B, how is a teacher to choose?

I have been at pains to avoid a spurious specificity—real or fictitious case studies that are at best only stereotypes for the actual children in any classroom, or simplistic solutions for complex problems. Instead I have tried to present ideas from which implications naturally flow, although I do not want to suggest that the process will be easy. Teaching is not a simple art and teachers warrant consideration for their intelligence as well as for their responsibilities.

The examples that I give are just that—illustrations rather than applications, guides rather than rules. If I have drawn most of my examples from language and reading, it is because I prefer to speak from experience, and because the points are highly generalizable. Besides, reading is more than just a core topic at school; it is the basis of much of the learning that is supposed to take place. Many of the "learning problems" with which teachers are faced fundamentally language problems.

My intention then is to provide a broad conceptual framework that will enable teachers to make their own decisions in the classroom, and also to interpret, evaluate, adopt or reject any research conclusion or item of educational theory with which they might be confronted (starting with this book itself). The aim is to encourage the development of a thoughtful and flexible teacher, rather than a programmed one. In other words, I believe that the most appropriate way to help teachers is precisely the same as the most appropriate way to educate children, by facilitating their search for information that is relevant to their attempts to comprehend and learn.

Outline

The first three chapters of this book are concerned primarily with comprehension, a topic and a condition that I take to be an essential precondition and logically prior to learning. In Chapter 1 I outline a definition of comprehension, and relate it to such diverse psychological topics as perception, attention, "thinking", knowledge and skills. The object is to show how a child employs a coherently organized system of knowledge or beliefs about the world in order to comprehend, to make sense of, experience. Chapter 2 is concerned with psychological factors that restrict comprehension of the world, limitations to which the brain itself is subject in its cognitive activity. In particular, there is a concern with the time that it takes the brain to make decisions about the world, and about limits that are inherent in memory. Chapter 3 picks up the theme of comprehension with particular reference to language.

The next three chapters are specifically concerned with the topic of learning, beginning with Chapter 4, which is an analysis of the manner in which learning is related to comprehension. In effect, children learn in order to gain comprehension when they are unable to comprehend. Chapter 5 becomes more specific about aspects of learning that are often thought to be of particular concern in school, including concept learning and memorization. Chapter 6 returns to the focal topic of language, considering first how children develop speech, and then examining the nature of reading and writing. Chapter 7 is concerned with how individuals, fundamentally identical, might come to demonstrate differences in both language and learning. Finally, Chapter 8 examines the nature of instruction, and includes a few observations about teachers.

I would like to conclude with a word of guidance to the reader: read to comprehend, not to memorize. As long as you understand, read on, and where you meet difficulty try to go forward rather than backward. If I were asked to summarize the message of this book in one sentence, it would be that the effort to learn is an effort to comprehend. The principal implication for teachers, therefore, is that the effort to teach must be an effort to make comprehensible. My aim has been to interest rather than teach, and I hope indeed that you will find much in the following pages that is both interesting and comprehensible.

CHAPTER 1

On Making Sense

Imagine a student rehearsing a phonic drill or a multiplication table, hearing that Paris is the capital of France, reading that 100 degrees Centigrade is the boiling point of distilled water at sea level, or examining a blueprint of an internal combustion engine. Several fundamental conditions must be met before the student can learn in any of these situations. Some requirements are self-evident, such as adequate visual or auditory acuity, a certain amount of motivation and attention, and some basic language ability. But there is another requirement so obvious that it is frequently overlooked: there must be a point of contact between what the student is expected to know and what he knows already. The student's need to comprehend what he is doing is no different from that of an adult trying to follow instruction in skiing or sailing, or the procedures for the assembly of a Christmas toy.

Classroom teachers know that comprehension is crucial. There is no way a child can learn without it; he will not even understand the instruction. Unless he comprehends what he is doing, a child will not be able to find his seat. School, like the world in general, is constantly making demands upon a child's capacity to comprehend.

So we shall begin by attempting to comprehend comprehension. And we shall find that the dictionary is not much help. Looking in a dictionary beautifully illustrates the fact that the most that can be offered by way of a definition for many words is a synonym. In my dictionary, "comprehension" is defined as "understanding" and "understanding" is defined as "comprehension"—a perfect circle. As a bonus, comprehension is also defined as "grasping mentally", a psychological conceptualization. Obviously, if we want to understand comprehension we shall require not a dictionary definition but a psychological theory.

Comprehension and Theories

Let me begin with an everyday language definition that I shall try to expand into a psychological theory: *comprehension means relating new experience to the already known.* Such a definition constitutes an interesting starting point because it can also apply to learning. Learning is something more than comprehension. It involves changing or elaborating on what is already known. I shall take up this topic a little later in this book. But comprehension and learning are basically inseparable; they both involve relating new experience to what is already known.

Before I get a little more technical there is another everyday language way of defining comprehension: *comprehension means making sense.* I shall in fact often use the term "making sense" rather than "comprehension" because "making sense" is more general. The word "comprehension" is often assumed to refer specifically to language. Making sense of what is going on is something all school children must do, if there is to be any chance that they will learn, and they must do this by relating the situations they find themselves in to prior knowledge. Anything they cannot relate to what they know already will not make sense; it will be nonsense. So a primary concern of teachers must be with what children know already, if only to avoid making impossible demands on them by confronting them with nonsense. This chapter is concerned with the knowledge that is the basis of the sense we make of the world. I am not so much talking about the specific contents of children's minds, about the particular items of knowledge that they might possess, because that to a large extent will vary from child to child. To know what an individual child thinks, you have to know the child. However, I shall be examining the way in which all children acquire knowledge of the world that is contained within their brains[1] and how they organize this knowledge and how they must endeavor to employ it in order to make sense of school and of instruction and of the world in general. We must all have such a store of knowledge in our heads, because without it all our commerce with the world would be devoid of meaning. It is what we know that makes our experiences meaningful.

Several psychological terms are available for labelling this store of knowledge in our heads. One very obvious term is *memory.* In fact, a reasonable working definition of memory might be the accumulated totality of all a person's knowledge of the world. A more specific alternative that I shall frequently use is *cognitive structure*[2], which is an appropriate label because it implies knowledge that is structured, or organized. Our heads are not just a collection of unrelated facts and figures; such a jumble would have no utility in enabling us to comprehend the world. What makes the difference between good and poor learners at school may be less the sheer amount of knowledge they possess than the degree to which they have it integrated and available for use.

But there is a third and far less common term that can be used to refer to the store of knowledge in everyone's brain, and I think it is particularly appropriate for children. The term that refers to what children, or adults, already know is a metaphor: a *theory of the world in the head*.

I offer three justifications for my predilection to use the phrase "theory of the world" for everything that we know. First, it is not precisely accurate to refer to anything in our heads as "knowledge", because there is always some possibility that we might be wrong. Besides, much of the content of our minds is more appropriately termed opinion or belief, not to mention preference, prejudice, taste, habit, hope, fear, love, hate and expectations, all of which contribute their share to how we comprehend the world, and all of which are closely interrelated.

My second justification for using a scientific term like theory is that it is a metaphor that can be extended. I intend to propose that a child at school is comparable to a scientist in a laboratory, not only because each has a theory, but because both learn by conducting experiments. The "scientific method of discovery" is the manner in which every child must learn about the world.

And finally, I want to suggest that the theory of the world that we all have in our heads is in fact exactly like a theory in science; it has the same kind of composition and serves precisely the same functions. To explain this final point, I want to begin by discussing not the child, but the scientist.

Functions of a scientific theory

A scientific theory has three functions, which are related to the scientist's past, present and future. The first function is to provide a useful summary of everything the scientist has learned. It takes the place of a long list of unrelated incidents and becomes the scientist's memory, the essence of his experience. The scientist does not try to remember data; he looks for principles.

These principles in turn influence how the scientist will perceive and interpret new data, the second function of theories. Astronomers who once held to the theory that our universe revolved around the earth perceived the motion of all the planets quite differently from Copernicus, whose own theory enabled him to perceive their movement in relation to the sun rather than to the earth. All astronomers were looking at the same data, at the same movements of the planets, but what they saw was determined by their underlying theory of how the universe was interrelated. Their theory determined how they made sense of their data, how they comprehended events in their world.

The third function of a scientific theory is to serve as a fruitful source of useful hypotheses about the future. Scientists do not wait passively for events to happen; they could never acquire useful knowledge in that way. Instead they go out to look for information, in effect selecting the experiences they will get, and the basis of this selection is their theoretical expectations. Scientists construct hypotheses, which become the basis of an "experiment", and they confirm or modify their theories in the light of the experimental results.

Functions of the theory in the head

Children try to make sense of the world by relating all their experience to the theory of the world in their heads, a theory they have been developing and testing since birth. This theory becomes the constellation of beliefs and attitudes and expectations that children bring with them to school; it constitutes the prior knowledge upon which they will depend if they are to make sense of instruction and instructors. It is the child's theory of the world that the educational process endeavors to build upon, modify and elaborate.

The theory of the world that all children develop functions for each individual in exactly the same way that a theory in science functions for scientists. The theory is a summary of experience; it is memory. It is the evidence upon which children will try to interpret new events—the only basis for any sense or meaning that they can impose upon the world. And finally the theory constitutes their expectations for the future; it is the foundation for learning.

Figure 1.1 is a simple diagrammatic representation of how cognitive structure—the theory of the world in the head—is related to the world around us. Anything in the environment that can be perceived or interpreted in the light of the contents of cognitive structure will make sense. Cognitive structure, in effect, imposes meaningfulness upon the world, as the direction of the arrow indicates. Anything that cannot be related to cognitive structure is nonsense, no matter how meaningful it might appear to anyone else. Does it make sense to say that Paris is the capital of France? At the very least it depends on whether you know (or can deduce) that Paris is a city, that France is a country, and the nature of a capital. A biologist peers through a microscope and sees cell structures that I cannot even begin

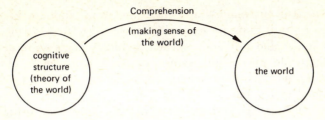

Figure 1.1   Making sense of the world

to discriminate, not because there is something wrong with my eyes, but because I have little prior knowledge of cell structures.

The Organization of Cognitive Structure

Whether we try to look directly into our minds (to examine the manner in which we organize our knowledge of the world), or whether we reflect upon our perceptions of the world around us (which are determined by the manner in which our minds are organized), we find that three aspects of this organization can be distinguished. First of all, we distinguish many categories or classes of objects, ranging from inanimate and manufactured items, such as ball point pens and styrofoam cups, to complex natural living organisms, such as fish, birds and human beings. Despite the fact that hardly any of these objects, and especially the nonmanufactured ones, can be said to be identical, we ignore many of their differences in order to treat large numbers of them as the same. We give personal names to human beings, and to a few other select objects in the world, such as pets, ships, stores and commercial products, but nevertheless there are always category names that pertain to them also. My friend Fred is a male, a father, a teacher, a chess-player and a radical humanist; his friend Rex is a Dalmation, a dog, an animal and a pet; and the *Queen Elizabeth II* is an ocean liner. Nothing, and no one, is ever treated as entirely unique.

In addition to organizing objects in our experience into categories, our knowledge of the world must also include rules for recognizing objects, for putting each of them into one category rather than another. If we can look into an unfamiliar classroom and see a desk and half a dozen chairs, then we must have some rules or specifications in our minds that enable us to recognize desks and chairs. This is the second aspect of the organization of cognitive structure, the rules for allocating objects into categories, a system of what I shall call *distinctive features*.

And finally, all the objects with which our internal and external worlds are furnished are interrelated in some way, whether directly or indirectly. All objects that can fall within the same category have something in common—at least in our minds—and there are many kinds of interrelations between categories. Cups, for example, are closely related to saucers, to hot drinks, to kettles and to teapots. Teachers and students share one kind of relationship, while other relationships are shared by teachers and textbooks, teachers and principals, and teachers and the internal revenue service. Gasoline is related to the internal combustion engine, to international politics and to naked flames. Try to think of two objects that are not related in some way, and you will appreciate the intricately complex manner in which we organize all our knowledge of the world.

These three basic aspects or characteristics of cognitive structure: (1) a system of categories; (2) sets of rules—or specifications of "distinctive features"—for allocating objects or events to particular categories; and (3) a network of interrelations among the categories themselves, are requirements of any system for imposing order on complexity.[3] I propose to elaborate upon my analogy, by examining such mundane organizational systems as postage stamp collections and supermarkets.

Systems of categories

The need for categories in any organizational system, including the human brain, reflects the need for some way of grouping objects according to whether they are to be regarded as the same or different. The basis upon which categories are established may be determined as much by the individual who is doing the organizing as by the objects being organized. Postage stamps are generally grouped first of all according to country of issue, but they could be arranged on the basis of shape, color, size, denomination or type of illustration; the collector makes the decision. A store manager could arrange his products according to weight, or whether they are packaged in plastic, paper or glass, but he usually chooses to arrange them by use. Even the distinction among "natural orders" that the zoologist observes, distinguishing fish from insects from mammals, is only one of many possible methods of classification that could be adopted. The fact that a particular method of categorization seems to "make sense" is a decision made by people.

Everything that a child can perceive—whether a piece of furniture, a dog or a cat, or a letter of the alphabet—must be represented by a different category within his cognitive structure. If he has no system in his mind that separates dogs from cats, then he will perceive dogs and cats as the same kind of animal.

A category is an abstraction in two senses of the word. In one sense we "abstract" categories from our experience by making a decision to treat one kind of object differently from another—the philatelist treats German stamps differently from French stamps and the supermarket manager treats detergent differently from ketchup. A child must learn that *A* should be treated differently from *B*. Abstraction in this sense occurs when we decide to ignore such differences as the color of stamps or packages and to respect certain similarities such as the country that issues the stamp or the contents of the packages. A category is an abstraction also in the sense that there is nothing concrete or tangible about it. You cannot point to a category, or pick it up, or weigh it, although you may be able to manipulate an "example" or "instance" of a category. A category is a decision to distinguish certain objects or events from others.

When the topic is the human brain, there is a natural tendency to talk about categories that have names. Categories that have unique names are often referred to in psychology as "concepts". But it is not necessary for a cognitive category to have a name. We can distinguish many kinds of objects for which we as individuals do not have a name; for example, certain types of vehicles or furniture or trees. Infants distinguish classes of objects from each other long before they have names for them; in fact it is generally necessary to have a cognitive category before a name can be learned. Words like "product" or "mass" are literally meaningless to a child unless he has a category in his cognitive structure that he can attach them to.

As we get older, obviously, we tend to partition our experience more; we acquire more and more categories. Some of the butterflies we used to see prove to be moths and we treat them differently. Our culture determines the general lines of our category system, but individual interests and preferences also dictate how differentiated particular areas of cognitive structure might be. The philatelist may be able to distinguish more categories for postage stamps than I, but on the other hand I may be able to distinguish more kinds of trees.

Distinctive features

A category system is necessary but insufficient for the imposition of order on any collection of objects or sequence of events. The philatelist who has an album with different pages reserved for stamps of different countries has the possibility of systematic organization but needs something else. So also does a child who has simply been told that there are in the world some objects called "dogs" and "cats", or letters called "a" and "b", that he should differentiate from each other.

In order to identify any object, something about it that is distinctive must be discriminated to permit its allocation to a particular category. German stamps must be distinguishable from French stamps, detergents from ketchup. For every category, whether in the system in the head, in the stamp collection or in the supermarket, there must be at least one set of rules to specify the objects that may be allocated to it. These are the rules that make identification possible. Such rules must be based on some combination of properties that is unique to the objects that should be allocated to the particular categories and that will serve to distinguish them from other objects that should not be allocated to that category. These distinguishing properties or significant differences of objects may be termed *distinctive features.*[4]

The number of distinctive features that must be discriminated in order to allocate an object to a category depends on the number of alternative categories to which the object might belong. If we know that an animal is either a camel or a dromedary, then we need to look for only one significant difference—the number of humps. If we know that a letter is either *O* or *C* then we must look for only one distinctive feature, obviously related to whether the circle is open or closed. The more alternatives there are, however, the more distinctive features we must be able to discriminate, while different distinctive features will be required depending on the alternatives that are to be considered. The distinctive feature that distinguishes *O* from *C* will not distinguish *O* from *D*.[5] Unless we have adequate specification of distinctive features for every category we shall not be able to make our theory of the world work. A child who confuses two letters of the alphabet may not know what he should be looking for.

To make a cognitive category system functional, then, some kind of specification or set of rules is required for every category. This specification may be regarded as a cognitive list of distinctive features, which shall be called a *feature list* for short. When we tell a child "That is a dog", or "That is the letter *K*", we are not so much giving him information as presenting him with a problem. We are really only saying "There is a category of objects which we call 'dogs' or 'K'; now you must find out how to identify one in the future. You must discover its distinctive features". And the child must go ahead and try to construct a feature list that hopefully will enable him to identify these objects. To make the whole matter more complex, the nature of the relevant distinctive features can rarely be specified to the learner, because they are not usually subject to anyone's awareness. Fortunately, children do not need to be told the solution to solve such problems.

Distinctive features are not exclusively visual. Objects or events can be allocated to cognitive categories on the basis of any property detectable by our sensory systems. For example, color, shape, size, texture, weight, smell, and taste are all part of our knowledge of oranges.

Interrelations among categories

Lists of distinctive features permit a category system to be put to use, but they do not ensure that it makes sense. The philatelist is not satisfied to say that two stamps are the same or different, nor is the store manager content simply to stack soap in a different location from sardines. There must be some way in which the different categories can be related. A child does not want only to distinguish cups from saucers, or mothers from fathers, he also wants to know what each has got to do with the other and with him. Just as our category system becomes more differentiated as we develop, so the richness of all the interrelations among categories grows. A child literally lives in a less complex world than adults.

It is through the manifold ways in which our cognitive categories are related to each other that we make our environment meaningful. These interrelations are the core of the entire cognitive system of our theory of the world. They enable us to summarize past experience, make sense of the present and predict the future. Nothing in our lives would be comprehensible if these interrelations were absent. The fact that we can compartmentalize various aspects of our experience would be devoid of purpose and sense without interrelations, just as if we were to partition the world into such arbitrary categories as men with green eyes, dogs less than twelve inches high, or cups with floral patterns—categories which for most individuals at least would relate to nothing, and which would therefore be pointless and meaningless.

Cognitive Interrelations

Any tabulation of the different kinds of interrelations among cognitive categories must be illustrative rather than exhaustive. The fundamental question of how knowledge is organized in the human brain has engaged philosophers and psychologists for centuries, and might well be ultimately insoluble, because at its roots human thought defies language. But we can acquire an idea of both the kinds and complexities of interrelations within cognitive structure if we reflect once again upon the manner in which our minds arrange our comprehension of events in the world.

Class inclusion

One important clue, to which I have already alluded indirectly, is that almost all the objects of our experience have more than one name and can be placed into more than one category. Usually when we are asked to explain what something is, we begin by giving it another name. If asked to explain what a trout is, for example, we describe it as a fish. A finch would be described as a bird, the Boy Scouts as a youth organization. Each time we put the object into a broader category: there are more fish than there are trout; more birds than finches; more youth organizations than the Boy Scouts. The effect of such a description is to point to the similarities between the object being "explained" and other objects that fall within the same larger category. Thus by saying trout are fish, we are saying that trout have something in common with salmon, mackerel and marlin.

In short, when we specify a larger category into which a category of objects can be placed, we indicate that there are ways in which this entire category can be regarded as the same as other fish or birds. On the other hand, if we specify a smaller subcategory to which an object belongs, such as when we refer to a canary as being a particular kind of finch, then we are indicating that there are ways in which the object can be regarded as different from other objects in the same category. (You will note that a widespread view that every kind of object has one name and that every name refers to just one kind of object is, fortunately, incorrect. By giving objects a variety of names that can be used on different occasions, much more can be said about them.)[6]

Categories that can be "embedded" into each other, in the way that canaries and certain other kinds of birds are all finches, and finches and still other kinds of birds are all "birds", are sometimes said to have a *hierarchical* relationship. This is the first kind of cognitive interrelation for us to distinguish. The broader categories, in which many objects are clustered despite many possible differences between them, are called higher-order or superordinate categories. Any category that can be fitted into a more general category is regarded as a lower-order or subordinate category. So you can see that whether a particular category should be regarded as higher-order or lower-order depends on what it is being compared with; finch is a superordinate category as far as canaries are concerned, but a subordinate category with respect to birds. Synonyms for higher-order category and lower-order category that are coming into vogue are *superset* and *subset*, respectively. Finches are a subset of the superset of birds, which in turn is a subset of the superset of vertebrate animals.

A diagrammatic representation of the way in which different categories or sets of objects can be embedded hierarchically within each other is given in Figure 1.2 (a). Figure 1.2 (b) shows exactly how the same relations can be represented in the form of what is commonly termed a "tree structure", although it is an odd kind of tree that has its roots at the top and branches proliferating towards the bottom. The two forms of representation, embedded sets and tree structures, are logically equivalent, but representations like the tree structure are usually preferred by cognitive psychologists for a variety of reasons. For a start, tree structures are "networks", and it is in the form of neural networks that knowledge is often conceptualized as actually being represented in the brain.[7] It is also in the forms of logical networks that computer theorists try to "wire up" their organizations and manipulations of information within computers.

Furthermore, networks offer a way of representing hierarchical relations that overlap, or that go in divergent directions. For example, my friend Fred

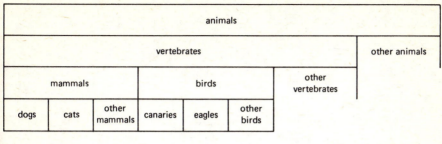

(a) Embedded sets

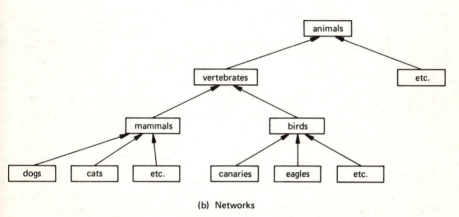

(b) Networks

Figure 1.2   Representations of hierarchical relationships

is a man and thus he is human, a mammal and a vertebrate, and so forth. However, he is also a teacher and thus an employee; he is a baseball player and thus an athlete. There is no way in which all these different hierarchical relationships can be represented in the same set diagram, but they can be represented in a network with no difficulty, as shown in Figure 1.3. It may be necessary for the lines in the network to cross occasionally, or to go from one side of the diagram to the other, so that the network finishes up looking like a heap of spaghetti, but all the connections are properly made. We can trace our way through the network of Figure 1.3 to find that Fred and Freda are both athletic, but that only Freda plays tennis. (In Figure 1.3, I have begun to follow the convention of making category names like "animal" and "vertebrate" singular rather than plural.)

The network type of diagram is useful also because it permits the representation of alternative connections among categories. For example, as illustrated in Figure 1.3, the categories human, dog and cat may have a direct relation to the category animal without having to "go through" the

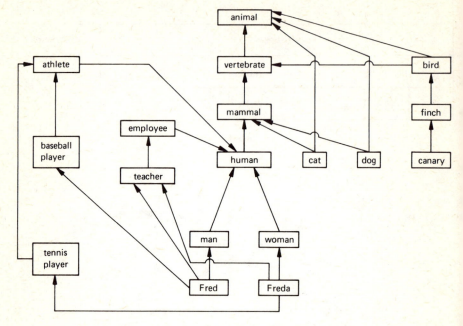

Figure 1.3   More hierarchical interrelations

categories mammal and vertebrate. After all, this is a model of how an individual might organize his knowledge of the world, not a biological taxonomy. We may realize that a finch must be an animal because finches are birds and birds are technically part of the animal kingdom, but in the human brain, at least, finches are not normally regarded as animals.[8] On the other hand, everyone recognizes that a dog is an animal, without first having to work out that dogs are mammals and mammals are animals. Children usually learn that dogs and cats are animals before they have ever heard of the terms mammal and vertebrate.[9] The embedded sets of Figure 1.2 (a) would again not be a very realistic representation of how knowledge is organized in our minds; a network like Figure 1.3 is at least able to indicate cognitive "shortcuts" where direct connections exist between categories logically very much apart.

The hierarchical relation I have just described is formally termed a *class inclusion relationship*—the lower-order categories or classes are included within the higher-order ones. In the opposite direction, the lower-order categories may be termed "exemplars", "examples" or "instances" of the higher-order categories. Finches are "examples" of the category of birds; Fred is an "instance" of the category of teachers. There is a less formal term for the class-inclusion relationship; it can be called an *isa* (pronounced "izza") relationship. Fred *isa* teacher; a finch *isa* bird.[10] Sometimes the relationship sounds a bit ungrammatical—a dog *isa* animal.

Property relations

The term *isa* is useful, however, because it distinguishes class-inclusion relations from a second broad type of cognitive category interrelation that is often indicated verbally by the word *is* without an article. For example, we can say that a canary *isa* finch but that a canary *is* yellow. Fred *isa* teacher but Fred *is* tall. We usually use the word *is* when the object we are referring to has a property that is some kind of quality, such as color, size or shape. Sometimes the property seems to refer more to something that is appended to the object, in which case we express the relationship verbally with *has* rather than *is*. A dog *has* four legs and *has* a tail. Fred *has* red hair and *has* two arms. Some property relations extend into veritable chains —the human body *has* two arms, each of which *has* a hand which *has* fingers, each of which *has* nails. It is not difficult to show that in some sense the property relationships which verbally may be expressed by either *is* or *has* are the same, because the two terms can often be used interchangeably; we can say that a dog *is* furry or *has* fur.

Once again there is an advantage to conceptualizing the organization of knowledge in the human brain in the form of a network. The *is* and *has* property relations can be represented on the same diagram as *isa* relationships (see Figure 1.4). But here an interesting psychological problem arises, the question of where and how many property relation arrows should be represented. As Figure 1.4 indicates, Fred has an arm which has a hand which has a finger. But if someone asked you whether Fred has a hand, you would not have to ask yourself first of all whether Fred has an arm.

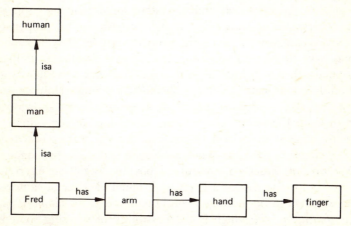

Figure 1.4 Some class-inclusion and property relations

Although Figure 1.4 represents the anatomicial relationships among arms, hands and fingers, a more accurate representation of human knowledge would no doubt be to put arrows directly from Fred to arm, from Fred to hand and from Fred to finger. Our knowledge that Fred has a hand would seem quite independent of our knowledge that hands are attached to arms. Similarly, Figure 1.4 could indicate that the category "man" has the property of having an arm, a hand and a finger; these surely are among the things we know about men. And exactly the same direct representations ought to be given for the superordinate category "human being". If you were to be asked if human beings have arms, you would not have to go through the following reasoning process: "Men are one kind of human being; Fred (and George, Harry, etc.) are men; Fred, George and Harry have arms; therefore, it is probably correct that human beings have arms." Instead, the fact of having arms seems to be directly related in our knowledge of the higher-order categories such as "human being" and "man" as well as to particular instances such as Fred.

It might seem then that the arrows in our conceptualized network of knowledge ought to go everywhere and in all directions, but in fact there are many gaps in our knowledge where we can be said not to know something directly, although we can work it out. Not everything is directly related to everything else in cognitive structure. Much of the knowledge that is available to us was never specifically taught nor even worked out or thought about in the past. Do canaries have blood? Do canaries breathe? We can answer these questions but must pause a little longer than we would for questions like "Do canaries sing? Are canaries yellow?" Our knowledge about singing and color seems to be related directly to canaries while our knowledge about blood and breathing is related more to higher-order categories.[11]

Logically, the most economical system for organizing property information in a system of knowledge would be to relate all properties to the highest-order category to which the property applies. If you know that all mammals have lungs, and you know that dogs and cats and human beings are mammals, then you logically need not store the redundant specific information that dogs, cats and human beings have lungs. However, as I have said, we are concerned with the organization of human knowledge rather than with logical systems. The way in which human individuals organize their knowledge of the world in their heads is a matter of what is convenient to them, rather than what is logically the most economical or elegant. We do not directly represent all possible cognitive interrelations in our minds, but we represent a good deal, much of it technically redundant because we seem to be more generously endowed with *memory space* than with *computing space*, which is the possibility of working something out. If a fact might be useful, we prefer to have it at our mental fingertips.

Other cognitive interrelations

I have tried to simplify, but complexity is unavoidable in even the sketchiest outline of the intricacies of the mind. Class-inclusion and property relations represent only a fraction of the ways in which the categories of our experience are distinguished and interrelated. For example, many categories of objects do things; fingers grasp, arms bend, canaries sing, dogs bark and cats drink milk. Furthermore, many of the same or other objects have things done to them; canaries are caged, dogs are chased by small boys and cats are chased by dogs. Many objects have a functional relationship to us personally, especially when we are young; dogs are to be petted and stones are to be thrown. Some objects use objects to act upon other objects: birds use twigs to build nests; artists use paint to produce pictures. Some objects may be transferred from one person or location to another, sometimes intentionally, at other times not: I can give a book to Fred; he may steal it; or I may leave it on a bus.

Just to give a flavor of how involved and complicated a human mind must be I have tried in Figure 1.5 to illustrate the very tiniest fragment of what the organization of cognitive structure might be like. The example represents little more than a few basic facts related to the circumstance that my friend Fred has a pet dog. See whether you can find out if Fred's dog has lungs, and try to put a whale into the network.

As I have said, no one has yet hazarded a guess about the totality of the different ways in which our cognitive categories are interrelated. Certainly language does not exhaust the possibilities about all the different ways in which aspects of our thought may be organized. Words are the observable peaks rising from unexplored ranges of thought.[12] Since the argument is being presented in language, all of the relationships, like all of the categories, must be labelled by words, generally verbs for the former and nouns for the latter. But it should not be thought that the network of interrelations in cognitive structure is a language system. A cat knows that dogs chase cats, and an infant comprehends the connection between thirst and milk, and neither needs words to represent these relationships in its mind. Actions and images are as much a part of cognitive structure as words. The names that I have attached to categories in the figures should rather be considered a particular kind of relationship—what I really mean by saying "the category dog" is that there is a category of experience, specified by certain lists of distinctive features, that for some humans has the name-relationship "dog". Language is just one of the many forms of human behaviour developing out of the theory of the world in cognitive structure. Language obviously has a lot to do with the way human beings develop and organize their cognitive structure, but it is far from all there is of it.

Many cognitive relationships are causal or explanatory. We know or

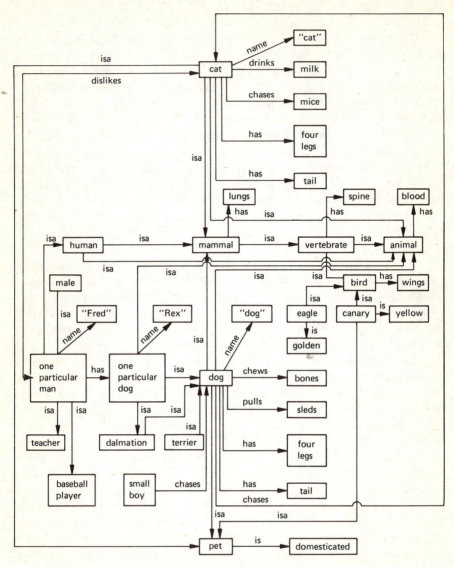

Figure 1.5   Some category interrelations in a cognitive network

believe that objects in one category may have an effect on objects in another
—unsupported bodies fall, rain causes seeds to grow. Such are the kinds
of relationships that enable us to employ our theory of the world for prediction, that form the basis of our expectations about the future.

The term "event" that I have been using so loosely might be defined
as a particular relationship involving a change among categories. A traffic

accident is a particular combination of vehicles and a football game a particular organization of people. Births, marriages and deaths are all relationships among categorizable objects. Events may be treated as the same or different just as objects are treated as the same or different, provided we have learned and can determine both the relevant distinctive features that specify the objects and the relevant relationships among the objects that constitute a particular event.

Some cognitive interrelations reflect relatively permanent states of affairs. The fact that Fred is a man, and that Toronto is in Canada, are most unlikely to change. Sometimes, however, we must be ready to modify our knowledge of the world: Fred is currently unmarried; he teaches in Toronto; and he has a full head of hair. None of these facts can be relied upon to persist indefinitely. Some organizations of cognitive structure are notably provisional: My dentist is on vacation; Fred owes me a lunch. Others may be completely hypothetical: If I accuse Fred of stealing my book, he may admit it; on the other hand he may punch me in the nose or sue me. Not all the events that can be represented in our minds, for longer or for shorter periods, need be representations of actual events that have already occurred in the world around us.

A ubiquitous kind of cognitive structure to which we shall give further attention can be called a "plan" or a "routine"—a particular sequence of events intended to bring about a specific state of affairs. Some precisely organized and productive plans are so important that we call them skills. The nature of human skill is just one of the topics to which we now turn as we close this rather analytic discussion of the form of cognitive structure, and consider how it all might function both to help us to make sense of our environment and to impress our own intentions upon the world.

Using Cognitive Structure: Perception

Common sense tells us that our eyes see, our ears hear and so forth. This is an oversimplification. It is the brain that sees, hears and feels, making perceptual decisions based only partly upon information received from our sensory systems. The brain resides in silent darkness within our skulls, insulated from the world outside. Majestically parasitical on the rest of the human organism, with no feelings of its own, the brain does all the hearing, seeing, tasting, smelling and feeling for the entire body. Like the president of a vast and complex organization, it is the center to which all information flows and the source of all cognitive decisions. The pleasures and pains that are felt at various points of the body, even the sights and sounds that are located outside the body, are all creations of the brain. Our eyes may be closed but the brain can still produce images. Pain may be felt where an amputated limb would have been. Deaf Beethoven heard his own symphonies.

The world as we perceive it cannot be the world as it actually is. We perceive a world furnished with houses, trees, automobiles, men, women, children and animals, precisely because this is the way our minds choose to organize the world. But in order to see a house, a tree, an automobile or a person, we must have some idea of what it is about each of these categories of experience that distinguishes it from other categories of experience. We must have some basis in the mind upon which to perceive our environment, otherwise it would be full of unidentifiable and unrelated objects, a mosaic in time and space of completely irrelevant events, of random "happenings".[13]

Eyes, ears and hands are devices for getting information on behalf of the brain, for looking, listening and touching, not for making decisions. Their signals to the brain are basically all the same—the presence or absence of impulses along nerve fibers. The eye does not send photographic reproductions to the brain, any more than the ear sends little recorded messages. The only communications that sense organs can send to the brain are bursts of neural energy.[14] What makes the difference is the part of the brain to which these neural messages go. Strike the part of the head near the visual centers of the brain, and you see stars; strike the side of the head where the auditory nerves run, and you hear bells.

The brain takes these raw neural signals, decides how to interpret them and transforms them into sights and sounds and all the other fabric of our conscious experience. Some aspects of this miracle we can talk about, others go far beyond our comprehension. There is nothing that can be said about why a neural response to a certain frequency of radiant energy impinging upon the eye should be the stimulus for a sensation of color, or why perturbations among the molecules of the air, transformed into a waving movement of tiny reed-like hairs in the canal of the inner ear, should be heard as the sound of music. There is nothing at all that can be said about why we should be conscious of our experience. Neurophysiologists are beginning to identify some of the neural processes that underlie consciousness, or attention, but why these processes should result in our being *aware* of events impinging on the receptor organs, as opposed to merely *responding* mechanically, defies explanation.

Perception—a matter of opinion

It is important to grasp that the eyes merely look and the brain sees. And what the brain sees may be determined as much by cognitive structure as by the information from the world outside. We perceive what the brain decides is in front of the eyes. For example, look at the reproduction below of something that I wrote:

If I had asked what letter I had written you would have said "B". If I had asked what number I had written you would have said "13". It would be pointless to ask what I really wrote. What I really put on the paper were ink marks, which were what you looked at. What you saw depended on what you knew was there, a letter or a number. If you could make no sense of my ink marks at all—for example if I had written ꝋ; —it would have been nonsense. On the other hand if you know Pitman shorthand you would perceive the mark as "13", and therefore meaningful.

The brain is a decision-making mechanism, and our perceptions are among the decisions that it makes.[15] We become aware of the world around us because the brain is both executive and artist; it decides what we are looking at, then paints the subjective experience of the scene that we believe exists before our eyes. The brain makes its judgments about what the eyes are looking at (or the ears hearing or the fingers touching) by relating or comparing the incoming neural information to feature lists in the category system of cognitive structure that may be relevant, the feature lists for *1,2,3*, etc. if we believe we are looking at a number, the feature lists for *A,B,C*, etc. if we believe we are looking at a letter, and the lists for both if we are uncertain. Such a percept entails a category decision. And there is no possibility of identifying or categorizing any object unless there is a category to put it in. On the other hand, the brain may often generate perceptions without any sensory input at all, for example in fantasy or dreams or hallucinations.

Since what the brain "sees" depends on the decision it has made, and only indirectly on whatever stimulated our sense organs, our perceptions are colored by what we know, by what we expect to see, or by what we would like to see. We may mistake a stranger for a friend, an empty glass for a full one. A child does not necessarily see what the teacher presents to his eyes, he sees what he expects to see, and only as much as he can understand. If he does not have distinctive features for cats and dogs, he will not be able to distinguish cats from dogs, no matter how many times we tell him which is which. Unless he has worked out exactly why *A* and *a* and *ɑ* should be considered as the same, and how they significantly differ from *B* and *b*, and *ƀ* then there is no way that he will be able to see *A*s and *B*s as we do. The differences, significant and nonsignificant, between letters must appear quite arbitrary and purposeless until the alphabet is seen at work in words. What we see is limited by what we understand; the rest is meaningless.

Attention and uncertainty

Of course, we do not perceive everything that takes place or presents itself before our eyes. Our perceptions focus upon those aspects of our environment to which we pay attention, or that intrude themselves upon our attention, and there is a limit to how much we are able to attend to at any one time. Attention is perhaps best conceptualized as questions being asked by the brain, and our perceptions are what the brain decides must be the answers.

Perception has already been characterized as a decision-making process; the brain decides what is "out there" in the world on the basis of incoming information and prior expectations. Decisions generally involve a selection among a limited set of alternatives, which suggests that questions are asked on the basis of prior knowledge. If the decison to be made, for example, concerns which letter of the alphabet the ambiguous figure on Page X is supposed to represent, then the question for most of us would be to distinguish among the twenty-six alternatives, A through Z, that are specified by our prior knowledge. In attending to the perception of that figure, we would be asking a question that would relate the new to the known. Incoming information is matched with distinctive feature specifications of the alternatives we are considering, and we perceive the brain's decision.

There is another term that we can use for the range of questions that the brain might ask—the alternatives among which the brain will choose— that term is *uncertainty*. If our knowledge or expectation is that we are looking at a letter of the alphabet, then our uncertainty comprises twenty-six alternatives. If we know we are looking at a vowel, however, then our uncertainty encompasses only five alternatives. If we are not sure whether we are looking at a letter or a number, then the extent of our uncertainty increases and we require an answer to a more elaborate question. The question we are asking in effect constitutes the attention we are paying. We could be asking quite a different kind of question, such as how big is the letter, or is it upper or lower case, or what is its typeface or do I know someone with that initial? I shall refer to such questions as *cognitive questions,* to make it clear that they function at the level of cognitive structure and are not questions of which we are aware; we could not actually put them into words.

Most of the time when we attend to something we have in mind a limited range of alternatives—an upper bound of uncertainty—that is usually a reasonable estimate of the actual probabilities. We do not con-

sider alternatives that are highly unlikely, nor do we ignore possible alternatives that are highly likely. Such cognitive questions are usually quite accurate predictions. Here is an illustration. Look out of the nearest window,
or imagine looking out of a window, and catalogue what you perceive.
If you happen to overlook a main street, you will probably see automobiles
or a bus, pedestrians, perhaps a bicycle or even a horse. There will probably
be nothing very surprising about anything you see, and that is exactly the
point. The reason there is no surprise is that you have a reasonable prediction of what you are going to see before you look out; your uncertainty
lies among likely alternatives. Obviously, your theory about streets works
well. However, your expectation is not infinite; something *could* be there
that would surprise you, say a submarine, or a parade of elephants.

Now there is nothing intrinsically surprising about submarines or elephants. You would not be surprised to see them if your window overlooked
a naval establishment or a zoo. In other words, your uncertainty is constrained by what you would reasonably expect on a particular occasion.
Your implicit cognitive question on looking out of your window is: "Shall
I see cars, buses, pedestrians, horses or bicycles?" but not "Shall I see submarines or elephants?" Our predictions are not usually wild guesses, but
the well-informed elimination of unlikely alternatives.

Incidentally, our uncertainty usually has a lower limit as well as an
upper one. Your glimpse at the street may tell you that there are automobiles and people, but normally not the number of people in each automobile, or the brand name of the tires or whether the pedestrians wear
spectacles. You may or may not have noticed the make of particular cars,
unless such matters particularly interest you.

Between the upper and lower bounds of uncertainty a limited number
of alternatives remain, and this is the core of the question that the brain
asks: Which of these alternatives is confronting the eyes, or ears or nose or
hands? We typically like to keep the number of alternatives to a minimum,
without running too much of a risk of being wrong, as there is a limit to the
decision-making powers of the brain. Having to distinguish among too
many alternatives can be a strain. Paradoxically, however, we may also tend
to notice what we do not expect; when something occurs outside the range
of our expectations—the camel on Main Street—it consequently grabs our
attention with a compelling new question, "Now what on earth is *that?*"
The brain must now select from a much broader range of alternatives in
what is literally a "second take". The eventual recognition in such cases is
always accompanied by surprise. If the perception falls within the bounds
of our original uncertainty we are surprised if we find it was wrong. But if
the perception is outside the range of our original expectations we are
surprised when we find that it was right.

What determines the aspect of our environment to which we pay attention, the perceptual question that we ask? In other words, what establishes our uncertainty in the first place? There are three possibilities. First, an event may force itself upon our attention by its very unexpectedness—a loud noise, a sudden movement or flash of light. In effect, such an event poses us with a question that demands an immediate answer. Usually we experience at least a little difficulty in identifying unexpected events, simply because there is such a range of alternatives that they could be. More often, however, attention is self-directed. The brain, not external events, is in control of attention. If we walk down a street or listen to a lecture, we direct our attention to particular aspects of the situation that we know will help in relating what is going on to what we know already. These are the occasions when we know exactly what we are looking for. We are not gazing along the street to catalogue everything within sight, but to see if there is a taxi on the corner or if the crosswalk is clear. We may not be able to predict every incident precisely, but we have no difficulty within the range of our expectations and nothing occurs outside this range. As a result, perception is so effortless that we are not aware that judgments are involved.

Finally, attention can be externally directed; this is typically the case at school. We ask children to look at the board, or at a book or at a problem. Sometimes we are very specific, and ask them to look at a particular number or letter. But singling out a particular item for attention does not mean that the task will be any easier; the children must still formulate the cognitive question themselves. If they do not understand what they are being asked to look at, or why they are asked to look at it, the direction of attention is pointless. Small children often have difficulty in redirecting their attention, which tends to be held by the more prominent aspects of objects, such as their size, color or loudness, even when that prominent property is not a significant difference or is irrelevant.[16]

In general, inability to focus attention properly does not occur because children do not know how to look, but because they do not know where to look; they do not know what information to look for because they are not asking the right questions. A child's fixations may meander all over a page or a picture just as a teacher's eyes may wander aimlessly around the wiring diagram for the school air-conditioning system. In neither case will attempts to lead or even direct eye movements make any marked difference. Of course, children may not be interested in attending, which challenges the teacher with a completely different kind of problem.

Information and noise

I have been using the term "information" as a synonym for the signals or messages that come to the brain from the outside world in the form of neural impulses from receptor organs such as the eyes or ears, these impulses are the brain's only points of contact with the outside world. The brain must use this information to answer cognitive questions, to reduce uncertainty. There is a useful technical definition of information that can be adopted from a field of study called "Information Theory"[17] that is primarily concerned with the efficiency of communication systems. Information, in the technical sense, is defined as the reduction of uncertainty by the elimination of alternatives.

According to "Information Theory," a message or signal is informative if the receiver of the message knows more after receiving the message than he knew before receiving it, a proposition that sounds eminently reasonable. If a child correctly identifies as *B* a letter that his teacher has written on the board, and thereby eliminates the other twenty-five alternatives, then he has received information. His uncertainty about which of the twenty-six letters is written on the board has been completely reduced. But the neural message that his brain receives when his eyes look at the board is informative only if there is the possibility of uncertainty reduction. *B* might be one of the child's alternatives and he must have an appropriate feature list for making the identification.

The notion that information reduces uncertainty is highly appropriate for our consideration of perception because it underlies the need for information in or about the world at large to be related to something that is known already. Unless a message, or a signal, reduces uncertainty, it is nonsense. There is an alternative term to "nonsense", which Information Theory employs as a direct opposite of information; the term is *noise*. Noise is defined as a signal that conveys no information, that cannot be interpreted and can be in any sense modality. Acoustic noise in the technical sense is no different from what we normally call noise, a sound that is meaningless. But noise in the technical sense can also be visual. Like the static on a television picture tube, it is a visual signal or event that tells us nothing. To the uninitiated, contemporary art and music can be visual and auditory noise.

From the point of view of cognitive structure, noise is always a consequence of not knowing something. If children have a good mastery of French, then hearing someone read a poem in French is informative; the "message" reduces some uncertainty on their part, concerning what the poem is about. On the other hand, for children who know no French, the reading of the poem will be noise. Similarly the assertion $F(x) = f(x) \, dx$ may be visually informative, provided students are familiar with calculus, or it may be noise, depending entirely on what they know already. I make the distinction for one simple reason: What is mainly informative for one child—or for a teacher—may be mainly noise for another. Noise depends on what you do not know.

Using Cognitive Structure: Comprehension

The term "perception" is sometimes defined as the process by which we become aware of objects and events in our environment. Perception implies relating aspects of our experience to the category system in cognitive structure. We "see" a chair when the object we are looking at matches a feature list that we might have for the cognitive category "chair". Comprehension would appear to go one giant step further, by locking our identification of objects into the network of all we know, into the cognitive interrelationships which make our experience meaningful.

But it is probably rare that we perceive objects simply as objects, in the sense of making mental declarations like "There's a chair", "That's a man running" or "That's the letter D". Rather we assimilate objects or events into our current state of mind. We are aware of the relationships or purposes or possibilities that are the most relevant to us at the time. Instead of "seeing" a chair, we observe something to sit on, or clashing with the color of the drapes, or a pleasing shape. We do not notice a man running, we see him trying to catch a bus, or wonder if we should be running too. I am sure you did not notice that there was a word beginning with the letter D a couple of sentences ago, although you probably comprehended the phrase it was in—". . . the color of the drapes". We somehow respond to the *relevance* of an object or event, relative to our particular purposes, without having to identify *what* it is. If we are looking for somewhere to rest, we see a chair as something to sit on (a functional relationship) but not as a piece of furniture (an *isa* relationship) nor as a "chair" (a name relationship). In effect, our perceptions often seem to constitute answers to cognitive questions, which is one of the ways I have tried to characterize comprehension.

Comprehension is not in fact a process that arises out of perception, rather perception depends on the way we try to comprehend the situation we are in. This might appear to suggest that perception and comprehension to some extent are indistinguishable, that they are not completely independent processes. And indeed there is no clear way of separating processes of perception from comprehension psychologically, unless one imposes completely arbitrary limitations on the manner in which each of the two terms can be used. Which is as good a time as any to discuss what is called the nominalistic fallacy.

On words and referents

The words "comprehension" and "perception" are basically everyday-language descriptors that are applied to various aspects of human behaviour or experience. We say that a person perceives or comprehends something when he behaves in a certain way or says that he is having a certain kind of experience, such as "seeing" a bacillus through a microscope or "understanding" a mathematical problem. Often the two words can be employed interchangeably: "Don't you perceive/comprehend that there is muscle tissue on the slide?" or "Surely, you perceive/comprehend that like terms should be collected on the same side of the equation?". My dictionary offers "comprehend" as one of the definitions of "perceive" (though not *vice versa*). The fact that our language contains descriptive terms does not necessarily mean that these terms refer to distinctive psychological or physiological processes. This is the nominalistic fallacy—the assumption that because a noun form of a word exists, it must have a referent. Philosophy and psychology have been plagued by the multitude of words that cause no problems when used as adjectives or adverbs (when we say that a person is *anxious*, or behaves aggressively or acts *intelligently*) but become completely mystifying when we use them as nouns (when we try to identify some property of "anxiety", "aggression" or "intelligence" within the individual as something that he *has*, that might perhaps even be measured).[18]

There is no need to reject perfectly good everyday language in favor of an awkward arbitrary jargon, especially since the jargon must be retranslated into ordinary English for it to be understood. The notion that mentalistic nouns necessarily refer to discrete psychological processes must be repudiated, however.

Comprehending and noncomprehending

I would be tempted to refer to comprehension as a "state", except that that term might be taken to connote something unusual, or something that requires special circumstances to bring it about. Rather I prefer to suggest that our normal psychological condition is one of comprehension; it is so commonplace that most of the time we pay no attention to it in ourselves or other people. Only on those occasions when we do not understand some aspect of a situation we are in do we become aware of the difference between comprehending and not comprehending. Just as the inspiration of air is something we consciously attend to only when we suffocate, so our attention normally turns to comprehension only when something interferes with it.

Although the word comprehension can be applied to any situation in which we find ourselves, it is, I think, significant that the term tends to be used primarily with respect to language, usually in the context of a failure to understand. While the word comprehension is not widely used in nonlinguistic contexts, we can in fact talk about the absence of comprehension whenever a person does not know what to do or is unable to make sense of a situation. We may say, for example, that a person does not comprehend how to drive a car, operate a slide rule or paper a wall. We fail to comprehend whenever we have questions about a situation to which we cannot find an answer.

Here then is a definition, or rather a description, of how comprehension might be best conceptualized: *Comprehension is the condition of having cognitive questions answered, the absence of uncertainty.* Such a view of comprehension ties in with the earlier conceptualization of information as the reduction of uncertainty. As long as some alternatives remain—some choice among possible interpretations, some inability to identify—then the individual does not comprehend. But when there is no noise in the situation, when information reduces all uncertainty, then indeed he comprehends. Comprehension exists, in other words, when there is no residual uncertainty.

The preceding analysis may seem to make comprehension a relative matter, which I think it is, especially as far as language is concerned. If you say that you have comprehended a particular book or movie, then I must take your word for it. As far as you are concerned, there was nothing about the book or movie that remained puzzling, that left you with unanswered cognitive questions. If I then want to assert that you did not comprehend the book or movie because you failed to see some particular point that I feel was important, then you can argue that the particular point was not an issue for you; you were not asking that kind of question. You know whether you comprehended the book or not, because you would be the one aware of noncomprehension. I may persuade you that you did not comprehend the book, in my terms, by showing you that you should have been asking a different kind of question, but I can only do this by generating uncertainty in your mind.

The analysis also leads to the conclusion that comprehension is specific to the particular questions being asked, to the precise nature of the individual's uncertainty. It is true that we comprehend any situation, verbal or otherwise, by relating it to what we already know, to cognitive structure, but not by plugging the situation in to all of cognitive structure. Some rather simplistic psychological theories of language seem to assert that a word is understood if all the connections or associations to that particular concept in cognitive structure are activated in some way. But how often do we want to become aware of everything we know about a word or object that we see? If the topic of concern happens to relate to colors, then I want to recall that milk is white. If the concern is with the cost of living, then I want to remember the price of milk and the rate at which my family consumes it. Certainly if I am drinking milk for refreshment, the last thing I want to think of is the udder of a cow. In brief, we do not comprehend indiscriminately, but rather in terms of what we are looking for, in terms of what we want to know. We use what we know about the world in order to make sense of it, not blindly, but by seeking information that will answer specific questions. The true art of making sense of the world lies in knowing what can be safely ignored.

Using Cognitive Structure: Other Aspects

I have been trying to point out that words like "comprehension" and "perception" do not denote completely independent cognitive processes. Rather they are descriptive terms for aspects of human behavior and experience that are manifestations of the same underlying processes. There are a number of other terms that are employed for describing other aspects of mental functioning, such as "learning" and "thinking", which must also be examined. For the moment I want to do no more than discuss the relation of these terms to the concept of cognitive structure. The entire book might be regarded as a deeper analysis of their nature.

Learning

Scientific theories do not always work, nor do the theories of the world that we have in our heads. Theories may prove to be poor summaries of past experience, or may fail to provide adequate interpretations of present events (so that the environment confronts us with "noise"), or may lead us to make unreliable predictions about the future (the wrong kind of cognitive questions). When a theory does not work it must be revised, and the revision of the theory that is in the head is called *learning*. Human beings are innately predisposed to learn whenever the effort to comprehend fails and the world does not make sense. The nature of the learning process—the elaboration or modification of cognitive structure—is the theme of the second part of this book, beginning with Chapter 4. Learning particularly implies a reorganization of that aspect of cognitive structure that is our summary of past experience, the summary we often call *memory*.

Thinking

Thinking is another mentalistic term that has a multitude of meanings, so much so that I usually avoid using the term at all. Instead I try to be more explicit and specify the aspect of thinking that I am talking about. By avoiding the word "thinking" I try to keep clear of questions about whether perception is thinking, or if there can be any thought without comprehension. I hope you can see that these are fundamentally semantic questions about the way words should be used, and they are generally used

with considerable abandon. These are not theoretical questions about underlying psychological processes.

Whether or not you want to call perception and comprehension thinking, there is another broad aspect of our mental life that must be accounted
for and that would very often be described as thinking, perhaps as the
major definition of the word. I am referring to the covert life that takes
place within the privacy of the brain, often independently of events in the
outside world, a form of activity that cannot be observed directly. Very
often this internal activity is a substitute for behavior in the outside world:
"You may not be calling me a liar but you think it"; "What do you think
would happen if you joined these two wires?"; "Do the next problem in
your head, not in your workbook". Because mental activity of this kind
may be a substitute for actual behavior, I shall call it *vicarious experience*.

Vicarious experience

Having constructed a world in the head, human beings then proceed
to dwell in it. There are many such private aspects of thought, ranging
from the trivial to the sublime. We can rehearse poetry, recall telephone
numbers, calculate our taxes, hold imaginary conversations, visualize how
the kitchen will look with orange wallpaper, contemplate a chess move,
plan a vacation, design an apartment complex, compose a poem, tee off,
conduct a symphony, or even write a book, all in the mind. I have no wish
to catalogue all the different manifestations that vicarious experience can
apparently take. Instead I propose to make a very general statement about
them all: *All mental activity (or cognitive function) taking place wholly
within cognitive structure is a substitute for interaction between cognitive
structure and the outside world.* In even more simple terms, thought is a
substitute for action.[19]

Many theorists use more elaborate language to express what I consider
basically the same idea. For example, thought is often defined as "symbolic activity" or "symbolic representation". However, the word "symbolic"
is little more than an elegant synonym for "substitute"—a symbol "stands
for" something else. Thought may also be referred to as "covert behavior",
which again means the same thing to me—an unseen activity that substi-
tutes for actual experience.

Two important aspects of vicarious experience, memory and imagination, are very closely related to perception. Our memory for events is largely
a matter of reconstruction from fragmentary cues of experience in the past;
it is an exercise of imagination based in part on our expectation of what
a past event must have been like.[20] Our fantasies about the present and
future are similarly derived from what we already know. We may imagine
a three-eyed monster with green tentacles sprouting from rotating ears,

but we are familiar with eyes, ears, tentacles, rotating objects and green. The contents of dreams often provide vivid examples of the way familiar elements of experience may be conjoined into new and novel combinations. In fact, dreaming may represent the brain's experiments with different interpretations of the past and alternative plans for the future.

Many of the relations among cognitive categories to which I have referred, and the way in which these interrelations can be developed through learning, cannot be considered independently of vicarious experience. Our notions of cause and effect, of time and space, of how different operations may modify different objects and how these operations can be reversed, probably all depend initially on an internal representation of actual physical interaction with the environment. The process of "asking cognitive questions" obviously depends upon a mental reorganization as if we were affected by events in the outside world, or as if we already knew something.

Cognitive structure provides a mental arena, an internal world, through which an individual can move freely—organizing, examining, comparing and testing ideas rather than acts. We can in fact lead a much richer life in our world in the head, experiencing events that never could take place in the outside world, and even events that we would not want to take place. Creative individuals may draw their inspiration from freely running mental activity, in fact the ability to generate or visualize new possibilities of experience might be regarded as half of the artist's gift. The second half would have to be his critical selectivity, the ability and the will to recognize, reject or modify the less desirable creations of his mind.

The Dynamics of Cognitive Structure

My analysis of cognitive structure so far may have given the impression of a somewhat static state of affairs. Comparing cognitive structure with a network, a theory, even with a system, does little to encourage the image of a dynamic mechanism constantly in action.

But cognitive structure, if nothing else, is dynamic. Not only is it active, but for the most part it determines its own activity. It learns, and it largely directs its own learning. Cognitive structure is not only the source of our beliefs and expectations, our hopes and fears, but also of our motivations and abilities. Minds are not comfortable with passivity; the absence of uncertainty, which demands action, is boring and aversive.

I have already made passing reference to the active nature of cognitive structure when I characterized perception as the consequence of a decision-making process, and again when I talked of the self-directed aspects of attention. It is not appropriate to regard the human brain as passive, although that is the condition we often seem to expect to find it in at school.

If we consider human brains—and human beings—from an active point of view, we will better understand how being alive and having a functioning cognitive structure can scarcely be distinguished.

It is within cognitive structure that the roots of all behavior lie, except the most simple and instinctive of reflexes. Whether we act from habit or conscious decision, for some purpose of our own or in response to an external stimulus, every intention is generated in the fabric of cognitive structure. But not only does our theory of the world determine the ends that shape our acts, it also contains the means. Part of everyone's cognitive structure is a complex repertoire of integrated sequences of actions, each offering the possibility of accomplishing some desired end. These behavioral sequences can be executed directly in the world around us, but they can also be tested vicariously, in the privacy and security of the mind, so that we can examine and select among alternative courses of action. The fact that we can predict likely outcomes of potential actions is a critical feature of our ability to interact with our environment, as a simple example will show.

Plans and information

Imagine driving to school in the morning. From the moment you leave home, you know what you are going to do, the broad outline of where you are going and the detail of how to get there. You know where to find the car, how to get into it, how to start it, and how to drive. You know which route to take. None of this knowledge can be dismissed simply as habit; you might have to do something new, like make a diversion to pick up a friend. Even if you do not know the way, you know how you can go about finding the way. Let us call all of this knowledge *plans*,[21] some of which have relatively long range objectives, like getting to school, and some of which are routines involved in smaller steps on the way, such as turning the key in the ignition. All of these plans must be in your head, as part of cognitive structure. Even if you have to follow a map or a set of instructions to get to school, the route you must follow is meaningless until it becomes part of your knowledge (or theory) of the world. You will never get to school unless you are able to meet every possible contingency and to know which plans to follow and when.

Plans, in other words, specify procedures or routines for achieving certain objectives and may determine intermediate objectives. For example, you may have a very broad plan for driving to school, which you employ most weekdays but not on holidays. Within that larger plan are several alternative plans for different routes to take. None of your route plans completely specifies the way you will drive your car, however, because on the way you may have to exercise even smaller plans for turning corners, avoiding other traffic, changing lanes, starting and stopping.

In addition to plans within your head you need information from the world outside that these plans are being properly accomplished. You know where you want to park your car, but you need information to tell you whether you are succeeding in your attempt. Before you leave the car, you require confirmation that you have put on the handbrake and turned off the engine. Every step, or miniature plan, begins with a need for information concerning the execution of the previous step or plan.

The fact that you need information all the time to tell you if you are doing what you want to do implies that you know in advance the information you will require. You must know the information you need, or the cognitive questions to ask, before you can decide whether to overtake another vehicle or stay in your lane, to accelerate or slow down. You do more than predict the next event; you anticipate alternatives. When you make that familiar drive to school, your mind makes the journey at least twice ahead of the car itself. One of the vicarious journeys is your route; unless you know along which roads you should be going, there is no way of checking whether you are in fact going along the right roads. You know you are on the right route because of various landmarks you observe, but your mind must be ahead of the landmarks if you are to look out for them. But apart from your knowing the route, the car in your mind must also be a few yards ahead of the car on the road. When you see traffic signs or other vehicles around you, you do not relate their positions and other information to where your car is now, but to where you expect it to be in a few moments, and to what you expect its relation to them to be. You are constantly thinking ahead, which means you are driving ahead, always looking for that information which will tell you if your plan is or is not likely to be accomplished. To introduce another important term, the information that you seek is *feedback* that will assure you that you are (or are not) where you predicted you would be.

The information that you seek from the environment is always determined in advance. You will certainly pay attention to the road ahead, unless you plan to turn off to the right. And you will pay very little attention to traffic in the opposite direction, unless you plan to turn off to the left. You move from one situation of uncertainty to another, and in each situation there are alternatives among which you will have to choose. Is there or is there not a truck ahead? Can I or can I not overtake it? Have I or have I not gone past it? Can I or can I not pull in now? New information should not take you by surprise; it should always be relevant to a possibility that you are considering. In other words, it must be related to what you already know and expect, and it must be the answer to cognitive questions. You ignore anything you regard as irrelevant, but that is all you should ignore. Of course, events in the environment, which may or may not be a consequence of what you do, constantly modify your knowledge and need for information. If a ball rolls into the road ahead, you brake; if the road is under repair, you make a detour. But you always follow the underlying plan of getting to school.

All this information-seeking and decision-making usually takes place below the level of conscious awareness. You may arrive at school without any recollection of particular incidents on the way, although you may well remember news that you heard on the car radio. Usually we remember only the unexpected or something new. If the events of our drive to school were always within the range of our expectations, if our theory of how to drive to school worked, then nothing that occurred would have been unexpected, and therefore nothing would have been memorable. It is not the expected that demands our attention or stays in our memory, but the unpredictable.

Plans, it seems to me, should be regarded as a particular kind of interrelation among cognitive categories, which differ from the others I mentioned earlier in only one major respect: they involve change. Plans are concerned not so much with current situations as with bringing about new states of affairs and as a result their outcome is never certain. Whether we are tying a shoelace or driving a car, there are right and wrong ways in which the behavior can be carried out. Being able to do things the right way is usually characterized as a skill, which leads to another distinction that we must draw. Although the issue is as complicated and ill-defined as that of distinguishing between perception and comprehension, it is worth devoting some thought to possible differences between knowledge and skills.

Knowledge and skills

The extent to which our various uses of the terms "knowledge" and "skill" should be attributed to alternative semantic possibilities rather than to a deeper cognitive distinction is not clear. We can sometimes use the two terms interchangeably: We can say that someone knows how to play the piano or has the skill of playing the piano. Nevertheless there seems to be an underlying difference between knowing something (in the sense of knowing, or believing something about the world, such as the fact that there are 26 letters in the English alphabet) and knowing how to do something (in the sense of being able to identify the 26 letters or to put them together to forms words). These two aspects of knowing are sometimes characterized as "knowing what" and "knowing how".[22] I shall refer to both aspects as "knowing" when it does not seem important to make a distinction (or when

I am unable to make a distinction); otherwise I shall refer to the first as "knowledge" and the second as "skills".

There are important distinctions that can be drawn between knowledge and skills from a psychological (and educational) point of view. Knowledge can usually be talked about; it comes packaged in the form of "facts". In fact there is an interesting theoretical issue concerning whether knowledge in the "knowing what" sense is not completely dependent upon language. Skills, on the other hand, tend to defy satisfactory description in words. No matter how many lectures or demonstrations a child attends, he will not become a pianist without a piano. Skills involve action and require activity in their learning. Unlike skills, knowledge does not improve with practice. It would not make sense to tell a student to improve his knowledge that Paris is the capital of France, or that falling objects in a vacuum accelerate at the rate of sixteen feet per second, per second. Knowledge is also not generalizable. The fact that you know the capital of France does not help you to know the capital of Belgium. Skills, however, are rarely specific; if you know how to read music, you know something about reading pieces of music you have never met before. Knowledge is usually evaluated on the basis of truth or falsity, but skills are assessed on how well they are performed.

Despite these apparent differences, which are rarely as obvious or as clearcut as in the examples I have given, knowledge and skills, facts and acts, are very intimately related. Indeed, one very important set of skills can be identified in terms of the manner in which we acquire, organize, utilize and communicate knowledge.

Consider for a moment the way in which knowledge is acquired in the first place. There are just three basic ways in which we can obtain the information that we need to elaborate or modify knowledge of the world in cognitive structure: through experience (doing something); through observation (seeing someone else do something); or through being told. One might argue that a fourth way of acquiring knowledge is by thinking, or working something out in one's head. But I have already tried to characterize that kind of mental activity as "vicarious experience", so therefore I shall include it with the first basic way in which we can acquire knowledge—through experience—which can be either direct or imagined.

Now each of these three alternative ways of acquiring knowledge involves skills; in no case does the knowledge get into our heads directly and immediately. Sheer experience will not give us knowledge—we must interpret and analyze and comprehend. The process of making sense of the world by relating the unfamiliar to the known is a skill. Skill is also required in order to acquire knowledge from observation; merely watching an artist perform is not sufficient to enable you to perform similarly. And skill is obviously required in order to acquire knowledge by being told; a prior knowledge of language must be applied.

Despite all these apparent differences, I want to locate our skills as well as our knowledge within the organization of cognitive structure; I want to regard them both as part of the way in which we make sense of the world. Partly I want to do this because it seems awkward to try to account for knowledge and skills in terms of different mechanisms. Facts and acts are so closely related it is impossible to imagine one without the other. However, saying that skills are part of cognitive structure does not account for them, of course. It is still necessary to try to find some way of explaining what they are and how they function.

A few pages ago I discussed the dynamic nature of cognitive structure, and how it was the source of all our plans, of our predetermined routines for behavior. Plans involve both knowledge and skills, in fact plans might be regarded as the point in cognitive structure where the two kinds of knowledge, facts and acts, come together. Plans are certainly not static aspects of cognitive structure; they can vary from time to time, from moment to moment, and also include within their structure a temporal element. There is a right and a wrong time for carrying out plans, and the ability to do the right thing at the right time seems to me to be the essence of a skill.

Here then is perhaps the most reliable difference between knowledge and skills. Knowledge is completely independent of time—Paris is the capital of France and Brussels the capital of Belgium regardless of the order in which you make the two statements. Even if Paris ceases to be the capital of France at some time in the future, it will still make sense to say that Paris was the capital of France for a certain period of history. But while the time or manner in which you utter a fact makes no difference to the appropriateness of the fact, skills depend absolutely on timing. If the sequence is disordered or one part of a skill is performed at the wrong time, then the skill is disrupted. You know that a chair is a chair regardless of where a particular chair happens to be, but if you want to sit on a chair, then the time and place of your relationship to a particular chair is crucial. Familiarity with a certain complex move in chess, called castling, represents *knowledge*, and is independent of time. However, in order to make castling part of your *skill* at chess, you must know *how* to apply this knowledge at very specific times.

I do not want to imply that skills are simply facts set in motion. A far more intriguing notion is that facts are slices of the flux of existence frozen in time. Facts are artificial, constructed out of the constant change of our life through the time-binding properties of language.

All of these issues may seem abstruse and academic, but they lie at the very roots of many of our problems of instruction. From an instructional point of view, knowledge and skills are completely different. Skills are very poorly communicated through language, yet without them knowledge is use-less, an impediment rather than an aid to learning. Schools are supposed to be concerned primarily with developing a child's "abilities", his proficiency in a variety of skills, but when it comes to the point in the classroom we try to improve abilities by communicating knowledge. These are arguments that I will pick up again, but not until the very end of the book. Before we begin to think about instruction, there is much more to be considered about comprehension and learning.

These distinctions between knowledge and skills demand early mention for three reasons. First, because no description of cognitive structure would be complete without some attempt to integrate skills as well as knowledge; second, because the distinctions provide a necessary basis for much of the discussion of language and learning that is to follow; and third, because they underline that there is a difference between knowing something and being able to say what you know. And there lies a paradox. Cognitive structure is the source of everything that each of us knows—but it is not something that any of us knows anything about. We cannot look directly into our own cognitive structure.

Implicit knowledge

Everything I have said about cognitive structure in general, and every-thing any one of us might say about his own or someone else's cognitive structure in particular, must be based on inference. Cognitive structure is not open to inspection; our implicit knowledge or theory of the world is not accessible to our awareness. Theories in the head are *"implicit knowledge"*.[23]

By way of illustration, take a young child who has the word "dog" in his vocabulary. Learning how to use the word "dog" in the same manner as everyone else is far more complicated than simply learning or remembering the name. Dogs come in a variety of shapes, colors and sizes, and it is impos-sible to say what they have in common that cats, cows and other animals do not have. We certainly do not give this information to a child when we tell him "There's a dog". In effect we present the child with a problem. We say: "There is something that I call 'dog' and it is up to you to find out what exactly there is about this something that makes it one". It may transpire that the child believes that anything with four legs is a dog, or even any moving object. But it is unlikely that he will ever be able to say why it is that he calls some objects "dog" but not others. In other words, he will not have conscious access to his theory about dogs. He learns something but cannot say what he has learned. His knowledge is "implicit".

Inability to articulate underlying knowledge does not indicate any in-tellectual deficiency on the part of a child; adults suffer the same handicap. Simply pointing to a dog and saying, "That is what I call a dog", is to dodge the issue; the point is how you can tell it is a dog in the first place. If we all had direct access to how we know what we know, psychologists would very soon be unemployed, just as linguists would quickly become redundant if they could say what it is they "know" that enables them to comprehend language.

None of the processes of thought, however, appear to be immediately accessible to awareness, any more than we are directly aware of the category system, its feature lists or its interrelations. We may easily distinguish a cat from a dog, or a grammatical sentence from an ungrammatical one, but we are still unable to say what it is that we know that enables us to tell the difference. Similarly we may be aware of the products of cognitive activity —we "hear" imaginary conversations and "see" chess moves and nonexistent monsters—but we cannot be aware of the processes by which these creations are constructed. The solution to a problem may flash into our mind, but we will have no idea of where the solution came from or how it was conceived.

However, the fact that cognitive structure is completely shielded from direct examination does not mean that we cannot make theoretical statements about it. There is one simple way we can postulate and even explore its contents, and that is by putting it to work. It is by its products that we can get to know cognitive structure. Do you want to know if a child's concept of a dog is adequate to distinguish between a Pomeranian and a Persian cat? Show him both, and see if he can tell the difference. Do the cognitive interrelations in an infant's brain contain the notion that a given number of candies increase in amount as they are spread out over a wider area? Offer him the same number of candies in different arrays, and see which he prefers. Do you want to know what you think about world population control, or the consequences of gasoline rationing? Write or say something about these topics (or make a speech to yourself in your mind); it is only by pulling information out of your brain that you will be able to see what is in it.

The phenomenon of consciousness provides a compelling but almost completely impenetrable puzzle for all who like to contemplate such matters. My favorite conjecture about the function of consciousness is that it enables human beings to examine the products of thought so that, for example, they can transfer thoughts from one sense modality to another.[24] We would not be able to relate in our mind, or talk about, the sound of horses hooves and the sight of horses galloping unless we had the consciousness to be aware of the products of our own brain processes. Consciousness enables us to transform at least some of our knowledge into explicit form and therefore to make it communicable.

But as we shall see in the following chapter, most of what we know cannot be consciously examined and communicated, even when that knowledge is language itself. The fundamental riddle of learning, and therefore of education, is how it is possible for a child to learn so much when we can explain so little.

Comprehension in the Classroom

Fundamentally, a child is no different from an adult. The manner in which a child must look for information to help him make sense of his environment is no different from the teacher's. Whether or not they will share the same perceptions and understandings, whether in fact a particular experience will constitute information or "noise" in their environment, will be determined by the cognitive questions that each is able to ask.

When a teacher writes a sentence on the board, he knows what he is putting there. But the sentence that makes sense to a teacher does not necessarily make sense to the child. The teacher may see that a particular letter is obviously *A*, because that is what he wrote. But if the child does not ask the cognitive questions the teacher assumes he must be asking, then he will not perceive what is written on the board in the same way as the teacher. If the child asks the wrong questions—the wrong implicit cognitive questions—then he will not comprehend; nothing will make sense.

Furthermore, directing the child's attention will not lead him to see as the teacher does. Attention is not a matter of looking or listening in one way rather than another, but of asking specific cognitive questions. A child at school is constantly having his attention directed, without necessarily having any clue to the cognitive questions he should ask. If his uncertainty is not reduced, then directing a child's attention will not only fail to give him information, but it may inundate him with "noise".

A specific example: The teacher chalks *K* on the board and a child says it is "H". The teacher says "wrong" and chalks a series of *K*s on the board, asking the child to understand that each is an example of a "K". But the child may not know what he is supposed to be looking at. Does "K" mean a chalkmark on the board? Or a particular location on the board? *H* is not so very different from *K*, not so different perhaps as the lower case *k*. So what is it about *K* that makes it a "K"? To be precise, what are the distinctive features of *K*?

Let the teacher go further. He writes *H* on the board and instructs the child "That's an 'H'. Can't you see the difference between *K* and *H*"? Now the opportunity to inspect differences between *K* and *H*, and between *K* and every other letter of the alphabet will eventually enable the child to distinguish *K* from other letters. But asking him to *see* the difference between *K* and *H* before he has been able to identify the significant differences between the two, before he has acquired distinctive features for them both, is to assume that he has solved his problem in advance. The child's attention has been directed but he does not know the cognitive question to ask. The child may not see the difference because he does not know the difference the teacher is looking at. Until they look at the two letters in the same way, teacher and child will perceive *K* and *H* in different ways. What will be obvious to a teacher will be noise to a child, until the child is making the same distinctions as the teacher for the same reasons as the teacher. The difference between two letters is no more self-evident to a child than the difference between port and claret, obvious to an expert, is necessarily self-evident to a teacher.

Another example: A child experiences difficulty in understanding the commutative property of multiplication, that $3 \times 5 = 5 \times 3$. The teacher presents the simple analogy that three rows of five beans are the same as five rows of three beans:

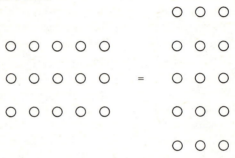

The teacher can "see" that this obviously proves the point, but the child cannot. The child may have a conceptual difficulty, for example with the relationship between the mysterious $\times$ sign and the arrays of objects. In what sense is 3×5 the same as

$$\begin{matrix} \circ & \circ & \circ & \circ & \circ \\ \circ & \circ & \circ & \circ & \circ \\ \circ & \circ & \circ & \circ & \circ \end{matrix}$$

? Perhaps there is an even deeper cognitive problem: The child does not see that the two arrays of beans are the same. The tall thin array may appear to have more beans than the short fat array. From the perspective of the child, taller means greater; in his eyes 3×5 is not the same as 5×3. And the teacher's demonstration has helped to prove this to him.[25] The child's comprehension of the problem is again quite different from that of the teacher.

I must now reiterate the point that comprehension is relative—it depends on what we know already and the cognitive questions that we ask. The individual who reads a novel for its logical consistency or narrative power will comprehend it quite differently from one who attends primarily to its poetic qualities. Which one is reading the book "properly"? The answer is in the realm of value judgment, not of fact. How then can comprehension ever be measured in school? The question is a vexatious one, since it is quite possible that no answer exists. How could there be an answer, if what constitutes comprehension varies from individual to individual? Teachers who are anxious to measure comprehension are often quite unclear about what they want to measure, or about the conclusions they could draw from a comprehension test score (except to assert that Johnny does or does not comprehend very much). It might be better to acknowledge that the tests we call comprehension tests at school always measure something else, and to be explicit about what is being measured. Comprehension tests often appear to gauge the ability to acquire certain facts, to obtain particular kinds of answers, on the basis of implicit questions that the teacher (or test designer) has decided in advance the student should ask. But if ability to get answers to questions is at issue, then it might seem appropriate to give the student the questions in advance.

Comprehension tests in reading are usually tests of memory; they are taken with the book closed and measure how much the student can recall. But if you want to conduct a memory test, you should presumably ensure that the information the student is supposed to remember has been acquired in the first place. It is true that ability to recall depends, among other factors, on the original comprehension, but the effort to memorize can in fact interfere with comprehension. Have you ever tried to comprehend a Russian novel while attempting to remember the patrinomics, relationships and rank in the civil service of all the characters? It is what we know in advance that enables us to comprehend a book in the first place, yet questions that the reader might have been able to answer without reading the book first are usually zealously eliminated from comprehension tests.

Whether or not it makes sense to measure comprehension, the fact remains that most children do not comprehend what is going on in school some of the time, and some children seem to comprehend very little most of the time. It might seem reasonable to ask, therefore, how comprehension might be improved.

But I hope I have already said enough to show there is no simple answer to such a deceptively simple question. At least two questions would appear to be involved, one concerning how children might be changed to make them comprehend more and the other concerning how the school might be changed to make it more comprehensible. The basic need is for teachers, and others responsible for education, to understand how children think and learn, their capacities and their limitations. Problems in education are rarely solved by the discovery of a magical technique that suddenly makes everything right. More often, everyone involved needs to attain the insights to understand what has been going wrong, in this case to understand what makes comprehension—and learning—difficult. To take a more positive view, teachers are very often effective in their work—after all, many children do in fact succeed in learning at school—without being able to specify what exactly they have been doing right. This entire book is an effort to shed light on these enormous issues, not in order to tell teachers what they should do, but to further their understanding, and thereby their underlying competence.

CHAPTER 2

Limits to Comprehension

You can lead a child to a textbook, but you cannot make him see. None of us is able to see everything in front of the eyes, and much of the time we can see very little at all. In fact there are severe limits to how much anyone can see, or hear, or experience in any way. The brain, marvellous instrument that it is, does not have an infinite capacity for coping with the world. A child makes sense of the world by relating the unfamiliar to the known, but if very little "known" can be brought to bear on a particular occasion, little will be comprehended or perceived. Seeing and hearing are not simple matters of "acuity"; there are limits to comprehension.

The particular activity that I shall examine will be reading, or at least the identification of letters and words in written English. There is a good deal of experimental evidence about visual aspects of perception, partly because it is easier to monitor what the eye is doing compared with the ear or nose or tongue. The arguments are not exclusive to vision; a child may be temporarily deafened in the classroom as well as blinded, but for a start, we shall look at how little, relatively, the eyes have to do with reading.

Between Eye and Brain

Of course, reading is a visual activity. In order to read it is necessary to have text in front of the eyes, the eyes open, and some illumination. But reading is far more than an exercise for the eyeballs. The art of becoming a fluent reader lies in learning to rely less and less on information from the eyes. Any reader who struggles to absorb more visual information than his brain can handle becomes a slow and hobbled reader, not a fluent one.

Visual and nonvisual information

Two quite different sources of information are involved in reading; one source is the author (or the printer) who provides what might be called *visual information*, which is the ink marks on the page. This is the kind of information that is lost if the lights go out. The other source is in the reader himself, who provides nonvisual information, which is available even when his eyes are closed. Put in another way, reading involves information that the reader receives through his visual system and information that he already has available in his head, in cognitive structure.

Suppose, for example, that even a skilled reader looks at a book written in a language that he does not understand. There will be very little reading, but not because there is a shortage of visual information in any way. Knowledge of language is crucial nonvisual information that the reader himself must supply. Similarly, very little reading will take place if the subject matter of the text is completely removed from the experience of the reader, for example an article on subatomic physics for most teachers of English. A good deal of prior knowledge is required if any piece of text is to be read. Everything the author takes for granted must be supplied by the reader in the form of nonvisual information. And the only source of nonvisual information is what the reader knows already.

The distinction between visual and nonvisual information in reading is important because they have a reciprocal relationship; readers can trade-off one for the other. The more nonvisual information a reader can use, the less visual information he needs. And the less nonvisual information a reader can supply, the more visual information he must get from the page. Instances of this reciprocal relationship will be immediately apparent: we read faster when the material we read is familiar or "easy"; we can read smaller type, and in dimmer light. Familiar names and words can be perceived from a greater distance than unfamiliar ones. On the other hand, we tend to peer more closely, and read more slowly, when the going is hard, when our own contribution to the understanding of what we are reading is limited.

The trade-off between visual and nonvisual information in reading is critical because there is a limit to the rate at which the brain can "process" incoming visual information, a limit often overlooked because we tend to think that we see everything that happens before our eyes. We are not usually aware that the sole function of the eyes is to pick up and transmit information from the visual world to the brain. The brain has the job of making the perceptual decisions about what we see.

THE BRAIN SEES WHEN THE EYES ARE INACTIVE   The eye picks up useful information from the visual world only when it is at rest—unless it is locked on to a moving object—and it can move from one position to another to pick up new information no faster than four or five times a second. All of the visual information that can be picked up from a single glance, or fixation, is acquired during the first one hundredth of a second or less. For the rest of the time the eyes are essentially nonfunctional while the brain works on the information it has received. In fact if a new burst of visual information arrives from the eye before the brain has finished with the previous input, then either the first or the second may be disregarded completely. If two different pictures or sequences of letters are briefly flashed on a screen within about a tenth of a second of each other, a viewer will be able to say something about the first scene or about the second, but not both.[1]

The fact that the eye is limited to about five fixations a second does not mean that the amount of information the brain gets from the visual world could be doubled by increasing the rate of fixations to ten a second. No visual activity can be improved simply by speeding up the eyeballs. It takes a full second for the brain to process all the information available in a single fixation. The eye need make just one fixation a second for all the visual information the brain will be able to handle. Instead the brain uses only a fraction of the visual information that could be available from four or five fixations a second.

These information-processing limitations apply to all people, incidentally, adults as well as children, good readers as well as bad. The difference between a fluent reader and a poor one lies not in what his eyes do, but in the way his brain utilizes the information through the eyes. Of course, none of this information processing can be consciously observed. We are usually quite unaware of the interruptions or disruptions of visual information that constantly occur, for example when we blink or when our eyes leap suddenly from one part of the page or room to another. But then we do not see what is happening at the retina of the eye. Our perceptions are constructed by the brain.

THE RATE OF VISUAL INFORMATION PROCESSING   It is not difficult to gauge the rate at which the brain processes visual information. I shall describe a classic experiment demonstrating the limitations of the brain in identifying letters.[2] Imagine that you are a subject in an experimental laboratory seated facing a clear white screen on which an experimenter is about to flash a sequence of letters from a slide projector. The actual period for which the letters will appear on the screen is relatively unimportant as long as it is not much less than a hundredth of a second (which is about all the time the eye needs to register the information) and not more than a fifth of a second (so that the eye cannot move to a second fixation). In other words, the experimenter will restrict your brain to one input of visual information.

Imagine that the experimenter will flash on the screen a sequence of about twenty-five random letters, such as:

K Y B V O D U W G P J M S Q T X N O G M C T R S O

Your task as a subject is to report the letters you saw immediately after the brief presentation was over. You focus your eyes on a faint marker in the middle of the screen and flash—the presentation is over. What did you see? On the average you would be able to report just four or five letters from the middle of the sequence projected on the screen. Most probably you will have an immediate recollection of something like:

J M S Q T

Thus we have an indication of how many unrelated letters can be identified from a single fixation, about four or five. We also have evidence of how many unrelated letters can be identified in an entire second, because it took your brain a full second to process all the information that it required to come to its decision about the letters. If you had been required to make a report about a second presentation flashed on the screen less than a second after the first one had been completed, or if something else had distracted your attention within that time, then you would probably not have been able to report the full four or five letters.

You could participate in a similar experiment at home with letters typed on an index card placed face upwards, but covered by a sheet of cardboard, in front of you. For the test, ask a friend to remove the cover just long enough for you to get one glimpse of the card, then cover it again.

USING NONVISUAL INFORMATION   We shall do our imaginary experiment again, but this time the twenty-five letters will not be selected at random but arranged into five or six unrelated words. The display will look something like this:

READY   JUMP   WHEAT   POOR   BUT   SEEK

Once more you focus on the fixation point and there is the same brief flash. This time, on the average, you will not see four or five letters but a couple of words. You will see something like:

WHEAT   POOR

The problem now is to explain how it is that you see only four or five letters if the display is random, but nine or ten if the letters are organized into words. The same amount of visual information was available to the eyes on both occasions, and presumably the same amount of visual information processing was done, but twice as much was seen on the second occasion. How could that come about?

It is no answer to suggest that words were identified rather than letters; that is the problem to be explained. When confronted by words you are able to process visual information extending over twice the width you were able to see when the letters were unrelated, but with the same amount of visual information.

No one gets anything for nothing in the cognitive world, and if you were able to identify letters in the second experiment for half the visual price, it was because you got the rest of the information somewhere else. And since that additional information did not come through the eyes, it must have been nonvisual, a part of what you knew already about the way in which letters go together to form words in English. We can be more precise; since four or five letters' worth is as much visual information as the brain can handle in one fixation, it must have been employing an equivalent amount of nonvisual information to see ten letters' worth of words.

It may seem a little surprising that letters require different amounts of visual information to be identified on different occasions; our usual impression is that we either see something or we do not. You may also find it surprising that the brain can make such economical use of prior knowledge about the way letters are organized into words, knowledge of a kind that we almost certainly have not been taught. I shall say a little about these two phenomena before going on to explain how the brain can make a little bit of visual information go even further, provided sufficient nonvisual information is available.

USING MINIMAL VISUAL INFORMATION   It is surely rare that we have to have need for all the visual information that is available before we can recognize an object. We can usually identify something as a car or house or horse even if we glimpse only a part of it or if details are lost in the distance. Most lines of print are readable whether we look at only the top half or the bottom.

There is a simple psychological demonstration that letters of the alphabet can also be identified on the basis of partial information.[3] Letters are projected on a screen, one at a time, so that subjects must try to identify them on a minimum of visual information, either because the presentation is very fast—a few thousandths of a second—or because the contrast between the letters and the background is very low. A similar effect is obtained by covering printed letters with several layers of tissue paper or otherwise partially obliterating their detail.

The idea is to force subjects to make errors. It can then be seen that such errors are rarely based on a random or reckless decision. Rather the errors are highly predictable, which suggests that if a subject does not know exactly what a letter is, he has a good idea of what it is not. If he mistakes the letter *A*, for example, he is likely to say (and see) *H*, *K* or *R*, but rarely *L*, *O* or *T*. Lower case *a*, on the other hand, tends to be mistaken for *e*, *o* or *s* but not *h* or *r*. In other words, some letters look more alike than others, which of course is not surprising. The demonstration shows that different letters have elements in common. If a subject is not able to distinguish all the elements of a letter, he may make an identification based on the few that he is able to discriminate. The identification—and the perception, because the subject is usually quite convinced about what he saw even if he was wrong—is based on partial information.

I have been talking about the "elements" of letters and other objects or forms, and also about "partial information", but I shall prefer to use the term *distinctive features* that I have already introduced. In the previous chapter I suggested that for every category in cognitive structure there must be at least one set or "list" of distinctive features specifying how members of that category should be identified. Now I propose that it is frequently not necessary for all the distinctive features in a particular list to be identified; often we can identify a letter of the alphabet, or any other visual form, on the basis of a few features only, just as we may identify cars, houses or horses from a glimpse. The number of features that must be discriminated—that is, the amount of information required to make an identification—depends on the number of alternatives we think the object or form we are trying to identify might be. The amount of visual information processing required, in other words, is our uncertainty. To distinguish between just two alternatives, such as two letters, only one distinctive feature need be examined by the brain. One feature would suffice, for example, if we knew that a letter was either *A* or *B*, although a different feature would be required if we had to distinguish *A* from *C*.[4]

If more than two alternatives are possible, then more than one distinctive feature is required. However, the number of features that have to be examined increases at a much slower rate than the number of alternatives that can be distinguished. Two distinctive features will distinguish four alternatives: one that has both features (++); one that has neither (——); and two that have just one (+—) (—+). (More for reasons of convenience than knowledge, it is conventionally assumed that one letter has the distinctive feature and the other lacks it.) Every additional distinctive feature will double the number of alternatives that can be distinguished. Three features, for example, would suffice to distinguish among eight alternatives, four among sixteen, and five would be more than enough for the entire alphabet. Even if we take into account the alternative forms available for some letters of the alphabet, such as *A*, *a* and *a*, *B* and *b*, six distinctive features (sixty-four alternatives) would appear to be ample. Just as many thousands of written words can be put together from an alphabet of only twenty-six letters, so the twenty-six letters can be constructed from barely half a dozen distinctive features.[5]

An alternative way of looking at the situation is that a child learning to recognize the letters of the alphabet must include in his cognitive structure at least one feature list of at least six distinctive features for each letter. It is probable that each letter comprises more than six features that could be distinctive, since many letters can be identified with much of their structure erased or obliterated, and letters must be distinguished from digits and other written symbols. But in any case, six features is the maximum that need be discriminated if the problem is to decide which letter of the alphabet is being looked at. In the first imaginary experiment we conducted, for example, five or six distinctive features were presumably required for each letter, making a total of twenty-five or thirty features for the five or six letters you were able to distinguish in one fixation, in one second of information processing.

If I could now show that you were still processing only twenty-five or thirty features when you were able to identify a couple of words in the second experiment, then I would have a demonstration of how the trick of reading twice the number of letters with the same amount of visual information was accomplished. The same amount of visual information was getting you twice as far. But do you know enough about the way letters go together in words to reduce your uncertainty by half in advance? We must now look at how much nonvisual information we have about letters in the English language.

THE USE OF PRIOR KNOWLEDGE   As everyone knows, including the youngest child who can talk, some words occur far more often in the language than others. Letters also have a very unequal distribution. If you were asked to name the letter most frequently used in written English, you would probably reply *E*, or perhaps *T, A, O, I, N,* or *S,* which happen to be the seven most frequent letters, in that order. You can also probably guess the least frequent letters, *Z* and *X*. Our prior knowledge of these differences in the relative probability of letters in the English language is an example of nonvisual information that can greatly simplify the brain's information-processing burden in reading English words.

For example, if you had to guess the first letter of the twelfth line of the next left-hand page of this book you would be reckless to suggest *Z* or *X*. The letter *E* occurs forty times more often than the letter *Z*, so you would be forty times more likely to be correct if you guessed *E* rather than *Z*. Of course you would not be right every time, but on the average, or in the long run, your best bet would be one of the half-dozen letters that are the most frequent. You could profit from this prior knowledge if you were reading, because the elimination of unlikely letters in advance would reduce your uncertainty and leave you with less visual information to process in order to make a decision.

But we know far more about the English language than the overall unequal use of letters. I have been talking about your knowledge of letters when there is no clue about the other letters around them. However, letters do not occur independently of each other in English words. If you know what one letter is, then you know a good deal about the letter that follows.

For example, I have tried to show that you would probably make one of just a half-dozen guesses about what the first letter of a word was likely to be, and most of the time one of those half-dozen guesses would be correct. If I then told you that the first letter was *T*, you would almost certainly guess that the second letter would be *H, R, W, Y* or a vowel. You would not even consider more than half the letters of the alphabet. By the time we get halfway through most English words, there is scarcely any uncertainty left. Certainly we would never consider twenty-six alternatives for every letter, some would have no uncertainty for us at all, a few would have a lot, and the average number of alternatives would be about six.[6] You may recall that three distinctive features would be sufficient to distinguish among eight alternatives; therefore, it looks as if we might indeed be able to make visual information go twice as far for letters in words. At an average of just three distinctive features per letter, we could identify two five-letter words with the amount of visual information required to identify five letters that had nothing to do with each other.

PRIOR KNOWLEDGE AND MEANING   I must ask you to participate in my imaginary visual experiment for one last time. Once more the experimenter will briefly flash twenty-five letters or so on the screen, but this time they will be words organized into a meaningful sentence, such as:

KNIGHTS RODE HORSES INTO WAR

How much do you think you would be able to read of this presentation, given one hundredth of a second to look at it and a second to make up your mind? The answer, not surprisingly I hope, is that you would probably see it all. If the letters flashed on the screen are organized into a meaningful sequence of words, you will identify not four or five letters, but four or five words, a total of about twenty or twenty-five letters. The number of letters that you will see is quadrupled, but still with the same amount of visual information.

The earlier explanation of why letters in words are easier to identify than random letters was that prior knowledge reduces uncertainty in advance. It must now be shown whether there is additional prior knowledge we can use when the sequence of words is meaningful, when it has grammatical structure and sense, to reduce uncertainty even further. Is it possible to stretch the twenty-five to thirty feature information-processing limit for one fixation or for one second of reading across twenty to twenty-five letters?

For a start, it must be obvious that words themselves are highly predictable in the English language. An author cannot select words at random when he writes. If you are reading a passage, and making sense of what you read, then you know in advance a good deal about the grammatical function and the meaning of words that are to come. In fact, one word in five can be omitted from most passages of English text (or English speech) without making much difference to comprehensibility.[7] Try it with a copy of yesterday's newspaper. If I asked you to predict the next word before you turned every right hand page of this book, you might not expect a large number of absolutely correct guesses, but most of the time you would have a pretty good idea of what the next word was likely to be. Certainly you should not have to make a wild guess among the fifty-thousand or more words in your vocabulary. Instead your average uncertainty would probably be down among two or three hundred alternatives,[8] which is a very big difference, and completely attributable to prior knowledge about language and about the topic being discussed.

The amount of prior knowledge that we can bring to bear for written English is even more striking when considered from the point of view of letters. Every other letter can be eliminated from many passages without a marked reduction in comprehensibility. If I asked you to guess every successive letter of a passage in a book, always telling you if you were right or wrong, you might need quite a few guesses for some letters, especially at the beginning of words, but very few guesses about others. In the long run you would not make more than one or two wrong guesses on every letter. Your uncertainty would be so low that you would barely need an average of more than one distinctive feature for every letter.[9]

In short, the brain's limited ability to make sense of incoming visual information, which restricts it to five letters or less per second if the letters cannot be related to anything known already, can be extended to twenty letters or more if nonvisual information can be brought to bear. A little simple arithmetic will show that when we read at a normal rate of about two hundred and fifty words a minute (four or five words a second), the brain must be supplementing its limited quota of visual information with four times as much nonvisual information. And when you read faster, which is often the case although you may not realize it, even more nonvisual information is utilized to take the burden off your eyes. Speed readers do not read fast by reading one word in ten—try *that* with yesterday's newspaper

—or even one out of five. Instead they make do with a tenth of the visual information that is available in every word, and compensate for the rest with nonvisual information.[10]

TUNNEL VISION   The imaginary experiments that you have just experienced vicariously demonstrate that there is a limit to the amount of information we can get through the visual system, and that the very breadth and detail of the scene that we perceive depends not so much on the eye as on how much the brain can contribute from behind the eyeball.

Consider the experiment once more from an opposite point of view. When the letters flashed on the screen are arranged in a short sentence, we are able to see effectively across a range of about twenty-five letters. When the words have no grammatical or meaningful relation to each other, however, breadth of vision is restricted to barely half that width, and if the letters are not even organized into words, we can see no more than a few letters in the center of the display. The differences in angle of view are indicated in Figure 2.1.

The narrowest angle of view in Figure 2.1 occurs when the subject is not able to see more than two or three letters on either side of his fixation point, and is illustrative of a condition called *tunnel vision*.[11] A person afflicted with tunnel vision perceives the world as if he is peering through a narrow paper tube. Tunnel vision is not uncommon in the daily life of all of us, since it can occur whenever the brain is overloaded with information from the visual system. We may not be aware of this limitation, because the brain encourages us to *feel* that we see everything, but in fact we may detect very little. If you enter a crowded room, a single glance is usually sufficient to tell you roughly how many people are present. But if you are curious to see if there are more women than men, you may need two or three glances around the room; your effective angle of view narrows as you try to utilize more of the visual information in the scene. And, if you want to get even more specific information, for example, to ascertain whether most of the group are wearing spectacles, then you will go into a condition

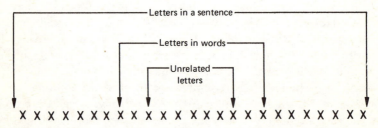

Figure 2.1   Effective angle of view for unrelated letters, letters in words, and letters in a sentence

of tunnel vision and make a large number of fixations around the room. In quite a different situation, the task of landing a modern airliner is so complex visually that one man alone cannot do it. It takes one tunnel-visioned crew member to look at the instruments, one to see that the plane gets on the runway and one to watch out for other aircraft.

And in yet another kind of situation, tunnel vision describes the condition of a reader, or a child learning to read, with relatively little nonvisual information to contribute to the task of interpreting print.

Any reader who is not able, or not permitted, to use nonvisual information to assist his brain with its burden of processing visual information from the eyes, may find that he has temporarily become functionally blind. Even adults may complain that a page of text is a blank, if they require too much visual information to comprehend it.

Nonvisual information in learning to read

It is generally assumed that a child who is just learning to read can see as well as a skilled reader, if only he looks hard enough. But a child lacking sufficient nonvisual information—unless he is helped to read with a minimum dependence on visual input—is inexorably and physiologically prevented from reading. Adults would not be able to read if they were shown only two or three letters at a time, and could not guess what the rest of the text was about. Yet this is precisely the situation in which young readers often find themselves.

Beginning readers are prime victims of tunnel vision because of the limited amount of nonvisual information they can supply, especially if the material they are confronted with is relatively nonsensical (which means unrelated to anything they already know) and when demands upon them for literal accuracy (emphasis on visual information) are high. Even advanced readers will be afflicted by tunnel vision if the material they are trying to read is too difficult for them to comprehend. A math book may be difficult to read simply because the student has an insufficient knowledge of math. And anxiety is a prime cause of overdependence on visual information and, therefore, tunnel vision.

Literal accuracy is something that few readers can achieve. Broadcasters and other professional speakers all deviate from their scripts from time to time although, because they are following the meaning, the words they insert or omit rarely offend the sense of what they read. A demand for literal accuracy on students at all levels may force them to believe that the marks on the page are all-important, that if they get the words right the meaning will take care of itself, or even that meaning is of secondary importance. But over-attention to the words, or to the letters of the words, will simply clog the visual system with visual noise, information that cannot be used.

To be able to read a child must be encouraged to predict, to use prior knowledge, or even have nonvisual information provided. It is not necessary to tell a child that he should use prior knowledge, he has been doing this all his life. The limitations of his visual system are not unfamiliar to him (implicitly, of course). One obvious way to offer nonvisual information to a young child is to familiarize him with a story before he reads it, perhaps even read it to him first. We should remember that the way he will eventually learn to read, if he is to become a fluent reader, is by making optimal use of everything he already knows, not by being profligate with the small amount of visual information his brain can handle.

Teachers may object that accuracy is important and that guessing should be discouraged. But accuracy will never be achieved if the reader ignores everything he knows already. Reliance on the purely visual leads to incomprehension, not accuracy. Of course, reckless guessing is not to be recommended, but that is likely to be the condition of the child who believes that he must identify every letter and word, even to the exclusion of making sense of what he reads. The child who predicts in the way in which I have been using the word, by eliminating unlikely alternatives in advance, by making use of meaning and everything he already knows about language, is the only one likely even to recognize foolish mistakes if they are made.[12]

Looked at from another point of view, readers have, or should have, three skilled routines for reading letters in isolation, for reading words, and for bringing meaning to words. The third routine is the best, even if word identification is all that is required, since it makes optimal use of nonvisual information.

Some hallowed classroom ideas must be turned upside down. While it is true that knowledge of letters may help a child to identify words, and knowledge of words facilitates reading sentences, nevertheless letters in words are easier to recognize, and learn, than letters in isolation, and words in sentences that make sense are easier to recognize than words in isolation. When we ask children to identify letters or words on flashcards, or written in isolation on the board, we are asking them to make the most difficult identification possible, because the number of alternatives (i.e., the children's uncertainty) is at a maximum. This is *not* the way children will have to identify words when they read them in text.

A child who cannot give a correct answer, especially in reading, may not be completely wrong, and it may not be necessary to spoonfeed him with an appropriate response. A child who says he does not recognize the letter *H*, or who confuses *H* with *K*, need not be absolutely ignorant about *H*. Perhaps he knows enough distinctive features to distinguish *H* from a dozen other letters, although *K* is not one of them. Being told he is wrong may force him to throw out what he does know and start again, or to give up in despair. A probing teacher will try to find out what a child does know, and build upon that. A child may not be able to read a particular word on a flashcard, but may have no trouble with it in a sentence, or if he is given a clue. Judicious prompts do not tell the child what the word is, nor do they encourage him to guess wildly; they merely offer an opportunity to eliminate unlikely alternatives and free the visual system of information overload. No word is readable, and no text is comprehensible, if it is looked at with tunnel vision.

Limitations to hearing

I do not want to recapitulate a lengthy exposition, but the point must be made that everything that has been said about vision applies to hearing as well. The brain is just as limited in the acoustic information that it can process from the ears as it is with visual information from the eyes. The brain cannot make sense of what is said just by listening. Acoustic information must be supplemented and interpreted with the aid of what I was about to call nonacoustic information, which, of course, is the same as nonvisual information, our prior knowledge of the world, of language, and of the context in which the particular communication to which we are attending is produced.

The sounds of spoken language are constructed out of acoustic distinctive features just as there are visual distinctive features for writing.[13] And the number of acoustic distinctive features that the brain must process to comprehend speech is directly related to the amount of prior uncertainty.[14] The more you already know, the less closely you have to listen, but the more you will hear. There have even been auditory experiments comparable to the "brief exposure" visual experiment that I reconstructed. Isolated syllables, whole words, and words in meaningful sentences can be recorded against a background of random sounds, literally embedded in noise.[15] As you would now expect, far more can be heard when the message has a meaning, even though it may be enmeshed in a babble of a dozen other voices.

Thus there is an auditory analogy to tunnel vision. If we have trouble in making ourselves understood, then a listener will have difficulty hearing what we say. He needs more acoustic information. Therein lies a possible explanation for the tendency to raise our voices when we are talking to a foreigner, or to a child who fails to comprehend our language. It may not be lack of goodwill that causes the well-known phenomenon of the child who is deaf in class but who can hear perfectly well outside.

Taking Chances with Perception

Every decision made by the brain to perceive or comprehend something in the world requires the processing of information, and there is a limit to how much information can be processed at any one time. I now want to show that the amount of information an individual processes before making such cognitive decisions is partly determined by the individual himself. Perception, and the effort to comprehend, is an inherently risky business; there is always a possibility of error. But because he can choose how much information to seek before making a decision, the individual can to some extent determine how much of a risk of being wrong he will accept.

A useful term for the degree of assurance an individual requires before he will come to a decision may be termed his *criterion*. If the amount of information about a particular letter, word or meaning reaches a reader's criterion for making a decision, then he will make a choice at that point, whether or not he will make the decision correctly. Individuals vary in the criterion level they prefer, ranging on particular occasions from a supercautious demand for almost absolute certainty to a reckless eagerness to decide on mere scraps of evidence. To understand why a particular criterion level is established, we must consider the effect of setting the criterion high or low.

Signal detection theory

The concept of a criterion in decision-making comes from a relatively new area of study called *signal detection theory*,[16] which has overturned several venerable ideas about human perception. It is traditional to think, for example, that either one sees an object or one does not, and that there is no area of freedom between within which the observer can decide whether or not the object is present. Signal detection theory, however, shows that in many circumstances the question of whether an object is perceived depends less on the actual visibility of the object than on the attitude of the observer. It is also conventional to think that there is a simple relationship between correct responses and errors, that the more often you want to be right, the less often you will be wrong. But in fact, the more often you want to be right, the more often you must tolerate being wrong. The paradox can be explained with a little more detail of what the theory is all about.

Signal detection theory was originally concerned with the literal detection of signals, with the ability of radar operators to distinguish between the "signals" and "noise" on their radar screens in order to identify aircraft presumed to be hostile. As far as the actual situation is concerned, there are only two possibilities: a particular blip on the screen is either a signal or noise; an enemy aircraft is present or it is not. The operator must decide.

If he decides that the blip is a signal, and there is in fact an enemy aircraft in the area, then he has made a hit. If he decides that the blip is just noise, and there is in fact no aircraft present, he has also made a correct decision. However, there are two less desirable possibilities that must both be considered errors. The first error occurs when no aircraft is present but the operator decides that there is, a contingency that may be called *false alarm*. And the other error occurs when there is an aircraft present but the operator decides there is not, a contingency that can be termed *miss*.

The problem for the operator is that the number of hits, false alarms, and misses are not independent; he cannot change the probability of one without changing the probability of another. For example, if the operator is anxious to avoid false alarms, and wants to get maximum information before he decides to report an aircraft, then he will have more misses. More hostile planes will get through. If, on the other hand, he desires to maximize the number of hits, reducing the possibility of a miss by lowering his criterion, then he will produce more false alarms.

Of course, with increased skills of discrimination, the radar operator can step up his level of efficiency and increase the ratio of hits to false alarms, just as any increase in the clarity of the situation will make the task easier. But in any given situation the choice is always the same between maximizing hits and minimizing false alarms. Always the observer has to make the choice, to decide where he will set his criterion for distinguishing signal from noise, friend from foe, or *A* from *B*. The higher the criterion and thus the more information required before making a decision, the fewer will be the false alarms, but the fewer also will be the hits, while misses will increase. There will be more hits if the criterion is set lower, if decisions are made on less information, but there will also be more false alarms.

What determines where the observer will set his criterion? The answer lies in the relative costs and rewards that he perceives to be attached to hits, misses and false alarms. If the radar operator thinks he will be heavily penalized for false alarms, then he will set his criterion high, risking an occasional missed identification. If he is highly motivated to get hits, then he will set his criterion low and ignore the false alarms.

THE STUDENT'S DILEMMA   The problem is general. A skilled reader cannot afford to set his criterion too high because if he demands too much visual information, he may be unable to get it fast enough to overcome information-processing limitations and to read for sense. Readiness to take chances, by eliminating unlikely alternatives in advance, is critical for beginning readers; however, they may feel they pay too high a price for "errors", and inhibit their use of nonvisual information. The child who stays silent in class, who "misses" rather than risk a "false alarm" with an incorrect response, may please his teacher but develop the habit of setting his criterion too high for comprehension or learning. Anxiety to avoid error may reduce the likelihood of being right.

There is only one circumstance that permits a child to establish realistic criteria for reading, or for any other aspect of making sense of events in his life, and that is the experience of actually making sense with a minimum of incoming information. Teachers cannot set a child's criterion level for him, but they may persuade him to set it too high or too low through the way they distribute rewards or "charge" for mistakes. They may force him into tunnel vision, and thus ensure that his comprehension will be minimal. No one can make sense of everything in the world around him—or on the page in front of him—unless he reduces as much uncertainty as possible in advance. The brain is limited in how much new information it can make sense of, but it also has a powerful way of overcoming that limitation, by making optimal use of what it already knows.

Bottlenecks of Memory

An obvious disadvantage of tunnel vision (or, as this applies to hearing, the inability to hear more than fragments of what is said) is that it is difficult to make sense of anything if you cannot grasp the whole. A reader with tunnel vision must try to keep in mind a handful of letters, perhaps a few parts of words, while his brain is busy interpreting the next fixation. But the limited rate at which incoming information can be processed is only one of the handicaps confronting the brain in its efforts to make sense of the world. There are also severe limits to how much new and unrelated information we can hold in our minds, while we decide what to do with it. And there is also a limit to how much can be stored away for future use at any one time. There are bottlenecks in memory.

Defining "memory"

Like many words with a high frequency of use in psychology and education, "memory" can be employed in a variety of ways, some rather more metaphorical than others. Sometimes the word seems to specify a *place* in which information is stored, such as when we admit that our memory may be cluttered. At other times the word tends to denote the *content* of such a store, for example when we say we have a happy memory of an event. And if we claim to have a good memory or a poor one, we appear to be using the word to refer to a *process*.

Certainly memory is not a place in the sense that it is a particular location in the brain; rather our memories seem to be distributed across large areas of the brain and always to involve many more than one specific part of the brain at a time.[17] And the particular memories that come into our conscious mind should more appropriately be considered as the products of memory processes rather than contents from a store; our recollections seem often to be reconstructions by the brain based on current knowledge and expectations rather than a literal recall or revival of events.[18] Such remembering seems basically little different from perception, with the brain making decisions based on limited information but generating a subjective experience of a complete and meaningful whole. The notion that memory is a process at least acknowledges its dynamic characteristics, although as a definition it fails to do justice to the multifaceted richness and complexity of the entire phenomenon.

I think there is no choice but to regard memory as a complex *system* concerned with nothing less than the selection, acquisition, retention, organization, retrieval, reconstruction and utilization of all our knowledge and beliefs about the world, including our past experience. All of these "processes" or "operations" constitute a single, coherent, interactive system, and that system *is* memory. There is nothing more. Memory is not something that does all these things, nor is it the place where they are done, nor is it the elements to which they are done. And when the word "memory" is employed in our everyday language, it can refer to any aspect of this complex system for selecting, acquiring, retaining and so forth.

The "contents" of memory, the objects of all these operations, are indistinguishable from cognitive structure, while the operations themselves are performed on cognitive structure; these are cognitive skills. It is no more possible to distinguish our "memories" from our knowledge of the world than we can distinguish "memorization" from learning.

The fact that we can ask quite meaningful questions like "Isn't learning something more than memorization?" or "Why can't you remember everything you've learned?" demonstrates that words like "memory", "memorization", "remembering", and even "learning", can be used to denote many different aspects of the system, but not that the system as a whole can be broken down into separate parts. Because memory (as a system) can be looked at from many points of view, at different times and in different circumstances, it may appear to have quite different characteristics. Some memories seem to stay with us for most of our lives, for example, while others we are unable to retain for more than a few seconds. Some aspects of memory seem vulnerable to the sudden disruption of ongoing brain activity, such as a head injury, electric shock treatment for psychiatric conditions, or even when our attention is allowed to wander. But other aspects of memory seem to be much more stable: I may have forgotten where I left my shoes last night, but I have not forgotten how to tie them.

Three aspects of memory[19]

Such differences are easier to comprehend if we consider the theoretical distinctions between *short-term memory*, which serves as a working memory for transient information that we want to remember only briefly, and *long-term memory*, which is the relatively permanent accumulation of all our knowledge and beliefs about ourselves and the world. A third aspect of memory has already been introduced in this chapter—the persistence of incoming information for about a second while the brain makes its perceptual decisions; this is sometimes referred to as the *sensory store*.

These three aspects of memory should not be considered as separate locations or "stores" within the brain, despite the way they are labelled. Certainly it is very difficult at times to distinguish short- and long-term memory, and all three are closely interrelated. It would also be misleading to regard the three aspects as different stages in a process of memorization, although diagrams in some psychology texts suggest that information comes into the brain through sensory store, and passes through short-term memory on its way to long-term memory. But, as we shall see, the content of short-term memory seems more often to come from long-term memory than from the outside world, and long-term memory certainly determines what we extract from sensory store.

In other words, it is probably better to consider the three aspects of memory I am about to discuss as different "operating characteristics" of a single memory system, as the way memory looks if its operation is analyzed at different intervals after an event—after a few seconds, a few minutes, or after hours, days or years. All this should become clearer as we examine each of the three aspects in turn.

SENSORY STORE   That there is some kind of holding area or holding stage in the head for new information about the outside world is an obvious theoretical necessity. In the imaginary letter and word identification experiment that I conducted earlier in this chapter, there was no necessity for the visual information to remain on the screen longer than a few thousandths of a second, although the observer's brain would labor over "processing" the information for about a second, and could have labored a good deal longer to make sense of everything on the screen. Since the "visual" information was not on the screen during most of this processing period, it must have gone somewhere behind the eyeball until it eventually disappeared or "decayed". Sensory store is one of several rather misleading terms psychologists have invented for what is obviously ongoing neural activity. Experiments can be conducted to see how long this activity will persist, and the answer is about a second, two seconds at the most. After that, the observer requires another exposure, another glimpse or fixation to recharge his sensory store.[20]

A person who is staring is not so much looking as thinking about what he has seen.

All our perceptual systems seem to have some way of maintaining a representation of new experience for a brief period after the original event. When the visual system is involved, the sensory store is sometimes called a *visual image*, a term that I think is particularly misleading because it suggests there might be another eye in the head looking at internalized pictures. (In general, it is better to regard *all* the images we may feel we can conjure up in our heads as the *result* of cognitive activity, not its basis.) Besides, the contents of the visual sensory store are not something we are aware of until we have processed the information it contains, and we can in fact be selective about the information we shall process before it disappears. In our imaginary experiments I could have instructed you to say what you saw in the left, center or right of the random-letter display immediately *after* the letters had been represented, and the four or five letters that you saw would have been in these particular parts. Of the rest you would have seen nothing, or just the broadest details. However, this would not have been because you were *looking* at different parts of an internal image, but because you were *constructing* different parts of one.

The acoustic aspect of sensory storage, incidentally, is sometimes given the rather graphic label of *echo box*. Acoustic sensory storage helps to account for the fact that we often do not realize what someone has said until several moments after he has said it, when we may hear it being said in some kind of auditory retrospect. The raw acoustic information must have stayed around in our heads for a while, even though we did not immediately interpret it, and therefore did not hear it as something meaningful.

Important though the concept of sensory storage may be from the point of view of experimental psychology, it raises few issues that are of practical concern in school. We do not usually present children with information for only a few thousandths of a second, and children normally change their fixation point four or five times a second, unless they happen to be bored, thinking or asleep. There is nothing we can do or need do to extend the persistence of the visual image, nor can we train anyone to process the visual or acoustic information faster, although we can help by making it more meaningful so that it goes further. Having introduced sensory storage as an act of theoretical good manners, I can move on to matters that should make a considerable difference to our expectation of how children will learn the relative strengths and limitations of short-term and long-term memory.

SHORT-TERM MEMORY   Some information we can put into our heads practically on demand and retain for a relatively short period. If we are sorting our small change in a store, for example, we usually do not have to write down the amount we are trying to make. We can usually remember where we are going while we are trying to get there. Much of the information necessary for the everyday task in hand can usually be held in a "working memory" that we do not want to keep. But there are limits to how much we can put into this working or short-term memory, which is very easily overloaded.

The capacity of short-term memory is very limited indeed. Six or seven digits, for example, would appear to be as much as we can hold in our head at any one time.[21] It is almost as if a benign providence provided us with sufficient short-term memory capacity to hold a telephone number, and then failed to predict direct dialing and area codes. Most of us can retain an unfamiliar seven digit number in our heads as we walk to the telephone to dial it, provided no one asks us what time it is on the way.

If we try to put more into short-term memory than it can accommodate, something has to come out. It is rather like pouring liquid into a glass that is already filled; the amount you try to put in above its capacity will overflow. And in the case of short-term memory there are only two possible fates for information that does not get in, or that overflows—either it must go into long-term memory or it is lost altogether.

In fact, information is lost from short-term memory almost as soon as it goes in, unless we make an effort to "rehearse" it, for example, by repeating the telephone number over and over to ourselves. Short-term memory, in other words, persists as long as we pay attention to what we have in it. As soon as our attention is distracted, then its contents are erased. Indeed, there are reasonable grounds for asserting that what is often called "attention" and short-term memory are the same.

The other two characteristics of short-term memory to be considered are wholly in its favor. The first is that information in short-term memory is immediately available. If the telephone number we want is in short-term memory, we can dial it straight away. There is no need to wait for information in short-term memory to come to mind; in fact, unless we can remember it at once, we have probably forgotten it for good. The second advantage is that information goes into short-term memory practically instantaneously. A name or figure must be rehearsed to keep it in short-term memory, but not to get it there in the first place.

The obvious practical implication of all these characteristics of short-term memory is that it should not be overwhelmed. Short-term memory can be loaded and unloaded with speed and facility, but it can also be very easily swamped. Anything that tends to cause information to be delivered to the brain in unrelated fragments—for example tunnel vision—is likely to overload short-term memory, and once this state of affairs is reached it is unlikely that any permanent learning will take place.

Because the limitations of short-term memory are under review, it would seem only proper to provide a convenient summary. Figure 2.2 encapsu-

	Short-term memory (working memory)	Long-term memory (permanent memory)
Capacity	limited	practically unlimited
Persistence	very brief	practically unlimited
Access	immediate	depends on organization
Input	very fast	relatively slow

Figure 2.2   Characteristics of short-term and long-term memory

lates the four points I have made, and also provides a comparison with long-term memory.

LONG-TERM MEMORY   At first glance our permanent or long-term memory would appear to be wholly superior to that of short-term memory—the capacity of long-term memory seems unlimited and its duration essentially indefinite. Long-term memory frequently surprises us by the sudden revelation of some fragment of its content. For example, the stainless steel probes of surgeons may elicit recollections of long lost childhood from patients in brain surgery. Brain surgeons like to have a conscious patient, and since the brain has no sensations of its own such surgery is possible with only a local anaesthetic. Equally likely to revivify old associations are the verbal probes of psychoanalysts, who ask the right kind of stimulating questions when their clients are in the right kind of responsive mood. There are also less expensive examples of effective probes. Little reminders that jog the memory like "You remember her—she wears square glasses", or "I think the name began with *K*" may spark the recovery of something we think we have forgotten for good.

We are usually unaware of the extensive capacity and persistence of long-term memory because of the difficulty we have in getting information out. "Access" is by no means as automatic with long-term memory as with short-term. The ease with which we can retrieve from long-term memory seems to depend upon the extent to which the information we seek is integrated with everything else we know. Unlike short-term memory, long-term memory does not hold itself open for our continual inspection. To retrieve something from long-term memory, we must find a route to it.

Another reason that we are usually unaware of the tremendous capacity of long-term memory is the severe limit on how fast we can get information in. While the limited amount of information that we can hold in short-term memory is established practically instantaneously, information cannot be accommodated in long-term memory faster than one thing every four or five seconds.[22] The seven-digit telephone number that just exceeds the capacity of short-term memory takes about half a minute to commit to permanent memory.

This ultimate limitation on the efficiency of long-term memory is so critical that I shall reiterate it at once together with the limitation of short-term memory with which it should be jointly considered. The capacity of short-term memory is restricted to about a half dozen items and if this capacity is exceeded information from short-term memory must either go into long-term memory or be permanently lost. *But only one item can get from short-term to long-term memory every five seconds.*

Once again, consider these limitations from the point of view of a beginning reader handicapped by tunnel vision. What good is it to see only fragments of words and individual letters if only one letter can be retained every five seconds? If all a child can perceive at one time is four or five letters, or even a couple of unrelated words, what chance is there that he will be able to make sense of them when they represent unassimilated nonsense in short-term memory and serve only to clog entry into long-term memory?

The combined limitations of short-term and long-term memory and of tunnel vision can be critical in reading. For example, it is probably impossible to read with comprehension at slower than 200 words a minute—the units we are trying to get into short-term and long-term memory will be too small to be of any use.[23] Similarly it is impossible to read for meaning if we stop to read every individual word; short-term memory will soon overflow with a meaningless clutter of disconnected words and bits of words, and it would be most impractical to try to cram such "information" into long-term memory. To read with comprehension we must use visual information parsimoniously and memorize economically; we cannot read sentences as if they were sequences of unrelated words. In fluent reading, individual words come last rather than first.

Overcoming limitations of memory

It may have been noted that I have used rather colloquial and ill-defined terms in the discussion of memory. For example, I said that short-term memory can hold five or six "items", and that it takes about five seconds to get "something" into long-term memory. What are these "things"?

The answer depends on the extent to which the brain can organize incoming information into larger units. Or more precisely, it depends on the implicit "questions" that the brain is asking, the level at which it is processing information. If a reader is looking for individual letters on a page, then it is individual letters that go into short-term memory and one individual letter that he must try to put into long-term memory every five seconds. A reader operating at the level of words can hold up to half a dozen words in short-term memory at one time, and put one entire word rather than a single letter into long-term memory once every five seconds. This process of making larger units out of smaller ones is sometimes referred to as *chunking*.[24] It obviously would be difficult to remember the sequence of digits 71421283542495663707784 for either a short or long period unless once noticed that they are multiples of seven up to 84—7, 14, 21, 28 and so forth.

Finally, a reader looking for meaning is able to put into short-term and long-term memory units of information that are not as easy to specify as letters or words, but which are clearly at a much higher level of chunking or integration. Meaning lies beyond words, and it is not possible to indicate with examples of language how a single meaning can be a condensation of several words. But it is obvious that the meaning of a twenty or thirty word sentence can be held in short-term memory, even though the actual words of the sentence are lost, because we can usually repeat its "gist" or say whether it paraphrases or contradicts another sentence.

In other words, the "size" of the units that can be accommodated by short-term and long-term memory depends on the prior knowledge of the reader or listener, the kind of cognitive question he is asking. If his questions are at the fragmentary, particulate, fine-detail level, then memory will be grossly overburdened. The more an individual is able to make sense of a situation in advance, the less the processes of perception and learning are likely to overload memory.

This matter of the level at which new information can be organized in advance is also the cue to getting it out of long-term memory again. The better we can integrate new information with what we already know, the easier it will be to recover. New information that is essentially meaningless, or that is contrary to our more cherished beliefs about the world, is the hardest to get into and out of long-term memory.

There is evidence that organization and memorization are in fact the same process. Anything we attempt to organize, by bringing some existing knowledge to bear, in effect becomes part of that existing knowledge. In one experimental study[25] three groups of people were asked to inspect a set of 52 cards, each of which had a word written on it. One group was told that they would later be asked to recall as many of the words as they could; the second group was asked to look at the cards and sort them into as many piles (or "categories") as they liked; and the third group was asked both to categorize and recall. After each group had examined the cards for the same period of time, however, they were all given exactly the same task— to recall as many of the cards as they could. In the test the second and third groups did equally well; the instruction simply to categorize took care of memorization, and the additional instruction to organize *and* remember made no difference at all. On the other hand the group told simply to re-member performed worse than either of the other groups. The key to better recall lay not in telling people to remember, but in telling them to organize, to try to relate in some way what they were doing to what they knew already.

The implications for classroom practice are so important, yet so self-evident, that I think I can do no better than to paraphrase the previous sentence: The key to better recall lies not in insisting that the learner memorize, but in ensuring that he can make some sense of what he is doing.

THE RELATION OF SHORT-TERM AND LONG-TERM MEMORY   Perhaps it is clearer now why I proposed at the beginning of this section that short-term and long-term memory should not be considered as distinct and separate memories, and that the three aspects of memory were not "stages" in the development of a memory. Whether we put letters, words or meanings into short-term memory when we read depends on our uncertainty—on the cognitive questions we are asking—and our uncertainty is determined by prior knowledge and expectations that must come out of long-term memory. In fact, short-term memory might in some respects be regarded as a kind of spotlight, or battery of a half-dozen spotlights, focussing upon particular categories within long-term memory. If we are trying to identify words, then we attempt to relate incoming information to word categories in long-term memory. If we are trying merely to identify letters, then it is the letter aspect of cognitive structure on which we focus. It is in these respects that short-term memory is difficult to distinguish from what is often called attention. If we are attending to words, then words are what we see and keep in mind; if we are attending to letters, then our perceptions and immediate recollections are of letters.

Sometimes short-term memory, or our attention span, can be filled with information that comes directly from long-term memory, without any input from external sources at all. For example, we fill short-term memory with items from prior knowledge when we rehearse a shopping list or plan a nonhabitual sequence of activities that might be forgotten the moment they are released from attention—mailing a letter, delivering a package or buying a copy of a new magazine while on the way to school.

But even when we are primarily concerned with putting into short-term memory information derived from the outside world, from sensory store, it is not distinctive features that go into short-term memory but cognitive decisions about the letters, words or meanings that we are looking at. The brain does not process information in sensory store indiscriminately, otherwise our perceptions of written language would always be at the five-letter tunnel vision or worse. Instead the brain samples, or *selects*, just the incoming information that it requires to decide among the alternatives it is considering. If we identify letters rather than words, or words rather than meanings, it is not because letters or words are all we can see or put into short-term memory, but because they represent the level at which we are getting our cognitive questions answered. The most effective form of chunking to overcome the limitations of memory is done before we try to perceive the world or interpret experience, not after.

The structure of memory

How is long-term memory organized? In what form is new information about the world represented? Both "long-term memory" and "cognitive structure" are labels for the totality of our knowledge of the world, or rather the accumulation of the decisions that we have made about the nature of the world, including our own place in it. In the previous chapter I conceptualized cognitive structure as a system of interrelated categories that constitute the basis both of our perception of the outside world and of the ideas, images and fantasies that we can create within the mind. The system must also include specifications of distinctive features that enable the world outside the mind and the cognitive world in the head to be related.

But the discussion of memory raises more specific questions about the way in which categories of experience and their interrelations are represented in cognitive structure. For example, developmental psychologists are generally agreed that an infant's first items of knowledge about the world are laid down in his mind in the form of his own actions and their consequences. What a child knows about drinking from a cup or about the effect of banging one block against another is embedded in a memory of his behavior of drinking from a cup or banging blocks. An infant starts to make sense of the world by acting upon the world, and he can remember these acts by repeating them, overtly or in his mind. Piaget refers to this kind of knowledge as "sensorimotor", a combination of acts and feelings about acts, and has called such "interiorized" sequences of acts *schemes*. He argues that it is these first "schemes" of interiorized or mental activity that form the original basis of thought.[26] There is a similar idea behind the suggestion I have already made that the aspects of "thinking" that appear to take place wholly within the head, independently of any external event, should be regarded as "vicarious experience".

Remembering events in terms of what we had to do to bring these events about, or to avoid their consequences, may be the first kind of memory to manifest itself, but it should by no means be disparaged as "childish" since it persists throughout our lives. In many circumstances, memory of specific acts may be by far the most efficient. A variety of skills from tying shoelaces to open-heart surgery depend for their effectiveness on knowledge that seems to be laid down more in the muscles than the mind (or in the mental "routines" that orchestrate muscular activity). These routines are difficult to describe, and no description will guarantee adequate performance. When it comes to having to *do* something, there is no substitute for knowing *how* to do it, for a memory that is in the form of action.

However, other modes of representing knowledge in the mind rapidly develop. Our most vivid memories often seem to be perceptual, in the sense that we can re-create our experience of an object or event in precisely the way that we perceived it originally. Perceptual memories of a visual kind often seem to be particularly powerful and useful. For example, you will probably refer to a visual representation if I ask you how the dials and gauges are organized on the instrument panel of your car. In order to answer this question you somehow must conjure up an image of the interior of your car.

The apparent ability of some individuals to provide themselves with particularly graphic and detailed mental images of past events is sometimes known as "photographic memory". This capacity to conjure up a scene, at least for a short while after the event, is by no means as rare as one might imagine, especially among young children. In fact it looks as if large numbers of young children, possibly all of them, are able to do this early in their lives.[27] Like their innocence, the ability disappears as children grow older. And like innocence, photographic recall may well disappear because it is not particularly adaptive for the world in which we live. "Total recall"of past events in any form is by no means advantageous.[28] Normally we do not want to recall everything that happened to us in the past, nor every detail about particular events, but just those important aspects that are likely to be relevant to our reason for wanting to recall the event at all. You will remember that the first function of the cognitive theory of the world in the head is to summarize past experience. Total recall is not a summary; very little of it can be informative, and the rest will be noise. Total recall or photographic memory suggest that information was not properly processed at the time of the original experience, so that the brain must start working on it now. The advantage of reducing experience to a more condensed form is not simply that it is easier to get into memory, but also that it is easier to get out again and it is more immediately useful when recalled.

I do not particularly like the term "image" for the kind of perceptual memory that I have just described, although it is well established in cognitive psychology.[29] It is misleading to suggest that recall can be in the form of a "picture" that is looked at by some inner eye (just as the term "visual image" that we earlier met as a synonym for sensory store should not be taken literally). There is nowhere inside the head for pictures to be displayed and there is no internal eye to look at them. The images that we seem able to conjure up of earlier events are the product of memory, not its basis. The same underlying constructive process would appear to be involved, whether we are perceiving an event, remembering the event, or imagining it. If we can see this morning's breakfast in our mind's eye, it is probably because we are replaying in our brains some of the process by which we perceived breakfast this morning.

The word "image" is also deceptive because we might forget that perceptual memories are not necessarily visual. But of course we can remember how our breakfast tasted, smelled, sounded and felt, as well as how it looked. We can in fact remember, or imagine, in any way that we can perceive. Our emotional reactions to an event also seem to claim part of its representation in memory. We not only remember the smell of the dentist's surgery, we recall and even reexperience the sinking feeling in the stomach. Sometimes it seems that the emotional reaction is all that remains to us of a particularly significant event; the reason we had such a reaction is forgotten. Therapists of a variety of theoretical persuasions are avidly sought by individuals who cannot forget that they fear (or love) snakes, heights, examinations, telephones, their parents, certain street corners or sundry articles of clothing for reasons that completely escape their awareness.

There is a third and final kind of memory representation to be mentioned, one to which great store is attached in school. I refer to knowledge that is *symbolic*, which usually means knowledge that is represented in our minds in the form of language. Examples are the "facts" that Paris is the capital of France and that the square on the hypotenuse equals the summed squares of the other two sides. Knowledge may be represented symbolically in other ways than through language—for example, in diagrams, formulae and even ritual. But knowledge that a child has acquired and can reproduce in verbal form is obviously a central consideration in school, where so many of our tests concern a child's ability to retrieve "facts".

THE INDEPENDENCE OF MEMORIES   The manner in which knowledge is represented in memory does not necessarily reflect the form in which the knowledge was originally presented to us, or of the original event. Our recollection of a visual experience is not necessarily visual, any more than our memory of something that was told to us need be in the form of language. People, including children, frequently translate pictorial information into words; when they examine a picture or scene they put a verbal description of it into memory. If asked later what they saw, they may recall specific details, such as a lighthouse and a couple of jetties, and perhaps four or five fishing boats at rest, but they will not be able to say on which jetty the lighthouse stood and whether the boats had sails.

On the other hand, many psychological experiments have demonstrated that for many people the process of understanding sentences involves translation into visual form. Ask someone to listen to a sequence of sentences like "The rock was at the top of the hill", "There was a house in the valley", and "The rock rolled down and demolished the house", and he will often be quite ready to assert later that he *heard* such sentences as "The house was smashed" or even "A large stone rolled from the top of the hill and hit a building at the bottom". These sentences are quite different from the ones he actually heard but agree with the mental "image" he created. On the other hand he will probably deny having heard anything like "The house was at the top of the hill"—a sentence very similar to one he actually heard but contrary to the picture he has constructed. Sentences that do not lend themselves to such visual representations are usually harder to remember.[30]

Furthermore, it is quite impossible to provide any kind of general rule about which form of knowledge representation is best. Everything depends ultimately on the purpose for which the knowledge will be required, the way in which the memory is to be used. If you want a lot of very general information (for example, to paint a picture, construct an object, or repair a piece of machinery), it is advantageous to have a visual representation in your mind as well as a verbal description. The visual representation may be able to provide you with much of the specific description that you need. On the other hand, if you want to remember particular items of information, such as the quickest route from one part of town to another or the measurement of an object, then a verbal description is likely to prove more useful.

A verbal description can contain much more information than a picture (or a visual image). If I ask you to go to the staff room to pick up a brown coffee cup with a broken handle that I left there, I not only tell you something about my coffee cup but a lot about the staff room. You know, for example, that there will be other coffee cups there, otherwise I would not have described mine. And you know there will probably be other brown ones, otherwise I would not have mentioned the broken handle. But you know there is not another brown one with a broken handle, otherwise I would have mentioned some other characteristic of mine. If I had just shown you a picture of my coffee cup, however, you would have known nothing about the other coffee cups in the staff room and would have had to carry more information in your head, much of it irrelevant. On the other hand it is not altogether false that one picture can be worth a thousand words, especially if it represents something that is difficult to describe uniquely, such as a human face.

Frequently all three forms of knowledge representation in the brain complement each other, just as instruction may be incomplete without all three. If you want to become proficient at sailing a boat, it will be helpful to have a "muscle memory" of the feel of the craft in various situations, images of how to move around the boat adjusting various pieces of gear and "rules" or verbal descriptions concerning specific procedures. As I have already pointed out, retrieval of knowledge from long-term memory is by no means as automatic and immediate as our access to short-term memory. We get to our long-term memories through *organization*. The more complex and integrated the network of interrelations in which a particular memory is embedded, the more likely we are to retrieve that memory when we need it. Our recollection of the location of the lighthouse, missing from the visual representation, may be triggered by the mental reconstruction of a walk along one of the jetties or the verbal memory that it was to the south of the harbor. We may recall the name of the painter of *Guernica* through our remembrance of how the painting looks.

Finally, individuals have preference about how they represent their knowledge of the world or their memories of events. One person will remember the sights of a vacation, another the food, a third the music and a fourth the fragrances. These differences are not necessarily a simple matter of interest; some people find it easier to recall events through imagery, others prefer verbally represented knowledge. Such preferences can probably be attributed to past experience, but it would be difficult to deny that none of them are innate, and from a practical point of view there is not much point in arguing about it. From another point of view, our preferences for representing knowledge should be determined by what is most useful to us, and what is most useful depends on circumstances. To illustrate some of these points, we can turn our attention directly to children.

Children and memory

It is common knowledge that younger children have poorer memories than older children; there are even items on intelligence tests to prove it. While adults on the average can recall a series of seven digits read aloud to them, each of which fills one of the seven "slots" of short-term memory, a child of nine or ten scores an average of only six on such a test and a child of four or five achieves only four.[31] It looks as if the short-term memory capacity of a child arriving at school may be barely half that of a twelve-year-old. There is, however, an alternative point of view, which suggests that the younger child might not have been tested fairly. Suppose he is being evaluated on the basis of a test that is incompatible with either his preferences or his experiences, and that his short-term memory is in fact as good as that of adults.

It might seem surprising that such an alternative has only recently been considered.[32] After all, children are not usually born with fewer pieces of vital equipment than adults; they have the same number of arms and legs, ears and eyes, even if a certain amount of experience is required for the development of strength and skill. Why should they have only half the capacity of short-term memory? Besides, children seem able to remember things that they want to remember very well, although obviously the younger ones are more distractable. At the rate short-term memory capacity seems to decrease, one might expect that a two-year-old would have none at all. Yet a child of that age is making tremendous progress in learning to comprehend the world, including making sense of language. Surely this could not occur without the benefit of an effective memory.

Think again of the test used to measure a young child's memory. It was a *symbolic* test, in which the child was asked to remember a sequence of digits. Despite the telephone is this the kind of task in which a child of five or six would be very experienced? Would he see very much sense in it? You might argue that digits are digits, and if a child's short-term memory were as extensive as an adult's, he ought to be able to pack the same number of items into it. If he has seven "locations" in short-term memory, shouldn't seven digits go in? But there are many reasons why one digit might occupy more than one location in memory. Perhaps a young child will try to remember the digits as meaningless sounds (they probably do not make very much more sense to him than that), so that "one" and "six" and "nine" will consist of three or four sounds each and "seven" consist of five. Even if each digit does occupy only one location, an anxious child might put each one in twice, or use up memory capacity with extraneous information, such as remembering "four *and* six *and* seven" instead of "four, six, seven".

There are alternative tests of memory than digit span. A fairer yardstick for a child might be a test of visual representations, which would certainly be more to his liking and experience. For example, show a five-year-old child pictures from a magazine; then show him the same pictures again one at a time, only this time pair each one with a picture he has not been shown before; then ask him to identify the picture he has seen before. Adults are extremely good at such a test, selecting the correct picture ninety-five per cent of the time or better. And five-year-old children are just as good.[33] In fact, on such a test three-year-old children are almost as good as adults. Children do not lack memory capacity, just familiarity with the very specialized—and for a young child not exactly critical—skill of handling symbols.

All this does not mean, incidentally, that young children are not able to represent ideas symbolically. The very youngest child can play with a block and pretend that it is a car; that is symbolic thought. Children are also quite aware of the symbolic importance of adult gestures: They know the meaning of a friendly pat on the head and of a withheld treat. The evidence should also not be interpreted to mean that it is better to show five-year-old children pictures than to read them stories, or to encourage them to read for themselves.

Remember that we are discussing how representations of knowledge are laid down, not how information is presented in the first place. There is no reason a child should not hear or read a story and represent it to himself in visual terms just like an adult; in fact small children love "graphic" stories. A child will have no difficulty in constructing images if the possibility is there. Many pictures, on the other hand, may be quite difficult for a child to interpret, since skill is involved in reading pictures just as there is skill in reading text. In most pictures there is a good deal to ignore, and most of what is important requires interpretation. Unless it is clear to a child what he should be looking for in a picture—something better than "Here is a coal mine"—the picture may be just as bewildering as written language to a child who cannot read.

I have been tempted to summarize by saying that young children do not have a memory capacity inferior to older children and adults—they are simply not as good at memory operations involving the acquisition, representation, organization and retrieval of certain kinds of knowledge. They cannot "chunk" as efficiently as adults,[34] for example, and may put unnecessary packing into short-term memory. But even these judgments may be biased towards an adult view of what is important in the world; they primarily concern the presentation of verbal knowledge with which children have been rarely concerned in their lives outside school, retrieved in a formalized manner with which they are also unfamiliar. One must assume that children's preferred strategies for acquiring, representing and retrieving knowledge are the strategies that have best enabled them to make sense of the world so far. And children do not usually try to remember anything that does not make sense to them, until perhaps they discover that this is expected in school.

Obviously there are differences, but they must be considered in the light of every child's previous experience. Younger children are closer to the age when the bulk of their learning is accomplished through direct experience, and they will not be familiar with situations where they are expected to acquire knowledge passively and reproduce it verbally. Most young children collect objects of one kind or another, but the collection of facts may not have the same appeal. And though they may have learned to talk and comprehend relatively fluently, children in the early primary grades have not developed a sensitivity to subtle overtones of language of which few adults are aware—for example, the "brown coffee cup" phenomenon, where the description of an object conveys information about the listener's alternatives. Children tend to describe objects as they perceive them, in terms most relevant to themselves, not as they might be viewed by others. Finally the near-total recall of perceptual memories that some young children might have could itself be a handicap, as their minds are inundated by the sheer amount of unorganized visual—and emotional—experience that they can revive.

MEMORY IN THE CLASSROOM   Many practical questions might seem to arise at this point. How can children be trained to use short-term memory efficiently, and to put into long-term memory only knowledge that will prove worthwhile in a form that can be most effectively retrieved and utilized? How can children be taught to look for the distinctive features of objects, to predict intelligently and to make the optimal use of everything they already know? How can the persistence of sensory store be increased, and other limitations in information processing be eradicated? In short, what are the implications of this chapter for specific classroom practices? What does my discussion have to say in favor or against particular instructional methods or materials?

Most of what I have talked about in this chapter cannot be changed. Children try to comprehend the world in the manner I have described and their efforts are constrained by the memory and information-processing limitations I have outlined. I have not been talking about anything that teachers can try directly to improve, although I have been talking about much that teachers should try to understand and bear in mind. The discussion has not been directed towards providing teachers with helpful hints about what they should do in class, but towards helping them make sense of what goes on in class, whatever subject they may be teaching and whatever methods and materials they may employ. It should lead them to more reasonable and reliable expectations concerning children, understanding better why any activity or material at certain times might make learning and comprehension easier, but why the same activity or material at other times might make them difficult.

I could be very general and make obvious statements about the advantage of ensuring that everything that goes on in the classroom can make sense to every child, that it can be related to what they know already. This is not simply because sense is interesting and nonsense aversive; nor is it because sense respects and nonsense demeans children. There are quite practical advantages—comprehension reduces tunnel vision; eases the burden on short-term memory; and facilitates the representation of knowledge in long-term memory and its subsequent retrieval.

There are also a few specific points that should be made. For example, that conscious effort to memorize always interferes with comprehension; the more we try to remember, the less we are likely to understand. This is one reason a textbook can be so difficult to comprehend the night before an examination and so transparent the morning after. The reason by now I hope is apparent—the effort to cram detail into long-term memory results in the clogging of short-term memory, and directly interferes with comprehension. Even if new information is retained in such conditions, there is a chance it will be nonsense, unlikely to be retrieved, and useless if it is. The more you try to memorize anything you read, unless you scan it first for comprehension, the less likely you are to comprehend. On the other hand, comprehension not only facilitates memorization by organizing the material to be memorized into meaningful chunks, but also improves the likelihood of subsequent recall.

The effort to memorize is not the only condition that will interfere with comprehension. The state of anxiety, all too common in educational situations when there is a particular desire to memorize, has the effect of interfering with comprehension and memorization together. If we are anxious we are reluctant to make mistakes; therefore we demand more information before making any kind of decision, perceptual or otherwise, and can overload our information-processing capacity. Requiring more information from the visual world, for example, produces tunnel vision and uses short-term memory inefficiently.

Does all this mean that children at school should never be required to memorize, and must at all times be shielded from anxiety or stress? Of course not. In reasonable circumstances a child's brain can cope very well with both. The discussion implies that both anxiety and the effort to memorize exact a cost, just as too great a discrepancy between what a child knows already and what he is expected to understand exacts a cost, and the teacher must understand the nature of the cost that is exacted. Simply asking a child to try harder will not make him a better student nor will it ensure that he comprehends more and learns faster. Trying harder makes demands on limited cognitive information-processing activities that can move the desired improvement even further out of range. The danger signal is always when the activity fails to make sense to the child.

Another objection that might be raised is that children will never progress if they are not challenged, which usually means if they are not engaged in an activity that is difficult and even somewhat unpleasant. According to such arguments, no one would advance beyond fairy stories and comic books without being pushed. The objection, however, is based on two misconceptions. The first is that nothing can be learned if a task is easy: a child who rereads a favorite book many times, perhaps till he knows it by heart, is wasting his time. In fact it is through such "easy" reading that a child becomes a fluent reader; he learns how to identify words and meanings with a minimum of visual information and to use short-term and long-term memory efficiently. He is practising all those essential skills of reading that are never taught. Once a child has really learned all there is to learn from any activity, he will move on without any external goad. The moment there is nothing left to learn the activity becomes boring, and boredom is aversive. That is the second misconception; that not-learning is preferable to learning. No child will hesitate to enter a situation in which he will learn, provided he is not motivated against that particular learning situation and he has a reasonable expectation that he *will* learn. Learning is not aversive to children, even when it requires effort. What is aversive is the expectation of failure, or that the learning task will prove not to make sense.

Children know how to go about making sense of the world, despite their limitations. Like everyone else, they have lived with their limited information-processing capacity and the bottlenecks of memory since birth, and they have learned to cope with the world on these terms. Children do not need to be taught to use short-term memory economically, to put only worthwhile knowledge into long-term memory, to look for distinctive features; teachers rather have to ensure that it is possible for them to exercise these skills. A child who does not learn, or who does not even comprehend, is not necessarily malevolent or stupid; he may simply be overwhelmed. The gap between what he is trying to do and what he is expected to do may be too great.

The brain I have tried to describe is the brain that a child must work with, whatever he is trying to comprehend and however you are trying to teach. You cannot change the kind of brain he has, but you can improve its performance, and make comprehension easier, by respecting its limitations and understanding the price that must be paid if its capacities are over-extended.

CHAPTER 3

Two Faces
of Language

In the previous chapters I tried to show there is more to perceiving the world than meets the eye; what we see is largely determined by what we look for. In this chapter I want to show that there is more to language than meets the ear; comprehension is not just a matter of listening. I shall begin with some general comments about language, and then I shall talk specifically about speech, demonstrating that comprehension is far more complex than it is usually assumed to be. Apart from specific differences of modality, hearing versus seeing, everything I shall say about spoken language will apply to written language, as well. But I shall leave questions concerning the relation between spoken and written language to a later chapter, when the topic will be learning to read.

Surface Structure and Deep Structure

There are two ways in which any piece of language, any sequence of spoken or written words, can be discussed. On the one hand, we can talk about its *physical characteristics*—about the sounds in the case of speech, or about the marks on paper in the case of writing. Physical characteristics can always be measured. On the other hand, we can talk about *meaning*.

These two ways of discussing language are completely independent of each other. For example, we can talk about the duration or loudness of a spoken utterance, or about the length or legibility of a printed sentence, without any reference to what the particular piece of language means. We do not even need to know the language; we could make the same kind of remarks about nonsense. But if we want to talk about meaning it is essential to know the language, and quite unnecessary to refer to the physical characteristics of the particular item. We might agree, for example, that *bachelor* and *unmarried man* have a common meaning, and that *Man eats fish* and *Fish eats man* are different, without having to debate whether the language is written or spoken, loud or soft, slow or fast.

Let me introduce two new terms that we shall be using a good deal: *surface structure*, which will take the place of the more cumbersome expression "physical characteristics of language", and *deep structure*, which will refer to meaning. Surface structure is the visible part of written language and the audible part of spoken language; it is accessible to anyone who can see and hear, whether or not he understands the language. Deep structure is appropriately named because meaning lies deeper than mere sounds of written symbols, which are literally superficial. In fact—and this is a cause of tremendous theoretical confusion and difficulty—meaning does not lie in the realm of language at all, but in the underlying thought processes of the language user.

The terms "surface structure" and "deep structure" have a number of advantages apart from their metaphorical value. One such advantage is that surface structure can be employed for both spoken and written language, so that it is not necessary to refer constantly to "the sounds of speech and the ink marks on the page". Deep structure, or meaning, is of course the same whether spoken or written language is referred to. The two terms are gaining a good deal of currency in educational publications and are used extensively in certain kinds of linguistic and psycholinguistic literature in a variety of idiosyncratic ways.[1] My definitions of these terms are somewhat simplified to avoid some controversial theoretical issues.[2] In terms of my distinction between the world around us and the theory of the world in the head, the surface structure of language must always be part of the outside world, while deep structure remains in the heads of the speaker and listener.

There is one simple but rarely understood fact about language that has enormous implications for psychology and for education, and that provides a basic understanding of the nature of the human brain. This fact applies equally to written and to spoken language, and can be stated concisely as follows: *there is no one-to-one correspondence between the surface and deep structures of language*. Put more simply, the sounds of speech are essentially meaningless, and so are the characters that we write. The basic question in the present chapter is how language can be used for communication if meaning is not directly represented in the surface structure of language—if it is absent from the physical signal that passes between speaker and listener, writer and reader. But first I must explain and defend the assertion that surface structure and sense are not the same.

Discrepancies between surface and deep structure

One way to illustrate the absence of a "one-to-one correspondence" between the surface and deep structure of language is to show that a single surface structure can have more than one meaning, and that a single meaning can have more than one surface representation. For example, the assertion *Flying planes can be dangerous* can mean: (a) it is dangerous to fly planes, as opposed to building or servicing them; (b) planes that *are flying* are dangerous; or (c) it is dangerous to fly *planes* as opposed to flying kites. Can you detect the ambiguities in sentences such as *Visiting teachers can be a bore*; *The shooting of the principal was terrible*; *The chicken was too hot to eat*; *She dives into the spray and waves*; and *Cleopatra was rarely prone to argue?* Double meanings are not always immediately apparent, a fact that will prove to be a clue to how language is actually comprehended. For an example of how a single meaning can be represented by different surface structures, think of any paraphrase: *The boy chases the ball* means the same as *The ball is chased by the boy* and *The juvenile male featherless biped pursues the spherical plaything* and so forth.

An interesting aspect of this fact that meaning and surface structure are not identical is that we rarely hear differences in the sounds of spoken language that make no difference to meaning. In other words, we listen for sense, not sound. For example the /p/ sound in *pin* is not the same as the /p/ in *spin*, which in fact sounds more like /sbin/. There are similar variations in the sounds of /k/ and /t/ when an initial /s/ is added to *kin* and *top*. The difference becomes even more apparent if you say the words with your open hand a few inches from your mouth; there is an expulsion of air at the beginning of *pin*, *kin* and *top* that is absent from *spin*, *skin* and *stop*. These variations do not occur because we could not pronounce the words otherwise. Both *pin* and *spin* can be produced with the same kind of /p/; the variation is a superficial rule of language which almost everyone follows, but which no one is taught and which makes no difference to meaning.

There is a special term for the many clusters of different sounds which do not make any difference to meaning in language and are therefore usually heard as the same. Each cluster is called a *phoneme*. A language could have thousands of different phonemes if all the variations in its sounds were employed to represent differences in meaning. But all languages of the world seem to make do with sets of relatively few phonemes, somewhere between thirty and fifty. English is usually considered to have between forty and forty-five phonemes, depending on how the counting is done and whose dialect is being tabulated. Ask a friend to write down the words *Mary, marry* and *merry*, or *cot, caught* and *court*, while you read aloud, and you may find that you do not have as many distinctive sounds in your own language as you think.

Not all languages organize their phonemes in the same way. The *pin–spin* difference that is not phonemic in the English /p/ *is* phonemic in Arabic. An Arabic speaker would hear a difference between the two sounds because Arabic words including the *pin* type of /p/ do not mean the same as Arabic words uttered with the *spin* type of /p/. On the other hand, the difference between /1/ and /r/ which is phonemic in English is not phonemic in Japanese. Not only does a Japanese speaker have difficulty in articulating the English words *link* and *rink*; he tends not to hear them as different. This inability is no reflection on Japanese hearing acuity; the English speaker is in precisely the same position with respect to the Arabic forms of /p/.

The point is that listeners do not hear the infinite variety of language sounds that speakers produce, but organize all these sounds into a few categories (phonemes) depending on whether they make a difference in the language. We do not hear the sound the speaker produces; we hear the sound as we have categorized it. We hear what we think the speaker has said. We are not aware of surface structure, but perceive deep structure, which is the way we make sense of environmental noise.[3]

In Pursuit of Meaning

The interesting question with which we must now come to grips is how it can ever be possible to understand language if meaning is not represented in speech or writing. To clear the ground for a solution to this problem, it may be illuminating to examine some conventional explanations of how language is understood.

The elusiveness of words

The most common account of the process by which we comprehend the meaning of sentences is probably that we comprehend the meaning of the whole by combining the meanings of the parts, of the individual words. Such an assumption underlies many endeavors to teach children to read. I want to try to show that quite the reverse occurs—we need to know the meaning of the sentence before we can decide anything about the meaning of individual words. There are several ways to make this point, perhaps the most basic of which is to dispute whether such a thing as a word exists in the first place.

Linguists generally prefer not to talk about words. The trouble is that they cannot define what a word is. A word is certainly not the smallest meaningful element of language, which is sometimes the way it is defined in school parlance, because some words appear to have no meaning when by themselves: What do *the, a, such* or *of* mean? On the other hand, some words can be broken down into smaller words or parts of words, so that they seem to have more than one meaning. *Unhappy,* for example, combines the meanings of *not* and *happy,* while *boys* contains the word *boy* plus an *s,* which means "more than one". Linguists have a different term for the smallest element of meaning, which they call the *morpheme,* a unit they much prefer to deal with than words. A word such as *boys* is assumed to consist of two morphemes, a "free form", *boy,* which can exist by itself, and a "bound form", *-s,* which must be attached to a free form. Sometimes a morpheme must be assumed to be present in a word although it is not physically represented: *sheep* in the singular is one morpheme, but two morphemes if plural. Sometimes the bound morpheme is embedded in the free form, for example, as in *man* (single morpheme) and *men* (two morphemes).

You might wonder why there is all this problem about defining words, when it is pretty obvious what they are in writing. And in fact the only rule any one has found for identifying words does come from written language —a word is a sequence of letters with a white space on either side. But no one can give the rule that explains *why* we put the white space on either side of certain sequences of letters. It looks as if the empty space between words might be an arbitrary artifact of our written language, which some other written languages have managed to do without. Certainly words are not part of the surface structure of speech. You may think a speaker is obviously producing clearly distinguishable words when you hear him; but that is because you, the listener, put them there. You hear words in a spoken sentence because you know what that sentence means.

Imagine saying "West end" to someone and asking your listener to tell you how many words you had uttered. You would expect him to answer "Two". And if you asked him to tell you what the two words were, you would expect the reply "*West* and *end*". But if you listen carefully to yourself saying "West end" you will find that the two words do not break in the way your imagined listener would hear them. You do not say /west-end/, you say /wes-tend/. The break in the surface structure is not heard by the listener, who hears instead a boundary that you have not produced. In fact, in normal fluent speech, breaks in the flow of words rarely occur. We-do-not-speak-one-word-at-a-time. When there are breaks within phrases, they tend to occur within words rather than between them.

The fact that boundaries between words are not represented in the surface structure of speech is one of the greatest difficulties confronting anyone trying to understand the speaker of a foreign language with which he is not familiar. Before he can even begin to translate the words that the speaker is uttering, the listener must find out what the words are, and the speaker gives him absolutely no help. It is impossible for anyone to listen to even a four- or five-word statement normally articulated in any language (including English) if he does not understand that language, and to say how many words were uttered. Meaning tells us what words are, not words meaning.

To make matters even more complicated, the things we call words in our written language never have only one meaning (or combination of meanings). Almost all words have more than one alternative meaning, and most of the common ones have scores of meanings. Think of the word *table*, for example, or *chair* or *dog* or *fish*; you cannot even tell if they are nouns or verbs. A word in isolation is absolutely meaningless. If you ask a child to tell what a word is on a flashcard, or singled out in a sentence, you are asking him for its name, that is all. There is no way he can give you a meaningful answer—unless he can guess what you have in mind. Speak the word *house* aloud and I would wager you are wrong. The word I wrote down was a verb, as in *Who shall house the homeless?* and your pronunciation was almost certainly incorrect. Did I trick you, or did our language?

Some well-intentioned people have thought they could make life easier for all of us, and even clear up many of the world's misunderstandings, if language could be reformed so that every word had just one meaning and every meaning—or every object at least—was represented by just one word. But a very good counterargument is that language would be impossible if it were arranged on that basis. Sometimes I call the family pet *Tito*, sometimes a *dalmatian*, sometimes a *dog*, sometimes an *animal* and sometimes just *that object over there*. It would be most inconvenient if all "isa" relationships were abolished, so that once we decided to call a certain class of objects dogs, we would never be permitted to refer to some of them as dalmatians and to all of them as animals.

Moreover, we certainly do not like to limit words to one meaning apiece, a most uneconomical process. Quite the reverse, the more common the word, the more meanings we make it serve.[4] Look up any common word in the dictionary—words such as *come, go, take, have, time, place, man, house*—and see how much space must be devoted to explaining all their meanings. Some of the most common words in our language have so many meanings that it is probably better to say they have no meaning at all; I am referring to prepositions. *At*, for example, has thirty-nine separate meanings listed in the *Oxford English Dictionary*, and so has *by*. *In* and *with* both have forty meanings listed, and *of* has sixty-nine.[5] The meaning of prepositions is so elusive that it is impossible to translate them. To translate any English preposition into French, or any French preposition into

English, you need to know what the other words are around it. The meaning comes first.

All the world's "natural languages"—the 3000 or 4000 different tongues the peoples of the world use for everyday communication and pass on to their children—have these two characteristics in common: Their deep structure is different from their surface structure; and the number of meanings a word has tends to increase with its frequency of use. On the other hand, "artificial languages" in which no ambiguity can be tolerated—such as the languages of algebra, formal logic or computer programming—are generally quite difficult for humans to learn, certainly at the age at which humans learn comfortably to talk. So it looks as if our languages may reflect something of the way the human brain is constructed, and we would be better off not to tamper with them too much.

Order and syntax

Once the status of individual words is undermined, someone is bound to point out that sentences (or statements) rarely consist of words in isolation, and that the way in which words are combined in sentences must determine both their meanings and the meaning of the whole. But sentences cannot be a simple combination of individual word meanings, otherwise a Venetian blind would be a blind Venetian, a Maltese cross a cross Maltese and hot dogs would have four legs and bark. Nor does the order of words necessarily eliminate ambiguity, since many sentences (such as *Flying planes can be dangerous*) obviously have more than one meaning.[6]

The next explanation might be that you have to take into account the part of speech of the word—that *blind* is an adjective in *blind Venetian* and a noun in *Venetian blind*. But how did you know whether it was a noun or adjective? You had to know the meaning of the entire expression first.

Takes a sentence we have already met, *Man eats fish*. If I asked you to parse that sentence you would almost certainly say that *man* and *fish* are nouns and *eats* is a verb. And so they are in that particular sentence. But each of the three words can play the role of noun and verb, so once again you had to know what the sentence as a whole meant before you could say anything about the individual words. And the order of the words in a sentence is not a clue to their parts of speech either. Here is another three-word sentence in which *man*, still the first word, would certainly not be identified as a noun: *Man the boats*.

It is often argued—and I am not going to disagree—that the bridge between surface structure and deep structure could be *syntax*, or the rules of grammar. It is our implicit knowledge of the syntactic rules of language that enables us to interpret and to produce grammatical sentences. However, it is not the case of a simple equation, surface structure + syntax = deep structure, because syntax itself cannot be determined without knowledge of meaning. Put in another way, syntax is also not directly represented in the surface structure of language; therefore, a sentence must be understood before we can ascertain its syntactic structure. I have already provided illustrations with simple sentences like *Man eats fish*; I shall now offer a more complex example.

Language teachers at least will usually have little difficulty in identifying a sentence like *Sarah was soaked by the sprinkler* as passive; if you ask how they know they will point to the *was* and the *-ed* and the *by*, and perhaps even refer to a reversible "passive transformation" that converts the sentence to its active form, *The sprinkler soaked Sarah*. But our set of syntactic clues will mislead us if we try to apply the same reasoning to a sentence which, apart from one minor change, appears to have an identical surface structure; *Sarah was seated by the sprinkler*. Note the *was*, the *-ed* and the *by*. But *Sarah was seated by the sprinkler* is not the same kind of sentence at all; and its transformation into *The sprinkler seated Sarah* does not work. How can we say one sentence is passive and the other is not? Because we know their meaning.

Here is another example to show that meaning must be consulted before we can decide whether certain grammatical rules are applicable. Most people would agree that the following four sentences are grammatical, meaningful and identical in structure (at the surface level, at least). Each sentence contains a subject noun, an auxiliary verb, a participle and an adverbial phrase:

(a) *Mother is cooking in the kitchen.*
(b) *Father is cooking in the kitchen.*
(c) *Meat is cooking in the kitchen.*
(d) *Cabbage is cooking in the kitchen.*

Now according to the rules of English grammar, subject nouns with identical predicates may be combined by the conjunction *and*. Thus we can say *Mother and father are cooking in the kitchen*, or we can say *Meat and cabbage are cooking in the kitchen*. We cannot say, however, *Mother and meat are cooking in the kitchen*, although there is no obvious grammatical rule that we seem to be contravening. *Mother and meat are cooking* is wrong, it would appear, because the sentence does not make sense—or at least because we are mixing up one sentence concerned with who is cooking and another concerned with what is being cooked. (To have the sentence make sense, we would have to imagine a special circumstance such as a cannibal cookout). In other words, what makes the sentence grammatical

is not its grammar, but its meaning. Once again we must give the priority
to deep structure, which is in the head.

Making Sense of Language

There is no need to belabor the point. You may understand a sentence
when you see it, but you do not achieve that understanding by putting
together the meanings of all the individual words. Not only is meaning not
represented in the surface structure of language, but syntactic clues are
missing as well. Nevertheless, we cannot avoid the fact that language, by
and large, is understood. How then does the listener (or reader) get meaning from the surface structure of language? The answer is that he does not.
The listener does not extract meaning from the surface structure of language because there is no meaning there. He must supply it himself. We do
not take meaning from the language we hear or look at; we bring meaning
to it.

Let me put the argument diagrammatically. Language is comprehended
not by extracting deep structure from surface structure, as in Figure 3.1(*a*),
but by imposing deep structure on surface structure, as in Figure 3.1(*b*).
Earlier in this chapter I proposed that surface structure was part of "the
world" and that deep structure reposed in the "theory of the world in the
head". Turn Figure 3.1(*b*) on its side and you will see that it is identical
with Figure 1.1. The arrow points in the right direction. The world, whether
or not it is language, is made sense of by having cognitive structure imposed

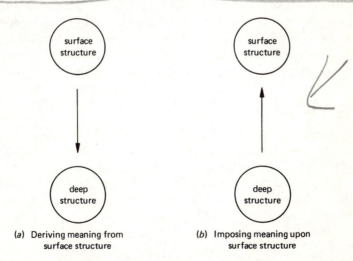

(*a*) Deriving meaning from   (*b*) Imposing meaning upon
surface structure   surface structure

Figure 3.1 Alternative representations of language comprehension

What abt. McLuen ?

upon it. Meaning does not travel from the message to the listener or reader; the receiver must bring meaning to the message.

Language comprehension, in other words, is a matter of *predicting* what the language producer will say or write. This may seem both an unnatural and an unlikely solution—but in fact any child of two will demonstrate that it can be done. We have already met the mechanism that performs the trick. The process by which we make sense of the world in general —relating the unfamiliar to the already known—is all we need to make sense of language as well. It is therefore not necessary to postulate new or special ability for comprehending language.

Comprehension and prediction

Put so bluntly, the argument may well sound absurd. If, for example, you can predict everything you are going to read in this book, why should you bother to read it? And if a child must predict everything a teacher is going to say in order to comprehend, doesn't that mean the child must know as much as the teacher?

But you will remember from Chapter 2 that prediction—in making sense of the world at least—does not mean making a wild guess or staking everything on the single most probable alternative. Prediction cognitively means the prior elimination of unlikely alternatives. When we look out of a window, you will recall, practically everything that we are likely to see —cars, buses, pedestrians—comes as no surprise to us, because our expectations of what we will see are realistic. On the other hand, unlikely alternatives—submarines or elephants—surprise us because they are beyond the range of our expectations; we do not predict them. Our cognitive predictions are neither too narrow nor too broad. We strive always to reduce the number of alternatives in order to ease the strain on our limited information-processing capacity, but not to the extent that we are likely to make a mistake, or become bewildered. And when we predict what a speaker is going to say, or what we will read in a book, we are simply excluding the improbable.

Furthermore, we are very good at predicting in language. As I also demonstrated in Chapter 2, we know a good deal about what we are likely to read in a word, a sentence or a book before our eyes get to work. I called this prior knowledge *nonvisual information*, and gave some examples. We know a good deal about the relative frequency of letters in words and of words in the language; we also know a good deal about the limitations that English grammar and the writer's topic place on the writer's selection of words. In fact, although there are at least 50,000 words in the English language which a writer could choose from in order to write a book, when it comes to the selection of a particular word in his text, the number of alternatives available is not 50,000 but more like 250. And that limitation upon the writer represents a tremendous potential reduction in uncertainty for the reader. The reader can predict that thousands upon thousands of words will not occur, and concentrate his attention on the 200 or 300 words that are likely—an economy that makes a considerable difference in reading.[7]

Finally, I am not suggesting that we predict entire paragraphs or even sentences in advance, certainly not on a word-for-word basis; that would be neither possible nor necessary. But we usually can make a reasonable job of predicting likely alternatives for the next few words, especially when we have a good general idea of where the writer (or speaker) is heading. And as our expectations about these words are confirmed or disconfirmed, we can modify our expectations about the next few words that follow them. The closer the reader approaches to any point in the text, the less uncertain he is about that point, and therefore the less uncertain he will be about other points further beyond.

Moreover, it rarely necessary to predict *precisely.* Our predicted set of alternatives need not include an exact match for a sentence that the speaker or writer will produce. The more we know, or believe we know, the less inclined we are to look for 100-percent similarity. If we know a speaker is telling us that he is on his way to school, home, or the theater, then *school, home* and *theater* are the only words to which we need attend—and we will need very little information to discriminate among the three. If we need little information because our alternatives are few, then we do not have to find a very complex fit between our prediction and what the speaker or writer actually says. Because it is rarely necessary to predict *exactly*, young children can understand utterances and grammatical constructions they could never produce for themselves; they are looking for certain elements only. If a child is waiting to hear whether he should stay or leave, open a book or clear his desk top, he does not have to understand or even hear the entire sentence; just a few sounds will give him the information he needs. Similarly, differences in dialect do not necessarily make a difference in comprehension. A child who says "I ain't got no money" in his own dialect may still understand "I haven't any money" or "I have no money" in your dialect. There is enough similarity for him to make sense of your statement; although if you ask him to repeat what you said, he will give you the meaning in his own dialect.

Occasionally this ability to comprehend on only a partial match works against a child. For example, children in the early grades of school may not have mastered the special nature of passive sentences and therefore will not predict them. They will interpret *Tommy was hit by his sister* as *Tommy hit his sister*, not because they have analysed the sentence incorrectly, but because they accept its surface structure as a sufficiently close match to the kind of sentence they would be likely to produce.

In summary, we are usually able to predict what a speaker or writer is about to say because we have the ability to make such predictions generally (we reduce uncertainty in advance in all aspects of our perception of the world), and because we have the necessary prior linguistic knowledge of how speakers and writers are likely to express their intentions in surface structure. We are therefore able to select among our remaining alternatives by *sampling* the surface structure, looking for limited "matches", or correspondences, with our expectations. Rather than decode surface structure exhaustively, we bring meaning, or a limited set of alternative meanings, to it.

Of course we are not normally aware that we are constantly predicting, eliminating alternatives in advance, either in our perception of the world or in our comprehension of language. Like most of our knowledge of the rules of language, the predictions that we can derive from this knowledge are not subject to conscious inspection. We are aware of what we comprehend, but not of the process that leads to comprehension.

Two questions remain. The first concerns the mechanism by which predictions of the meaning of what a writer or speaker is saying are tested. I have proposed that the reader or listener predicts alternative *meanings*, and that he tests to see whether the writer or speaker will in fact say what he has predicted will be said. But these predictions cannot be tested at the level of meaning—comparing the writer's meaning with the reader's expectations, for example—because meaning is not present in the surface structure the writer produces. If the writer's meaning were available in the first place for a comparison to be made, then no comparison would be necessary.

The second question concerns the role of grammar in comprehension. I noted earlier that grammar, or at least syntax, could be regarded as the bridge between surface structure and deep structure, although syntax is not directly represented in the surface structure of language. But I have not talked so far about grammar in the process of comprehension, except to suggest that we can comprehend some sentences whose grammar is unfamiliar to us, sentences we could not ourselves produce.

It is necessary now to show how grammar could be considered the core of comprehension. Just as the speaker or writer uses grammar to produce surface structures that represent his meaning, so the listener or reader must use grammar to comprehend. Although the listener or reader must predict on the basis of meaning, he cannot compare meanings directly; therefore he must use grammar to construct predicted surface structures. In other words, the listener or reader uses grammar in exactly the same way as the speaker or writer—to *produce* surface structure. It is time to take a closer look at grammar, and although our primary concern is with comprehension, it will be most convenient to first consider grammar from the point of view of the speaker or writer, as a mechanism for translating meaning into surface structure.

The Rules of Language

According to a view of language with a 2000-year history, grammar is a description of some kind of perfect language which all should seek but few will attain. The notion that the language people actually speak is a mere shadow, an inferior reproduction, of an ideal forever just beyond their grasp is rooted in classical Greek philosophy. And as classical Greek and Latin became more a memory than a viable means of communication, they were themselves beatified as models of everything that is best in language. Modern languages were analyzed and taught as if they had the same grammar as Greak and Latin. Not so many years ago one could still find school grammars asserting that English had a vocative case ("O table!").

An inevitable consequence of the assumption that everyone's language falls short of some mystical ideal is the belief that some languages or dialects must be closer approximations of perfection than others. And, naturally, the language closest to perfection for any culture or society must be the language spoken by the people who are in all other respects closest to God, namely, the dominating group. "Grammar", in other words, became the standard of good English, the language spoken by the governing classes, or of the teacher. Common people and children either did not use grammar or used only "bad grammar".

Modern linguistics has democratized grammar with the notion that grammar is a *system* that works to enable us to produce and comprehend sentences. No longer the mark of a particular caste, grammar has become a *set of rules* everyone uses to bridge the gap between surface and deep structure. And the rules of your language need not be an exact copy of the rules of mine. Even infants have grammar; they do not put words together randomly, but follow rules of their own. There are no longer good or bad grammars, just different ones. In principle, all languages and dialects are as good as each other; therefore all grammars are equal. Admittedly, the languages or dialects some people speak may have more prestige in a particular culture than others; but this inequality is economic or social, not linguistic or intellectual.

Generative grammar

I shall introduce you to a very simple grammar of English in order to demonstrate that grammars can be conceptualized as a set of rules, a "device" even, for producing sentences in English. I want to show that my grammar, small though it is, is very efficient, since with just three rules and a vocabulary of fifteen words I can produce over a thousand grammatical sentences. For the purposes of the example, it does not matter where I got this particular grammar from; it could have come to me in a flash of inspiration during the night, or I could have found it under a stone.[8] What matters is whether the grammar works. If it produces grammatical English sentences, and no ungrammatical sentences, then it may reasonably be considered as part of the grammar of English in the head of everyone who accepts the sentences it produces as grammatical.

Here is my miniature grammar, a representation of part of what you and I know about the English language:

A Miniature Grammar of English

Syntax	*Lexicon*
$S \rightarrow X + Y$	$A = a, the$
$X \rightarrow A + B$	$B = ball, bicycle, bird, cat,$
	$dog, girl, man, teacher$
$Y \rightarrow C + X$	$C = alarms, annoys, avoids,$
	$bites, chases$

You will notice that the syntactic part of my grammar looks rather like a set of algebraic formulae, except that instead of an equality sign there is an arrow. The arrow ($\rightarrow$) is known as a *rewrite sign*, and indicates that the symbol on its left should be replaced by the two symbols on its right. The starting point is S, which stands for *sentence*.

If I had attempted to write a more ambitious grammar of English, there would have been different choices for rewriting S, but my little grammar offers no alternative. $S \rightarrow X + Y$ tells me that to start constructing my sentence I must write $X + Y$. The second rule tells me that X cannot be kept, but must be "rewritten" as $A + B$, so that my sentence becomes $A + B + Y$. The third rule similarly instructs me to rewrite Y as $C + X$, so that my grammar grows into $A + B + C + X$. We have already discovered from the second rule that X must be rewritten as $A + B$, so that we are left with $A + B + C + A + B$. At this point, having exhausted all the possibilities of the syntax, I am ready to go into the lexicon. For expository convenience, I have put words into the lexicon, but—as I pointed out in the earlier section on the elusiveness of words—it would be more appropriate if I filled it with morphemes. Looking first for a word to replace the first symbol in my sentence, $A + B + C + A + B$, I find that I have a choice of *a* and *the*, and select *the*. My sentence now reads *The* + B +

$C + A + B$. I have eight choices for the first B; quite arbitrarily, I shall select the last, *teacher*. My sentence now reads *The teacher* $+ C + A + B$, and I shall hurry through to the end by selecting *chases*, as *a* and *ball* to replace C and the final A and B, respectively. My completed sentence reads *The teacher chases a ball*, which I hope you will agree is a model of grammaticality.

By selecting other items in the lexicon I could have produced many other sentences, such as *A dog annoys the cat*, *The cat alarms a bird* and *The girl avoids a bicycle*. And because I have two choices for A, eight for B and five for C, the number of different $A + B + C + A + B$ sentences possible is $2 \times 8 \times 5 \times 2 \times 8$, or 1280—all of them perfectly grammatical. In fact it is impossible for this little grammar to produce a sentence any speaker of English would regard as ungrammatical.

Additional rules of grammar would be required to enable us to produce and comprehend sentences such as the one I am writing now, which is far out of the range of my miniature three-rule grammar. But not many more rules would be required. No one has yet come anywhere near writing a complete grammar of any language; but it has been estimated that 100 rules should more than suffice for all the different kinds of sentences that can be produced in English. Some rules would offer alternative ways of re-writing S; others would concern X and Y and other "intermediate" symbols; and of course there would be many more items in the lexicon. But while an actual grammar in anyone's head (except perhaps an infant in the first few weeks of verbal life) would be larger than the miniature grammar I have described, its basis would be the same. The grammar would have to be *generative*, which means that it would generate sentences systematically. Words would not be put together arbitrarily, but in accordance with rules. The notion that everyone's language is generated by a set of underlying rules—(which may be different from person to person and certainly across cultural or social groups)—explains why a child who says "I ain't got no money" will also say "You ain't got no money" and "They ain't got no money". He is producing language systematically according to his grammar. An infant who may produce the sentences *Allgone big truck* and *Allgone red drink* will not produce sentences such as *Allgone truck big* or *Red drink allgone* because the rules of language he has acquired, or invented, permit the former combinations but not the latter.

The rearrangement, addition or deletion of sentence elements that would not be possible in a simple generative grammar is allowed for by a different and particularly powerful kind of grammatical rule. Such rules, called *transformations*,[9] permit the combination of such sentences as *The dog chases a cat*, *The dog is angry* and *The cat is mangy* into *The dog, which is angry, chases a mangy cat*. Transformational rules also enable a generative grammar to cope with what are called "discontinuities" in sentences. For example, English verbs consisting of two words, such as *look up*, sometimes must be separated by another word. A transformational rule permits *him* to be inserted in the appropriate place in *I looked him up in the library*, which I think you will agree is not the same as *I looked up him in the library*.

Grammar and sense

Let us return for a moment to the 1280 grammatical sentences that I calculated could have been generated by my modest three-rule, fifteen-word grammar. It may have occurred to you that while all of these sentences would be of indubitable grammaticality, many would not have much sense or utility. Sentences like *The ball bites a bird* or *A man alarms the bicycle* would not seem to be particularly meaningful in anyone's language. But I did not promise sense when I introduced the grammar, I merely promised grammaticality; and we all know that grammaticality is no guarantee that anything worthwhile is being said. Grammar is not concerned with making sense.

Who then is responsible for the sense of an utterance? The answer of course must be the speaker. When the speaker cranks up his grammar to produce an S, he will not be satisfied with any old sentence; he wants one that will represent a meaning he already has in his mind. He will use lexical items he has selected in advance. He begins with deep structure, and the grammar enables him to generate a surface structure for his meaning. Given that the speaker knows what he wants to say, he must be satisfied that the sentence he produces represents the meaning he wants to convey. If he decides it does not, he will try again. The speaker probably will not even be aware that what he says could mean anything different—unless he makes a particular effort to perceive how his utterance might be interpreted by someone who does not share the same deep structure, a self-critical skill not easily acquired. It usually does not matter to the speaker that other surface structures might represent the same meaning, or that the surface structure he produces could represent other meanings—as long as the surface structure he produces is compatible with the meaning he wants to express.

Grammar and comprehension

We can now return to the original question of how the listener or the reader uses grammar. The speaker or writer, as I have tried to show, begins with a meaning that he already has in mind, and uses grammar to generate an appropriate surface structure. But generative grammar would not appear

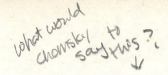
what would Chomsky say this?

to be a device that can be put into reverse. The grammatical function of many words is not manifest in surface structure. Nor will surface structure reveal which of a variety of meanings the majority of words may have. Even in my miniature three-rule grammar, the word *bites* could serve as both *B* and *C; The man avoids the bites.*

But the fact that generative grammar cannot be used to derive meaning from surface structure is not important as long as the listener or reader employs it in the manner I outlined a few pages ago—to predict what the speaker or reader is going to say. If the listener or reader is able to predict the meaning of *what* will be said, and he has a grammar similar to that of the speaker or writer, then he will be able to predict *how* it will be said.

If listeners and readers use grammar in the same "generative" direction as speakers and writers, then it is not surprising that the former are usually no more aware of the ambiguities in surface structure than the person who produces an utterance. Only very rarely are we not sure of what a sentence means, in the sense that we think it might mean one thing or another. Usually we either comprehend a sentence or we do not, which can only mean that we look for a specific meaning. If we do comprehend a sentence, then we think its meaning is self-evident and are surprised if we discover that it may have another. We expect that sentences will have one meaning only —which is why we can be outraged by puns. Our insensitivity to the multiplicity of possible meanings can only exist because meaning is in the head, not in the surface structure of language. Comprehension, in other words, takes place when our expectations are confirmed, and meaning to the listener or reader is the expectation that is confirmed, just as meaning to the speaker or writer is the thought he believes he has represented.

Borges!

To assert that language may be highly predictable in certain circumstances is to assert that it may be practically redundant—that the meaning may be comprehended with scarcely a word being uttered. And this is often the case with spoken language, especially in the experience of children before they get to school. Many remarks made in the home are closely related to events going on in the immediate environment at the same time. In fact young children would not be able to learn language unless they could intuit the meaning of utterances before they were capable of understanding the language itself.[10] Written language is rarely as closely related as speech to events in the immediate environment—which is one reason that print may sometimes be more difficult to comprehend than speech. And the language used in school may be the most difficult kind a child has ever had to comprehend—if he has no other clue to its meaning, if he cannot relate it to anything going on around him. No child will understand a teacher if he cannot predict what the teacher is likely to be talking about, or if the teacher employs a grammar radically different from that of the child.

SOME CONSEQUENCES OF PREDICTION   The idea that the listener may employ his knowledge of language in exactly the same way as the speaker is not confined to the matter of grammar. Several theories, variously labelled "the motor theory of speech perception" and "analysis by synthesis", propose that every aspect of our perception of speech involves a process of "generation" rather than of "decoding".[11] Such a perspective resolves a number of theoretical difficulties related to language comprehension, including our already discussed lack of awareness of the ambiguities inherent in language. For example, I mentioned early in this chapter that the boundaries between words are not represented in the surface structure of language; we hear /west-end/ when /wes-tend/ is spoken. But because /wes-tend/ is not something a listener predicts, it is not something he will hear. To hear /wes-tend/ it is necessary to listen deliberately for meaningless sounds.

Our ability to look for meaning in noise also explains how we can distinguish what one person is saying when twenty or thirty people are talking simultaneously in what psychologists call the "cocktail party problem".[12] Experiments have shown that subjects can follow a particular conversation or message even if successive words are uttered by different voices. It is our expectation of what will be said that enables us to relegate all irrelevant noise to the background.

Finally, by predicting what a speaker or writer will say we are able to *sample*, to follow his meaning on a minimum of incoming information. As I pointed out in the previous chapter, reading and listening would be impossible without large amounts of prior information because of the limited amount of new information the brain can process at any one time. I did not specify how a minimum amount of visual information could be made to go as far as possible, but this economy in information processing obviously could not be accomplished if language had to be processed "from the outside in". The way readers make use of prior knowledge, of nonvisual information, is to predict what the writer will say, and to "sample" the surface structure features only to the extent required to eliminate any remaining uncertainty.

The argument that a listener predicts what a speaker will say, even to the extent of generating possible surface structures in advance, should not be interpreted to mean that the listener actually produces sounds. There is a point at which the listener can stop just short of mouthing words, just as there is a point that the speaker must reach in the generation of sentences just prior to the production of sounds. In fact a more specific use of the term "surface structure" than the one I have employed regards it as an abstract level of language from which phonological representations are derived.[13] In other words, there is a level of language prior to sound for both speaker and listener; and it is at this level, before articulation actually takes place, that a listener can test his predictions. It is true that we may occasionally see a child's lips move when we talk to him; but this action is more likely to be an indication that he is having difficulty comprehending than to be a part of his comprehending. The recapitulation of what someone else is saying is probably a crutch to ease the load on the listener's short-term memory when his effort to comprehend is great. I think that this explanation applies also to subvocalization in reading.

An Alternative Point of View

Having gone to some length to describe and illustrate a miniature generative grammar in action, I must now confess that many linguists and psychologists no longer believe that this kind of grammar is the most appropriate conceptualization of the knowledge that every user of language possesses. An alternative point of view has arisen during the past few years which places more emphasis on semantics than on syntax, although it still perceives our mastery of language in terms of a set of implicit rules each of us has in his head. This opposing viewpoint is known as *generative semantics*.[14]

I make no apology for presenting an unresolved theoretical controversy; after all, very little could be written about psychology or education if we were to wait for certainty. Besides, the controversy throws light on the nature of the problem these opposing points of view are trying to resolve. And that problem is the relationship between meaning and grammar, which is precisely the topic we are concerned with.

One aspect of the controversy is quite technical and involves whether there is just one "deep level" of language, as the generative grammarians maintain, or whether there are a number of levels at which different transformational rules operate. Some linguists think that some of these metaphorical depths are so profound that they have coined the term "abyssal" to denote the fundamental level of meaning, far below anything to which words can be directly related.

A second issue, more critical to our immediate concerns, is whether any grammar will work independently of meaning. The fundamental question is whether language can be regarded as a closed system, unrelated to any other aspect of thought, or whether it depends on underlying thought processes that are not linguistic. Can a grammatical sentence be understood without knowledge of the circumstances in which it was produced? One of the boasts of the earlier generative grammarians was that meaning was quite irrelevant to their theorizing, that their grammars did not require any reference to a possible context or actual state of affairs in the world. They saw grammar, in other words, as a kind of algebra or self-contained logical system. However, I have already argued—with such examples as *Mother and meat are cooking*—that meaning must often be taken into account in the construction of a sentence.

Moreover, as I have also pointed out, meaning often takes priority over grammar; we use meaning to decide whether or not a sentence is grammatical. To take another example, if you ask most people what they make of the sentence *Zebras like horses,*[15] their first reaction is that a word has been left out, that you really meant to say *Zebras are like horses.* But *Zebras like horses* is not an ungrammatical sentence, any more than *People like horses* is ungrammatical. It just happens to make more sense to say that zebras (but not people) *are* like horses. So whether or not we decide that *are* should be in the sentence, whether or not we decide that the sentence is grammatical, depends on the meaning that we attach to it first of all.

I want to give a final example to show that sentences can be quite strange and unacceptable in their construction, although they break no obvious grammatical rule. I want to indicate once again that the way we put words together in sentences has a great deal to do with their meaning. This example is concerned with adjectives rather than nouns, and specifically with the fact that one can talk about *small boats* or *sailing boats* or *wooden boats* or even about *small wooden sailing boats*; but not about *wooden small sailing boats* or *small sailing wooden boats.*[16] Obviously a rule of language exists, exhibited by even the youngest children although never explicitly taught, concerning the manner in which adjectives are to be ordered. The rule seems to be that the adjectives most closely related to a noun—in the way in which the world is organized—must stay closest to the noun in a sentence. The characteristic "sailing" seems to be more specific to boats than the characteristic "wooden"—many objects other than boats are wooden—therefore we say *wooden sailing boats*, not *sailing wooden boats.* Would you say that having a color like "blue" is more typical of boats than being small or made of wood? Color seems in fact to fall between size and material, since most people would agree that *small blue wooden sailing boats* is the only grammatical way of ordering the adjectives.

Syntax is concerned with order, and semantics with meaning. The generative semanticists do not assert that our facility in language is not rule-governed, or that these rules are not "generative" in the sense illustrated in my miniature generative grammar. But the generative semanticists argue that the rules of language must be rooted in meaning, and related to meaning in all their operations. The syntax that determines the shape of our language is based not on how words can be put together with grammatical rules at the level of surface structure, but on how concepts are related at the deeper level of thought.

Generative semantics

There is not just one theory of generative semantics, but a number of relatively independent approaches that hold a few basic ideas in common.

The first general assertion is that all sentences of language are based on one or more propositions, reflecting the speaker's or writer's purpose in producing the sentence in the first place. (One of the problems of generative grammar is that it is just too productive. Even the simplest of rules will generate hundreds of sentences, all but one of which are presumably irrelevant, or even misleading, to the intention of the producer on any particular occasion.) The core of a proposition is an act or an event or perhaps just a state of affairs, such as *The dog is black* or *The dog is running*. Complex sentences are combinations of more than one proposition, and propositions are usually embedded in a context of time and place. For example, *The black dog was running in the park yesterday.*

The second general assertion of generative semantics is that the heart and pivot of a sentence is the verb since it is the word to which all the other words in the sentence are related. The relation between the various nouns which can be in a sentence and the verb is often referred to as their *case*. There are at least a dozen different kinds of case relations, several of which can be exemplified in the sentence *The cook was carving the meat with a knife in the kitchen on Friday*, where "cook" is the agent, "knife" the *instrument*, "kitchen" the *location* and "Friday" the *time*. *Mother is cooking* and *Meat is cooking* cannot be combined into *Mother and meat are cooking* because *mother* and *meat* have different case relations to the verb: *Mother* is an agent—she is cooking something; while *meat* is an object—someone is cooking it.

Case relations can be represented in the form of a network, as shown in Figure 3.2. The similarity to cognitive structure networks such as that shown in Figure 1.5 is not merely coincidental; the propositions of the deep semantic levels of language should be regarded as particular organizations of thought.

One reason that the surface structure of language does not have a one-to-one relation with the underlying deep structures of thought is that case relations can be represented in a variety of ways. In some languages, such as English, word order is important; the agent is placed before the verb and the object afterwards, so that *The man saw the woman* does not mean the same as *The woman saw the man*. In many languages agent/object relations are indicated by inflection, or change in the form of words. English does have inflectional changes for pronouns; we say *He saw her* but *She saw him*. Finally, and most importantly in English, case relations can be represented by prepositions, such as *at, from, by, to* and so forth. However, the same preposition may represent a number of different case relationships. We can talk about a letter that was written *by* hand (instrument) *by* a friend (agent) and left *by* the window (location) to be delivered *by* 5 P.M. (time).

Generative semantics tends to deal with such inconsistencies between surface and deep structures by wiping them out, or at least downgrading

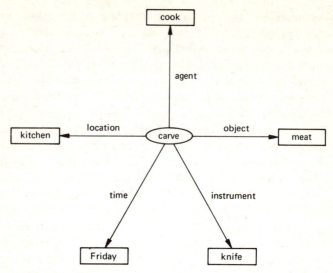

Figure 3.2   Some case relations underlying the sentence *The cook was carving the meat with a knife in the kitchen on Friday.*

them. For example, the fact that a single meaning can appear to have more than one surface representation may be regarded as merely an artifact of the linguist's bad habit of analysing words and utterances in isolation. Generative semanticists assert that in practise a speaker or writer can produce only one surface structure for any proposition; and this one possibility is wholly determined by what he wants to say, by the situation in which he says it (including his perception of his listener or reader's knowledge) and by the rules of his language. In fact, it is argued, the speaker cannot choose between alternative surface structures. Written in isolation on a sheet of paper, *The boy chases the dog* and *The dog is chased by the boy* may appear to have the same meaning grammatically, but in practice they can never replace each other. *The boy chases the dog* is an assertion about a boy. It is the answer to the question "What is the boy doing?" or the sequel to the statement I'll tell you something about the boy". *The dog is chased by the boy* can be used only when the previous topic has been the dog.

In other words, the speaker or writer has no choice in language in the sense that more than one sentence may represent the same meaning. Because there are always nuances, he must have a reason for using a passive sentence rather than an active one.[17] For example, saying "Take a seat please" rather than "Woncha siddown?" reflects the speaker's perception of the formality of a situation. And not even the words *oculist* and *eye doctor* are synonymous in their nuances, since use of the latter implies that the listener would not understand the former. The meaning of an utterance involves much more than the words spoken; it depends on the entire situation, verbal and nonverbal, in which the utterance is made.

In generative semantics, the fact that one word or sentence may represent more than one meaning is dismissed as a mere coincidence, of little importance in actual language use. Different semantic processes may lead by chance from different deep structures to an identical surface structure, such as *Flying planes can be dangerous*, but to the generative semanticist that possibility is no more a cause for consternation or theoretical wonderment than the fact that a type of fruit, two identical objects and the act of peeling happen to be represented by the same sound, variously spelled *pear*, *pair* and *pare*. Because language is embedded in meaning, and meaning is always limited by the prior purposes and understandings of both speaker and listener, or writer and reader, ambiguity is in practice a very rare event —a cause of amusement whenever it is detected.

Semantics, grammar and comprehension

The theoretical controversy surrounding generative grammar and generative semantics does not affect the conceptualization of language comprehension that I have outlined, with the listener or reader using his own knowledge of language and his expectations of what is being said to predict a limited number of alternatives, in much the same way that the speaker or writer produced the surface structure in the first place. In fact it is easier to explain "comprehension by production", or "analysis by synthesis", in terms of a theory of language in which everything is focussed on meaning. If indeed a speaker has little choice about the surface structure he will produce—given his intentions and the situation in which he makes his utterance—and if the listener also has a good idea of both the speaker's intentions and of the situation in which the utterance is made, then the listener should be able to make a sufficiently accurate prediction of the surface structure the speaker is likely to produce. ("Sufficiently accurate" means accurate enough for the listener to comprehend, to find answers to his implicit cognitive questions.)

Why then did I take up space and time in describing generative transformational grammar? The first reason is the ten- or fifteen-year time lag that seems to exist between the development of theories in such disciplines as linguistics and psychology and their dissemination among teachers as concepts applicable to education. Oversimplified notions of an outdated generative and transformational linguistics—dramatized on occasion by the label *new grammar*—have only recently begun to find their way into general educational thinking. I think it was never the intention of linguists to imply that children might be *taught* transformations by rote. But such has been the "practical" interpretation frequently made in education, where theoretical developments may be seized upon not as possible ways of enlightening teachers, but as justifications for new (or allegedly new) instructional materials and methodology. I have tried therefore to put generative grammar into its proper theoretical place.

Besides, some account must be taken of the fact that grammar does seem to make a difference to meaning, and that listeners and readers are often painfully sensitive to ungrammaticality. *The boy chases the dog* would seem to have the same meaning as *The dog is chased by the boy*, and a different meaning than *The dog chases the boy*, whether or not a boy is actually chasing a dog in the real world or whether we know anything about boys or dogs. (The argument is sometimes put in wholly abstract or nonsense form to prove this independence. It can be said *The wugs zak the vims* means the same as *The vims are zakked by the wugs* without any prior knowledge of wugs, vims or zakking.) But the power of grammar to handle such "intrinsic" meaning is severely limited to what the sentence entails by strict logic (for example, if boys chase dogs then dogs can be chased by boys), or by the denial of contraries (if boys chase dogs, then it is not true that boys cannot chase dogs). In none of these cases, most generative grammarians would argue, have you actually comprehended something you did not already know.

Compare the limited "logical" manner in which grammar handles intrinsic meaning with the richness of our normal comprehension. For example, I have just heard that a visiting speaker from out of town will be staying at a rather inconvenient hotel which I know is one of the cheapest in our neighborhood. I immediately comprehend that he must be paying his own expenses. Nothing in the grammar of *Professor Jelks will be staying at the Imperial Palace Hotel* tells me about his financial arrangements, but such is the information I derive from the sentence.

Why then does language have grammar if it is almost entirely subservient to meaning, both in production and comprehension? If I might speculate, I would suggest that grammar is probably a convenience to the speaker; it makes putting sentences together easier. The human brain is such that we normally prefer there to be just one right way of doing something; decision making is easier. But then why should the listener even be aware of grammar, if he scarcely uses it for comprehension? Because in fact the listener or reader uses grammar in exactly the same way as the speaker or writer: He checks his understanding of a sentence by seeing if its surface structure is the kind he would produce to represent the meaning. In other words, when an utterance has been tentatively understood—and only then —will the listener become aware of whether it contravenes his own ideas of what constitutes grammaticality.

Meaning and comprehension

The notion that the meanings of utterances—or at least important aspects of the meanings of utterances—lie outside the utterance, in the mind of the speaker or the listener, often causes difficulty. Does this mean that a sentence can mean anything at all?

Let us first look at meaning from the listener's (or reader's) point of view. To the listener, the meaning of a sentence must be the information he extracts from it, the answers he gains to cognitive questions. In part this information might be what the speaker wanted to convey, for example, that Professor Jelks is indeed staying at a hotel called the Imperial Palace. But the listener can extract or infer a lot of other information about Professor Jelks—and also perhaps about the producer of the statement. All this can be regarded as the meaning of the statement to the listener. The meaning is what he *comprehends*, and can go far beyond (and also fall far short of) what the speaker intends. There is no symmetry here. But it is not the case that any sentence could have any meaning. No listener is likely to deduce from the statement about Professor Jelks that he is staying at a hotel other than the Imperial Palace (unless part of the listener's prior knowledge is that the speaker is an inveterate liar). But the range of meanings an utterance may have is bounded and directed by the knowledge and concerns of the listener as well as by the intentions of the speaker.

Comprehension is not a simple matter of relating everything in a sentence or a discussion or a book to everything you already know. Such a procedure would merely swamp you in your own information. I may know the names of the historical figures depicted on all of our coins and bills, and even know when the particular individuals held office; but I do not want this knowledge to leap into my mind every time I am asked to make change for a parking meter. We extract from language the information that will be useful to us not by relating statements to everything we know, but by looking in them for what we want to know. And if we discover what we want to know, we "comprehend".

For a speaker or writer, therefore, the meaning of a sentence is inseparable from his original intention in producing the sentence: it is the information he wants the listener to derive, the knowledge he has tried to codify, the changed state of affairs he hopes to bring about. For the listener or reader, the meaning is the information he succeeds in deriving. And for the third party—the teacher "explaining" a passage in a novel or the linguist analysing a sentence—the meaning is *his* intuition of the intention of the original writer or speaker, very much affected by the particular point that the third party wants to make. When a teacher argues with a child "Don't you see what the author is trying to say?" the teacher is more likely to mean, "Why can't you look for the same kind of information that I do?"

Language and Thought

The intimate and complex relation between language and thought is a matter of critical concern in education for several reasons. First, language and learning are very obviously interdependent; most of the learning children are expected to accomplish in school is embedded in or surrounded by language. Second, a child's capacity to learn is often evaluated in terms of the language he speaks. The relation between language and thought is also a live and central theoretical issue both in psychology and in linguistics, and some points of view are diametrically opposed. For example, at one extreme is the assertion not simply that thought cannot exist independently of language, but that thought does not exist at all. According to the behavioristic point of view,[18] thought is a fictitious process invented to cover our ignorance or confusion about the causes of human behavior. No one has even seen or measured a thought, according to this view, and when we "think" we could simply be listening to subvocalized "inner" speech. Speech itself is an acquired habit, and—like all other forms of complex behaviour—does not require thought to explain it. A point of view almost as extreme as behaviorism proposes that thought exists largely as an internalization of speech. Thought, in other words, is socially determined. Initially adults talk to children in order to control children's behaviour. In due course children learn to talk to themselves in order to control their own behaviour. And eventually children suppress the sound of their own voices while they are still talking to themselves—and this is thought. This point of view, which is close to being the official position of Soviet psychology, is derived directly from the theories of the great Russian physiologist and psychologist Pavlov.[19] At the other extreme from the behaviorist perspective is the opinion that language and thought are completely separate and independent. Such a view would appear to be patently false. We may at times be tempted to assert that a person's statements seem unrelated to any prior thought, but we would be unlikely to claim that a person who has never thought could speak intelligibly. However, an eminently respectable linguistic point of view (now coming under increasingly critical attack) holds that language as a process can be studied and described without any reference to thought. This is the point of view that a grammar of language could be written without reference to meaning).[20] Its logic underlies many ill-founded attempts to write "grammars" that would enable computers to translate or to convert written language to speech.

The position taken in this book is more complex and generally reflects what might be called cognitive and psycholinguistic approaches to language and thought. This position asserts that the manner in which we learn, produce and comprehend language reflects human thought, and is basically no different from other cognitive activities. Nevertheless, many aspects of thought are not verbal; therefore it is inappropriate to assert that thought is dependent upon language. On the other hand, as we have seen, the surface structure of language cannot possibly be comprehended except to the extent that it makes sense in the realm of thought. Language, in other words, is founded upon thought. Despite this basically asymmetrical relationship between language and thought, thought is rarely unaffected by language, since it is through language that so much learning takes place. Like other mental activities, learning may indeed be possible without language. But all too often the spark that initiates learning, and directs its progress, is linguistic. The great handicap afflicting a deaf child in his labors to learn about the world has nothing to do with intelligence or motivation or will, but is so much simpler that incredibly it is often overlooked. The deaf child's basic problem is that he cannot *hear*, and therefore is denied access to much of the organized information available in the world of language.

Language: product, process and use

Some clarification of the relation between language and thought can be gained by remembering that the word *language* can be employed in a variety of ways, and statements about one aspect of language are not necessarily relevant to other aspects. Sometimes a generalization can be entirely misleading. For example, language is frequently described or "defined" as "a system of communication", as if repetition of what is already known in somewhat more impressive words would illuminate the issue. Everyone knows that language is *used* for communication; but so are winks, shrugs, nudges, whistles, flags, traffic signals and laser beams. The use to which an object is put may not tell us very much about the object itself. Buckets and sponges will both convey water, but they have little else in common. Feet and jet aircraft can both be described as systems of transportation, but such a statement does not throw much light upon anatomy or aeronautics. The asssertion that language is used for communication is not an answer to a question, but a statement that demands explanation. How is language employed for communication?

A good deal of mystification has been injected into the understanding of how and why children develop language skills by the popular assertion that children learn language "in order to communicate", or even because infants have a "need" to communicate (although children are rarely so well looked after as when they are too young to be told to wait, or to get something themselves). Such statements confuse use with motivation. They presuppose that children are aware of the uses to which language can be put before children learn anything about language. An alternative explanation for a child's initial moves in the direction of understanding language is simply that *language is there*, in his environment; it is part of the world he continually strives to make sense of. In other words, the child does not begin learning language to exploit it so much as to comprehend it.

A first step in any analysis of human behaviour must be to distinguish the *product* of that behaviour, or the observable behaviour—for example, the sounds of speech—from the *uses* to which that product is put. But it is also necessary to distinguish the product from the skills exercised to produce it. These skills are the *process* of language, which psychologists (and some psycholinguists) are usually talking about when they refer to a child's language development. On the other hand, the language produced—the way in which certain classes of words tend to be put together in sentences, and certain combinations of words tend to occur in certain circumstances— can be discussed quite independently of the human beings who produce the words in the first place, and of the use to which the words are put. Language as a product—the surface structure or physical manifestation of language—lies wholly in the outside world. The process by which language is produced or comprehended, on the other hand, is always in an individual's head; it is part of his theory of the world.

Another frequent assertion is that language is unique. In the light of the ambiguity of the word *language*, it is again advisable to look carefully at exactly what is being claimed. As we have already seen, there is certainly nothing unique about one major function language is supposed to fulfil, that of communication. Other forms of communication by humans or other creatures may be less flexible or efficient than language; but one must go a long way down the evolutionary scale to find an organism that does not communicate with others of its kind. Humans' use of *language* to communicate is unique, and so is their use of language for other purposes including the selection, acquisition, organization, storage, manipulation and retrieval of information in memory. But none of these purposes is unique. We can select, acquire, organize, store, manipulate and retrieve information from memory without language—and so can many other living organisms.

There also appears to be nothing unique about the skills human beings employ to produce language. As I have tried to show, the *process* of language comprehension seems to have much in common with the cognitive skills we employ in making sense of all aspects of our world. Our knowledge of language involves a category system, distinctive features and interrelationships among the categories. Exactly the same basic process seems to be involved in learning about language as in learning about other aspects of the world. A picturesque analogy suggests that it would be as fruitless to seek an "essence" of language as it would be to try to discover anything that makes cows unique.[21] Take a cow apart metaphorically, and it has no part that cannot be found in other animals. What is different about a cow is the way everything is put together. And what is different about language is the particular way it recruits and employs skills used in other aspects of cognition. The outcome is different, but the elements are the same. One of the basic assumptions of this book—an assumption which must obviously be examined critically—is that there are no thought processes unique to language. It is language as a product that is unique. No other species produces language; and language distinguishes man from other living creatures far more than his face, fingers or general physique. But other aspects of human culture are similarly unique, for instance, most of our technology. Language is part of the unique world man has constructed for himself.

LANGUAGE AS A PROCESS   While language as a product is located entirely in the outside world, language as a process, with rules for its production and comprehension, must be located entirely within the cognitive structure of the individual. The process of language is part of an individual's theory of the world—a part that enables him to make sense of the language (as product) in the world, and to produce language himself. How is this knowledge of language related to his more general knowledge of his environment, and how are language skills related to other cognitive skills?

Language, as we have seen, consists of a limited number of elements which can loosely be termed *words* (although it would be more accurate to refer to them as *morphemes* as noted at the beginning of this chapter), and a *syntax*, or set of rules, that determines the relationship these units have with each other in sentences. The various ways in which sequences of words are organized with respect to each other permit a speaker or listener to relate meanings to different word combinations.

This basic structure of language as a process—a fundamental set of units interrelated meaningfully by a number of rules—appears to be precisely analogous to cognitive structure, which might be defined as a system of categories, or discrete units of experience, which are interrelated meaningfully. In fact as a first approximation it might be asserted that words in language stand for categories in the cognitive system, and that the rules of grammar are the counterpart in language of the dynamic interrelationships among categories or "routines" of cognitive structure. Certainly the words of our language that seem to stand for objects or events in the world around us are in fact related to categories in cognitive structure. Whether or not a child calls an object by its "right name" depends on how his theory of the world is organized. A child who calls all four-legged animals "dog" or all men "daddy" has correctly associated a name with a category (in his own mind) but has not fully differentiated the category.[22]

However, not all words in the language can be associated with cognitive categories. Verbs often appear to refer to an interrelationship between categories rather than to the categories themselves. Two verbs of particular interest in this respect are *is* and *has*. As we have seen, the various parts of the verb *to be* often fit into a hierarchical system typical of one way in which cognitive structure seems to be organized. If you are told that a wallaby *isa* kangaroo, for example, you immediately know a good deal about wallabies. Anything you know about kangaroos—for example, that they have relatively short forelegs, powerful hind legs and long thick tail —applies to wallabies. In other words, *isa* indicates relationships inherent in the category system itself. The *has* relationship, on the other hand, extends outside of categories, or between them. A statement that a wallaby *has* a long thick tail tells you nothing more about wallabies.

Furthermore, many words have an exclusively linguistic function. They do not seem to be related either to categories or to their interrelationships in cognitive structure. For example, the word *by* in the sentence *The man was bitten by the dog* disappears in the sentence *The dog bit the man*, although the meaning is largely unchanged. It is very difficult to find a satisfying linguistic explanation of this phenomenon. If *by* has a meaning in the first sentence, then where has it gone in the second? Or is *by* simply a marker that a certain rule of language is being applied? In other words, we can see that some words—particularly nouns and pronouns—seem to be closely related to cognitive categories. Other words—often verbs, adjectives and adverbs—seem more closely related to cognitive interrelationships, while still others appear to have a purely grammatical function.

The uses of language

Communication—a complex term that might be defined as producing surface structure that someone else can make sense of in the way that you want—is usually regarded as the main, or even sole, function of language. Such a use of language demands a particular skill that may be lacking in many younger school children. This skill involves predicting the uncertainty of a listener (or reader), and organizing the surface structure so that just that uncertainty is reduced. For example, if someone asks me to pick up a book he has left in his car, which is parked near my home, then it is enough for him to specify the location if his car is likely to be the only one at that location. But if two cars are likely to be there, he will have to tell me the make of his vehicle or its color. And if more than one car of the same make or color is likely to be there, he will have to give me other information. The information he must give me must always be related to what the alternatives are.[23] Whether it is appropriate to refer to something simply as a car or a store or a book or a dog depends not on what the object being talked about is, but on what it might be confused with. Estimating how much prior knowledge on the part of a listener or reader can be taken for granted constitutes a major part of a speaker or writer's skill. Because children are usually not very practised at looking at situations from another individual's point of view, their language is rarely as informative as it might be—a fact that should be borne in mind given the current vogue of requiring children to read texts written by other children. It is true that children who are very close, like brothers and sisters, may understand each other when adults fail; but that is because of the knowledge these children are likely to have in common. In general, children find it easier to understand adult language than the language of other children simply because adults tend to be more experienced and efficient communicators. If children may on occasion be more effective tutors for other children than adults, it need not be because they know more or communicate better, but because they antagonize or intimidate less.

However, communication is not the sole purpose for which language is employed; and whether communication should be considered primary is a matter of debate. One very important reason for producing language is to change or control behaviour. We speak or write in order to achieve some end in the world around us. This may seem the same as saying that language is used for communication, or conveying meaning; but conveying meaning and changing behaviour may have nothing to do with each other. Someone may understand you without agreeing with you, or without doing what you ask. It may help you to achieve your ends if your meaning is communicated, but this is often not necessary and sometimes not desirable. A large measure of the propagandist's or advertising writer's art is his ability to change behaviour without having his audience comprehend his intention.

A related function of language, already referred to briefly, is the control of one's own behaviour by in effect telling oneself what to do. The control of many of our skills seems to have a verbal basis at least until they become habitual, for example, when we remind ourselves to keep the weight on the downhill ski, or to check that the car is out of gear before we switch on the ignition. Children can frequently be heard talking themselves through a task or telling themselves to stop doing something.[24] Perhaps it is a little less easy to regard language as communication when the person involved is talking to himself, or when he writes in a notebook or engagement book for his own future reference.

A second important function of language—at least according to the theoretical approach of this book—is its ability to put a person in touch with his own thought or knowledge. I have pointed out several times that we do not have direct access to cognitive structure or to the processes of thought that transpire therein. We have seen that it is difficult even for an expert to say exactly what he must know in order to perform certain skills, such as to distinguish cats from dogs, or to produce sentences. It is difficult even to specify what we are talking about when we refer to the representation of rules or knowledge in the brain. An anatomist or physiologist or neurologist cannot really say where or how a piece of information is stored in the brain. How could a pattern of neural activity or a particular organization of molecules within a cell be the same as knowledge of a friend's face or a piece of music? But if it is impossible to observe directly what we know, we can always find out whether we know something by testing to see if that knowledge can be translated into behaviour.

One form of behaviour is of course action. We say a person has a knowledge of car engines if he can repair one or strip one down and put it together. But another form of behaviour is language. We would also say that a person knows something about engines if he can talk about them, or describe how he would strip one down. Language is behaviour that can also be used to make knowledge manifest. It is a truism that we often do not know what we think or feel about something until we talk about it, either aloud or silently. Many speakers are genuinely interested and even carried away by what they hear themselves saying during spontaneous lectures. What they say is grammatical, and hopefully makes sense; yet they are not aware of what they are saying until they say it. And if the speaker is following notes, or even a draft of his lecture, then the notes or draft must have been generated from knowledge structures below the level of awareness. At some point in the language process (unless you are reciting something someone else has written) the thoughts that you are expressing must have been thoughts that you did not know you had. One of the tragedies of our educational system is that it seems to result in reluctance to bring ideas to the surface and expose them to criticism. We prefer our ideas to remain dormant than to be stated and possibly labelled wrong. Furthermore, something in the early experience of almost all of us seems to inhibit fluent writing. It is ironic that many teachers who themselves exhibit so much reluctance or anxiety when required to write reports and papers have no hesitation in imposing these demands—in highly anxiety-producing circumstances—upon their students.

LANGUAGE AND PERCEPTION   Because information acquired through language (whether or not represented in verbal form) comes to constitute a large part of everyone's cognitive structure, and because cognitive structure is the basis for the predictions we must make to make sense of events around us, there is an intimate connection between our language and the way we perceive the world. A common sense point of view might deny that the manner in which we speak could make any difference to what we see, hear or feel going on around us. Surely our experience of the world is determined by what goes on in the world, not by our language? But the fact that we seem to be living in a structured world of clearly defined objects is attributable more to our expectations and previous knowledge than to the noise that impinges on our sense organs. And there is a highly debated theory that our language, both in its lexicon and its grammar, has a very great influence on the way we perceive the world. In effect, this *linguistic relativity hypoth-*

esis[25] asserts that we do not all live in the same world, but in individual worlds largely structured by our language habits.

Typical examples of the way in which languages classify experience differently are that Eskimo has many words for snow, while English has only one; and that Arabic distinguishes many more kinds of horse than English. In fact Eskimo lacks a word that is a direct translation of the English *snow*, just as there is no one Arabic word for *horse*. If you want to talk about snow or horses in these languages you are forced to be more precise than in English. Of course it is not difficult to think of reasons why Eskimos and Arabs should want their language to be more specific about cerain topics than an English speaker. It is a general rule of *all* languages that the more important a concept, or cognitive category, is to a culture or an individual, the more names that concept is likely to have. Anyone interested in dogs is likely to have many more names for them than a person who has no desire to distinguish one dog from another. Wine tasters, wool buyers and other specialists have words in their vocabularies that the majority of us have never heard of. And, naturally, people with specialised vocabularies perceive the world differently from those of us who cannot tell an *amontillado* from a *manzanilla*. Eskimos cannot even see snow in the general way in which many English speakers see it, and an Arab never sees merely a horse. Experiments have shown that colors that fit into a familiarly named category (such as *red* or *blue* in English) are recognized and remembered more readily than colors with less common names (such as *salmon* or *puce*).[26]

But it would be misleading to suggest that we perceive the world in the way we do only because of language. If perception were wholly dependent on the way we speak, then infants and deaf-mutes would be blind. We perceive the world in terms of the cognitive structure we establish in our heads; and the language we hear spoken around us is not the only influence on the way our cognitive theories are developed. But our perception of the world depends on how we have organized our past experience; and language tends to ensure that all members of a particular community organize their experience similarly. Since it reflects cognitive structure, language becomes a distillation of a culture or community's experience, and the means by which this experience is transmitted from one generation to another. A consequence of this cultural transmission through language is that to the extent that individuals differ in their language—even within the same general language group—they are likely to organize their experience differently and perceive the world in different ways.

The linguistic relativity hypothesis does not claim that individuals are unable to see differences not represented in their language, merely that they are unlikely to pay attention to them. A speaker of English may have only one word for snow, unless he happens to be a skier, but he might well be able to see the difference if shown examples of the categories that Eskimos distinguish. One reason he has no special categories for different kinds of snow is that the language he has learned does not distinguish them; and one reason his language has not distinguished them is that no one in the group in which he moves has found it necessary or useful to do so. This apparent chicken-and-the-egg paradox is resolved by the fact that both cognitive structure and language reflect the way individuals have learned or chosen to organize their experience. Languages in general are suited to their users.

Language and school[27]

There is another link between language and perception that has particular classroom relevance. We perceive what we attend to, and language is frequently used to attract or direct attention. The use of language to manipulate the perception of others is one example of the way language can control behaviour. Children in school are constantly told to look at this or listen to that. But telling a child to look at something is no guarantee that he will see it, even if he looks in the right direction with what seems to be sufficient application. Perception does not depend directly on language, but on cognitive structure. And if a child's cognitive structure cannot make sense of what you think he is looking at, then his simply looking in the right direction will be useless. Even if a child says "Yes, I see" when asked to look at a picture or a word, he may still be in the same position as most of us if invited by a chemist to peer through his microscope at some polychlorinated biphenyls.

I have tried to show that while language and thought are ultimately linked, they should not be considered identical. Language is in the very fabric of our thought and greatly facilitates learning; but thought and learning underlie language and can proceed independently. All of this theory has important implications for the classroom.

For example, a child should not be evaluated simply on the basis of the language he produces—certainly not in respect to his dialect, nor even to his grammar. For a start, the language that a child produces may have little relation to the language that he can understand. All of us understand sentences that we could not possibly produce, and we understand dialects that we would make a poor job of imitating. Children are particularly good at understanding adult language, which is one reason why parents try to hold private conversations out of earshot of their offspring, and why children of all ages and cultures seem able to comprehend much "adult" programming on television. Anxiety, inexperience, embarrassment, group cohesiveness and even downright cussedness are all good reasons why the language a child produces at school may be only a pallid reflection of his ability to understand and retain. What a child can talk about is often not a reliable indicator of what he knows.

Furthermore, the fact that they may on occasion use language differently from adults does not mean that children's language or their thought is defective. Remember, most of the "content words" of our language are based on underlying cognitive structure. A child who calls all four-legged animals *doggie* has not failed to learn the word correctly; he has associated the word with the cognitive category to which he allocates dogs (and all other four-legged animals). From his cognitive point of view, he is using the word appropriately. He simply has not differentiated his category sufficiently. Alternatively, a child may refer to a cat as a *doggie* because that is the best word he has available (just as adults may call a moth a *butterfly*), but if you asked the child whether the cat is really a dog, or whether a dog and a cat are the same, he would say "No". He knows there is a difference, and his use of an approximate word represents his best attempt to make sense of it.

Children often seem to misuse "opposites", for example, *ask* and *tell*, or *more* and *less*. Such confusion does not indicate that a child has gotten such words entirely wrong, but that he has a good idea of what the word is related to (transmission of information for *ask* and *tell*, relative quantity for *more* and *less*), and needs just one more "feature" of meaning to be completely correct.[28] A child's language development is pretty much complete by the age of five.[29] But his underlying logical structures, or the manner in which he organizes his world, are far from fully developed at the same age.

A child's fluency in language is vital to his general intellectual development, but it is also one of the most fragile and personal aspects of his growth. A child whose language is denigrated will remain mute, and deny himself the massive boost that language provides for learning and thought. A child whose language is rejected will feel rejected himself. Reluctance to talk may be less a sign of stupidity than of lack of trust.

CHAPTER 4

Learning

After three chapters concerned mainly with the manner in which individuals succeed in comprehending the world around them, it might be objected that the main reason children come to school is not because they can make sense of everything, but in order to learn what they do not know already. It might also be objected that no explanation has yet been offered concerning the origin and development of the cognitive structure that enables us all to make sense of our worlds. If cognitive structure were present in the brain at birth, or if it developed automatically as a function of growth, there would be no need for schools or for teachers. How does our theory of the world arise in the first place?

It is now time to focus our attention upon learning, although we shall find that learning and comprehension are fundamentally inseparable. Cognitive structure is learned. What we learn about the world enables us to make sense of it; and our efforts to make sense of the world provide the impetus for learning. *Making sense* has been characterized as relating events in the world around us to cognitive structure; and learning is the process of elaborating and modifying cognitive structure when it fails to make sense of the world. Learning, in other words, is not simply the basis of our attempts to make sense of the world; it is itself a consequence of our urge to transform uncertainty into familiarity. We do not learn by chance; nor do we passively assimilate what others try to teach us. Learning is a product of experience, and (as we shall see) is best facilitated when that experience is deliberately and systematically sought by the learner.

Like comprehension, learning is an interaction between the world around us and the theory of the world in our head. The symmetry of our basic diagram, Figure 1.1, can now be completed in Figure 4.1.

The upper arrow represents our use of cognitive structure to make sense of the world; we perceive the world through the mental filter of what we believe the world to be like. But the lower arrow, pointing in the opposite direction, indicates that cognitive structure is itself modified as a consequence of experience. A learning situation arises whenever our cognitive structure proves inadequate for making sense of the world, when something in our experience is unfamiliar or unpredictable, when we are confronted by noise. And we learn—that is, we modify cognitive structure—so that our experience will become more predictable, so that in the future we will have a better match between our theory of the world in the head and our experience.

My representation of the interaction between cognitive structure and experience (Figure 4.1) should not be interpreted in static sense; it is not like a map or the blueprint of a house. The interaction represented in Figure 4.1 is dynamic; it should be regarded as an endless cyclical process, a revolving wheel—with cognitive structure constantly striving to make sense of the world, and learning constantly leading to the reorganization and development of cognitive structure.[1] Whenever we do not understand, we are motivated to learn.

Learning, in other words, is a process of problem solving. We learn because we do not understand, cannot relate, cannot predict. Everything we know, then—the current state of our cognitive structure—is a consequence of all our previous attempts to make sense of the world. Our present knowledge arises out of a history of problem solving,[2] or of predicting the consequences of potential actions.[3]

The present chapter will be primarily concerned with the nature of learning, and with how it is accomplished. We shall take a look at how every child is "equipped" to learn. And we will consider how learning is

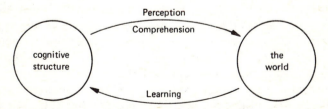

Figure 4.1 The interaction between cognitive structure and the world

a process as natural and continual as our efforts to comprehend, but a process that also demands a price from the learner involving risk. In the following chapter we shall examine some aspects of learning which are often of particular concern in school, and also a closely related topic that is equally critical in education, forgetting. Chapter 6 will then be devoted to what is perhaps the most central and important aspect of human learning —the learning of language skills including reading.

Learning and Memory

To demonstrate that many common English words have multiple and even overlapping meanings, it is not necessary to go beyond the everyday language of education and psychology. I do not want to imply that all theoretical issues are semantic, but our language does lead to confusion if a one-to-one relationship between words and referents is expected. Take for example the two topics (or is there just one?) with which we are now concerned: learning and memory.

Most introductory psychology texts treat learning and memory as entirely distinct; in fact there are often separate chapters or sections with these titles. But one looks in vain for an explanation of how *learning* and *memory* may be distinguished, for the simple reason that the terms do not apply to distinctive psychological processes, except when they are used in very arbitrary and narrow ways. One theorist[4] has observed that whether a study is referred to as a learning experiment or a memory experiment depends not on the experimental subject's task, but on the experimenter's mode of measurement. If the experimenter counts the number of "practice trials" given before the subject is tested for his acquisition of a particular item or skill, then learning is being measured. If the experimenter measures the time that elapses between the last practice trial and the test, then memory is being examined. For reasons largely of historical accident, the words *memory* and *learning* are used in large areas of psychological experimentation more as adjectives than as nouns, arbitrarily distinguishing one broad and undefined class of studies from another.

Of course the word *memory* is also used as a noun, especially by the "information-processing" theorists whose approach is generally represented in this book. In this use, memory is often treated as a store in which knowledge and skills are gathered and integrated. In such a metaphorical sense, I make no distinction between memory and cognitive structure. As a noun the word *memory* is also used to refer to a process, or to aspects of a larger process. In this sense, memory generally refers to the output of a system, to the "retrieval" of stored information, while learning refers more to the "input" of new information into the system. However, the word *memorization* is often used synonymously with *learning*, at least with respect to the input of unrelated names, telephone numbers, formulae and other "facts" not predictable from anything already known.

Obviously, examination of the way words are used will not cast much light on the underlying processes with which we are primarily concerned —the modification of cognitive structure. Nonetheless, it will be necessary to treat separately two aspects of such cognitive change that may sound suspiciously like a distinction between learning and memorization. We must distinguish learning that is "meaningful" from learning that is "rote".

The aspect of learning that I regard as by far the most important is that which can and often must be self-initiated by the learner. I shall call such learning "meaningful" because it involves a cognitive change that makes sense, because it is intimately integrated with everything else the learner knows about the world. I shall not pay so much attention in this chapter to rote learning, or rote memorization, partly because this is the least important aspect of learning but also because it should be the easiest. Rote learning is the least important cognitively because what matters is how well new information can be integrated into prior knowledge. In other words, what matters is meaningfulness. Besides, most of our knowledge of the world and all of our skills cannot be described with sufficient explicitness for direct instruction, and are therefore not amenable to rote learning.

Rote learning should be the least difficult part of learning because it seems to occur spontaneously as long as the learner can make sense of a new item of information. For example, children learn an average of over a thousand new words ever year of their school careers. When new words are not recalled, it is less because they were not learned than because they were not understood. The usual problem with rote learning is in fact not memorization but forgetting, and forgetting is determined by sense and relevance. As I shall explain in Chapter 5, rote learning is difficult only to the extent that it does not make sense, and when it does not make sense it should be avoided. Difficulty in rote learning is a clear sign that the enterprise is futile and a more meaningful approach should be employed.

The Modification of Cognitive Structure

I have characterized learning as the modification of cognitive structure; now I must be more specific. In Chapter 1 I distinguished three components of cognitive structure, or of any system for organizing information: (a) a set of categories, (b) lists of distinctive features to specify membership of each category and (c) a network of interrelationships among the categories. Learning may involve the elaboration or modification of each of these three aspects of cognitive structure, and I shall consider each one in turn.

Establishing cognitive categories

The development of new categories almost invariably involves the breaking down, or *partitioning*, of one established category into two or more parts.[5] For example, a child who had never made any distinctions within the category of drinking utensils might come to distinguish cups from glasses, or glasses from bottles. He will no longer treat all drinking utensils as the same, and some difference or feature to which he had formerly not paid attention will now become significant. A child who formerly called all four-legged animals dogs and now calls some of those animals cats has established a new category by subdividing an existing larger category. He is in exactly the same situation as the philatelist who discovers that he must now subdivide his German stamps into East German and West German, or a supermarket manager who must distinguish regular from decaffeinated coffee.

Often it is through language that we learn that a category should be modified or developed, for example, when we hear something we would call a butterfly called a moth. But language is not essential. Many of our basic categories are formed before we learn to talk; and new words remain meaningless until we have a category to relate them to. We rarely experience something that cannot be placed into any cognitive category. Even if we cannot identify the object we are looking at as an iguana, we may still see that it is a reptile, or at least an animal. But we often find that our categorization is too gross. We should treat some objects within a category differently, for example, by calling them by a different name; and so we subdivide the category. A particular kind of table should be called a desk; some camels are dromedaries. Our own interests also determine the extent to which we want to subdivide categories.

Although their category systems are less well differentiated than those of adults, small children rarely behave as if they are in the state of confusion or bewilderment that is sometimes believed to characterize their existence. A child may not distinguish the animals that we call dogs, cats, cows and horses from each other; but he probably has a category of his own to put them all in—perhaps with a name of his own invention or with no name at all. It is not necessary to postulate that children, or any other creatures, are born with cognitive categories formed in advance. Instead they must possess only the ability to establish categories at a very primitive level, for example, dividing the world into objects that can be approached and objects that should be avoided.

Learning distinctive features

Every cognitive category must be specified by at least one distinctive feature; otherwise there would be no way of distinguishing objects or events in one category from those belonging to another. So a second broad aspect of learning must involve discovering new distinctive features to permit the differentiation of objects into new or modified categories, and establishing appropriate feature lists for every category.

Sometimes the learning of distinctive features involves making a new list to help specify a new category. For example, the child who discovers that some object he has always called cup should be called glass must learn to distinguish one from the other by establishing which features of the two objects constitute significant differences. Sometimes the learning of distinctive features involves modifying existing feature lists, for example, when a child discovers that some objects that he would call dog rather than cat are in fact called cat by other people. The child then must modify both his dog and cat feature lists so that the way in which he allocates particular animals to these two categories is a closer match to the way in which other people organize their world.[6]

Learning can also involve establishing alternative feature lists for the same category. We all learn very early in life that there can be more than one way of identifying an object. We can recognize an orange by its taste and smell and feel as well as by its appearance. Multiple feature lists are also required when objects that look quite different should be allocated to the same category; for example, brick houses and wooden houses, or the letters A and a. Alternative feature lists that specify the same category may be termed *functionally equivalent.* The development of functionally equivalent feature lists for such visually diverse forms at *HAT*, *hat* and *hat*, is an important part of learning to read.

A most important aspect of distinctive feature learning is that there is a limit to how much visual or other information from the environment the brain can handle; thus the brain must make the most economical use of distinctive feature information. Children quickly learn to establish very small *criterial sets* of features within their feature lists so that identification decisions can be made with a minimum of incoming information, and objects can be recognized from a partial glimpse.

Learning relations among cognitive categories

Finally, learning can occur through the development or modification of the network of relationships among cognitive categories. Simply by increasing the complexity of the organization of what we already know, we can make our theory of the world infinitely richer. We may be able to distinguish water and fire, but the effect each can have on the other is something that is added to our theory of the world only when we construct a new relationship between the two categories. Of potential new interrelations there would seem to be no end, especially to a child in the first few years of life who has yet to learn that it might occasionally be better not to try to learn at all. He must learn not simply that certain individuals are called uncle, but that an uncle is the brother of a parent; not just that $2 + 3 = 5$, and $2 \times 3 = 6$ but the difference between addition and multiplication. He must learn that Paris is the capital of France, that the French word for *dog* is *chien*, that the prefix *un* in English connotes negation, that fresh water boils at 212 degrees Farenheit (in certain conditions) and that each degree Farenheit is worth just five-ninths of a degree Centigrade or Celcius. Our knowledge of the world contains a huge number of causal or propositional relationships, each of which must be learned. If there are certain kinds of cloud, then rain is likely; a particular tone of voice will provoke a particular response from a listener; a glance along the street will probably disclose cars and trucks, not submarines and camels.

All of our skills—from riding bicycles to speaking and comprehending language—involve dynamic cognitive interrelationships which must be learned. Particularly crucial are the skills that we employ in order to facilitate learning, our strategies for acquiring and testing new knowledge of the world. We learn to recognize the occasion when learning is likely to be rewarding and when learning may be too costly an enterprise to undertake. We learn to predict when the effort to learn is likely to succeed and when it will probably fail. We learn to limit our aspirations in learning, and we learn our expectations of how much or little we shall achieve.

An exhaustive list of cognitive interrelationships, even if it were possible to compile, would constitute a catalog of human knowledge and its representation in individual minds far beyond the scope of this book. Nevertheless, I propose that at the core of all these different aspects or manifestations of learning there is but one fundamental underlying learning process, a process the present chapter is intended to elaborate and explain. Whether the learning is explicit (as when a child is told that Paris is the capital of France), whether it is "guided", or whether it is an act of pure discovery, I shall try to show that this one basic process of learning—which is not so very different from the process of comprehension we have already met—is all that any child has or needs in order to acquire and organize his knowledge of the world.

Learning: The Child as Experimenter

In Chapter 1 I compared cognitive structure with theories in science in terms of three basic functions: summarizing the past, interpreting the present, and predicting the future. When a scientist discovers that his theory is inadequate in some way, or when he wishes to expand it, he conducts experiments. He constructs hypotheses about particular implications of possible modifications or elaborations of his theory, for example, that the addition of liquid A to substance B should result in outcome C. He then tests each hypothesis by conducting experiments in which liquid A is actually added to substance B. The experiments provide the scientist with *feedback* about the appropriateness of the tentative changes in his theory. If the predicted outcome occurs, then his hypotheses are supported and he is encouraged to stay with the modification of his theory. But if the feedback is negative, if the predicted outcome does not occur, then his hypotheses are rejected and he must look for an alternative modification of his theory.

Like the scientist, a child uses his own theory, or cognitive structure, to make sense of the world around him. And a child also conducts experiments in order to develop and modify his theory, following procedures similar to those of the scientist. The basic learning process of every human being involves the experimental testing of cognitive hypotheses.

The basic learning process

The basic process for modifying or elaborating cognitive structure, with which all normally endowed children and adults are innately equipped to learn, may be conceptualized as a four-stage procedure:

(a) Generate a hypothesis based upon a tentative modification of cognitive structure
(b) Test the hypothesis
(c) Evaluate feedback
(d) Confirm or reject the modification of cognitive structure

The first stage of learning—tentative modification of cognitive structure and generation of a hypothesis—is precipitated when an individual's current cognitive structure proves inadequate. For example, a child may find himself in a situation where an animal that he recognizes as a dog—because it meets with his internalized "description", or specification, of dogs—should be called some other name. His problem is to amend the list of distinctive features which specifies the category of dog in his cognitive structure so that this particular animal which currently fulfils these specifications will be excluded. He must find some additional features to distinguish this not-a-dog animal from dogs. To do so he constructs a hypothesis such as "This animal that is not a dog has soft silky fur instead of rough wiry hair; therefore any four-legged animal without rough wiry hair is not a dog". In other words, the nature of the animal's hair tentatively becomes a new distinctive feature for distinguishing dogs from nondogs.

Such hypotheses are normally implicit; we are not aware that we have made them. Children do not usually go to an adult with questions about the distinctive quality of the hair of cats and dogs; or at least it is not necessary that they should do so. Instead they test whether their hypotheses are good by putting them to work, which is the second stage of the basic learning process. They conduct experiments. There are a variety of ways in which the child in my example may test his hypothesis, but they all involve doing something. He can, for example, refer to the next wiry-haired animal that he sees as a dog, or alternatively he can assert that the next soft furry animal that he sees is not a dog. In either case, he puts himself into a situation where he can get *feedback* about whether his hypothesis is correct. If he calls a wiry-haired animal dog and no one corrects him, then his hypothesis is supported. The same applies if his assertion that a furry-coated animal is something other than a dog is challenged. But if his hypothesis is proved wrong—if he is told that a wiry-haired animal should not be called a dog or that a soft furry animal should—then he knows that his proposed modification of cognitive theory is untenable. The feedback that is the consequence of his "experiment" tells him whether his proposed modification of the distinctive feature list specifying the cognitive category "dog" is justified.

There is an important point to be noted here to which we shall have to return. Whether or not a child is "correct" when he tests his hypothesis —whether he calls a wiry-haired animal dog and is proven right, or whether he calls a soft furry animal dog and is proven wrong—the feedback he receives enables him to learn something. It is not simply by being right that a child learns; there must be a possibility that he could be wrong. Negative feedback can be at least as useful as positive feedback—provided a child is not required to pay a penalty for being wrong, and provided he is not so dependent on being right that he does not know how to handle his own errors.[7]

The situation that I have just described could also provide the setting for the learning of a new category. We might suppose that a child hears an animal that he has always considered as a dog referred to as a cat, or in some other way regarded as different from dogs, and therefore excluded from that category. Or perhaps he is told that some objects he has always regarded as cups are in fact glasses. He is now in a position where he must elaborate his category system. He must generate and test a hypothesis that some of the objects he formerly treated as the same, because he did not distinguish them within a single cognitive category, should now be treated differently. An existing cognitive category must be partitioned. Partitioning an existing category in this way, or establishing a new category, necessarily involves the modification of an existing set of distinctive features. It is one thing to establish a new category, another to determine how to distinguish the cats from the dogs, the glasses from the cups—that is, the objects which should now go into the new categories.

Language is perhaps the major medium through which children learn of the existence of new categories. When they are told for the first time "There's a battleship" or "That's not a camel, it's an elephant", or when they are taught to recite the alphabet, they are in effect being told that they should establish new cognitive categories, without however being told how to define or distinguish these categories. In other words, the children are not being given any distinctive features for these new categories. They are not so much presented with information as with a problem, which they must solve by hypothesizing and testing what the appropriate distinctive features are. A child who is told a name is not being taught very much. When a teacher writes the letter *A* on the board and says "That's an *A*", the child is presented with a problem he must actively solve through learning; this is far from a mere matter of memorization. The child must discover what distinguishes *A* from everything else which the mark on the board might be. The teacher knows that the mark is an *A* because the teacher knows all about *A*s and also about *B*s and *C*s and *D*s, but when a child is first told that the letter on the board is *A*, there is no way he can tell whether the teacher is making a statement about the size of the mark or that it is written in chalk or that it comes to a point on top or anything else. In fact, the child will not have learned to recognize the letter *A* until he can distinguish it from every other letter of the alphabet. He may quickly come to distinguish *A* correctly 100 percent of the time if the only letters he ever sees are *A* and *B*, but the first time he meets a *C* he will not know whether it is an *A*.

The names of objects or events are cognitive interrelations of the simplest kind, the association of a particular sequence of sounds with a cognitive category. But there is a difference between learning a sequence of sounds—a process perhaps better called memorizing—and using that sequence of sounds, or name, correctly. In order to use the word correctly, the child must learn both a category and a set of distinctive features; and these elaborations of cognitive structure require hypothesis testing.

GENERAL AND SPECIFIC INFORMATION   I have suggested that the basic learning process is innate. The process of generating and testing hypotheses about the world is all that any child has or needs in order to make sense of progressively more and more of the world around him. But in order to learn in this way, the child must interact with the world. Such learning is active; it involves deliberately seeking information that will facilitate the process of constructing a theory of the world. In order to learn, in other words, a child needs information.

This does not mean, however, that a child needs to be told specifically what he has to know about the world. Children would learn little if they had to wait for that much information from adults, since almost everything that all of us know about the world—from distinguishing cats from dogs to the rules of language—is known implicitly. Instead, children need information that will support the basic learning process, information that I want to characterize as general and specific.

General information basically provides exposure to a problem. The way in which an infant begins to learn language is by hearing language spoken around him—not organized in any particular way, not in the form of instruction—simply as an event in his environment. This general information about language in effect indicates to the child the nature of the problem he has to solve, and also provides the source of the hypotheses he will have to generate and test. Unless he can get some idea of the likely meaning or connotation of a word, for example, he will have no way of hypothesizing how his cognitive structure should be modified to accommodate that word. In order to begin to learn the differences between cats and dogs, or between letters of the alphabet, a child requires general information—exposure to large numbers of cats and dogs, or letters of the alphabet—so that he has an opportunity to analyse individual cases for possible distinctive features. Information that is too specific at this stage in learning—for example, acquaintance with only one kind of dog, or with a few letters of the alphabet —is not adequate to give a child even an idea of the learning problem he must solve.

A child requires *specific information* in his hypothesis testing—when he wants to know whether his hypothesized rules for distinguishing dogs from cats, or *A* from *B*, really do work. And he can only get specific information when he is doing something, when he is in fact engaged in a test. Such information is specific because it is directly related to the hypothesis the child is testing, not because it may be relevant to a point the teacher is trying to get across. If a child is trying to analyze in what significant ways the letters *A* and *B* differ, for example, information about the names or some of the sounds of these letters will be completely irrelevant to his purposes. Feedback in the form of specific information must always be directed to the hypothesis the child is trying to test. Such specific information may seem difficult to provide, until one remembers that it is provided automatically if the child receives feedback relevant to behavior in which he is engaged. As long as the child's activity determines the nature of the feedback, it is bound to be relevant. It is not always necessary for a teacher to provide such feedback personally and individually; for example, a child quickly knows if something he is reading does not make sense, as long as the material is potentially meaningful to him and he is concerned with reading for sense. On the other hand, the highly structured instruction characteristic of many efforts at education might be regarded as the systematic deprivation of information, since the teacher deprives the child of general information and offers him only specific information, which may be quite irrelevant to the hypotheses he is trying to test.

THE RISKS OF LEARNING   The fact that learning must involve tests—and that it can only take place when there is a possibility the learner will be wrong —points up the inherent riskiness of the learning process, particularly in a culture oriented towards "success" and accuracy. Success may generate pride in parents and teachers, and a certain instinctive satisfaction in children, but the road to knowledge can be fraught with frustration and inconvenience for all involved. A child acquires most of his knowledge of the world by asking questions, explicitly and implicitly, and by testing his hypotheses. To a large extent he learns by being wrong, because if he is sure he is right he can have nothing to learn. Asking questions or making observations that seem nonsensical to an adult may be just as important to a child as babbling and babytalk. Phrases such as "Don't ask silly questions", "Don't talk unless you've got something sensible to say", or "Don't bother me with your chatter" do not characterize the environment in which learning will proceed smoothly.

The fact that learning is risky, demanding and often a cause of frustration and inconvenience does not seem to handicap many children in their earliest years. Most parents accept that very young children will behave like babies. Problems generally arise when these babies arrive at school, and their self-oriented learning strategies become even more risky, demanding, frustrating and inconvenient in a less flexible world where adults may not be so tolerant of "childish" activities. Teachers should always consider the extent to which a school situation inhibits rather than facilitates learning.

No matter how much his cognitive structure tells him there is a need or an opportunity to learn, two critical conditions must be met if a child is to exercise his capacity for learning. The first critical condition is that the child must have the expectation that there is something to learn, that the uncertainty with which he is confronted is potentially reducible to sense. This fond expectation is generally fulfilled in the early years of a child. He is eventually able to make sense of the auditory noise that is language and of the visual noise that is all the changing events taking place before his eyes. The first time many children encounter pure nonsense, or noise without the potential of being related to anything that makes sense to them, may be when they arrive at school. The second critical condition for learning is that the learner must have some reasonable expectation of a positive outcome. Learning involves both cost and risk to the learner. Attempting to learn may be so unrewarding that a child prefers to put up with noise.

THE COMMON BASIS OF COMPREHENSION AND LEARNING   The basic process of learning I have outlined is not fundamentally different from the process by which children and adults attempt to make sense of the world in the first place. In the specific case of language and the more general instance of environmental noise, the perceiver tries to make sense of what is going on by relating it to his cognitive structure. The meaning of a sentence to an individual is the way he interprets that sentence by relating it to what he already knows. When we talk of the meaning of a sentence generally, we are referring to the way we would expect it to be interpreted.

The basis of comprehension—the generation and testing of predictions —is also the basis of learning. When one or another of the hypotheses generated by the listener or perceiver is confirmed by his sampling of surface structure, comprehension occurs. The listener has made sense of the acoustic noise in his environment. When a listener can generate no hypothesis that he can confirm because of inadequacy of cognitive structure, then he has only two alternatives. Either he can ignore the environment, letting it remain meaningless noise; or he can attempt to make sense of it by modifying his cognitive structure—he can learn. In the case of comprehension the individual's hypotheses will be based on existing cognitive structure; while in the case of learning his hypotheses must involve a change in cognitive structure. But in both cases the evidence for or against a hypothesis is acquired by sampling environmental noise selectively. The initiative must be with the listener or perceiver, whether he is comprehending or learning.

Learning is fundamental

The final section of this chapter is in the nature of a digression, but a digression which I hope will be illuminating. We shall be particularly concerned with the extent to which a newborn infant must learn to see, and with the manner in which he employs his innate learning ability to develop an understanding of the visual world. We will follow the development of an infant's cognitive structure through roughly the first year of his life, up to the time he begins to demonstrate that he has acquired some understanding of language. In other words, we shall be concerned only with the pre-verbal child, and the manner in which his knowledge of the world grows without the advantage of language.

It might be reasonably asked why a book primarily for educators should devote attention to the way a child learns and perceives the world long before he arrives at school. Most children have acquired a considerable mastery over language by the time they arrive at school, and all except those with manifest visual defects can obviously see. Why then should we not begin with the child's arrival at school or at kindergarten? The point I want to emphasize is that children should not need to be directed or motivated into learning; direction and motivation come from within themselves. It is in the nature of childhood to strive to make sense of the world, provided nothing has been learned to indicate that learning is unlikely, or will be too costly. Children are born ready and able to learn, and my purpose in the next few pages is to give some examples not only of how much infants have to learn under their own direction but of how brilliantly they accomplish this early learning. In order to comprehend the learning potential of a child, and the conditions under which this potential can be realized, we must consider the tremendous intellectual achievements of his first few years.

In one sense a newborn infant is like an explorer in a strange land with no idea of its geography, its vegetation or its inhabitants. The infant is like a linguist faced with the problem of finding structure and meaning in a totally incomprehensible new language. But in a deeper sense the infant's task is infinitely greater. The explorer and the linguist both have prior knowledge of the world, and of their own tongue, which gives them certain expectations of what new countries and people and languages will be like. An infant has none of these advantages. He has no knowledge of his new domain, nor any expectation of the possible nature of the events confronting him. Before he can start to make even the first rough map of his new world, he must learn to see.

Learning to see

No one teaches a child to see. This statement is so blindingly obvious that you may wonder why it is necessary to make it. We may assume that a child looks at the world through the eyes of an adult. But seeing is not accomplished without learning. Unlike breathing or sleeping; seeing is not achieved in the absence of any intellectual effort. A child learns to see without the benefit of instruction. To understand the magnitude of this achievement, we must examine what there is about seeing that has to be learned.

For a start, consider that we live in a three-dimensional visual world, that objects have depth as well as height and width, and that they may be located in front or behind each other as well as side by side. In other words, we perceive *distance*. Obvious, it might be said—except for the fact that distance is not directly represented on the retina of the eye. The retina, the layers of light-sensitive cells within the eyeball which transform optical information into nerve impulses sent to the brain, is as two-dimensional as a sheet of paper. The image of the world that the lens of the eye focuses upon the retina has lost a dimension, just as a photograph or drawing represents the height and width of objects but not their relative distance. Of course other kinds of clues indicate to the viewer how solid and how far away an object is, but these clues all require a fundamental understanding that we all take for granted—that the world is three-dimensional in the first place. But how does a child know this? Nobody tells him that the world is three-dimensional, nor is this information available from the pattern of light falling on the retina of his eyes. Moreover, a child does not learn about space by moving through it; he exhibits awareness that the world is three-dimensional long before he is able even to crawl.[8]

There is an even more fundamental question. How does a child get the idea that there are solid and permanent objects in the world? Adult "common sense" intuitions to the contrary, the world does not provide our visual system with the information that it is furnished with objects, many of which occupy space, persist through time (for a while at least) and maintain a certain size and shape. An obvious clue for adults is that objects tend to stay where they are put; they do not go away if we take our eyes off them. But this again is information that the eyes do not give. How do we know that we see the *same* object on two different occasions? Certainly a child does not know this; if a blanket is thrown over a toy just as an infant is reaching for it, he will probably stop reaching. As far as the infant is concerned, an object that he cannot see has gone from the world completely. He seems to begin life assuming that if he cannot keep his hands or mouth or eyes on something, it will go away.[9]

Later, as is frequently the case, a child's discovery that the world is not quite what he first thought may lead him to the other extreme. An older child, a toddler, tends for a while to think that all objects that look alike must be the same. If he sees a chair in your house that looks like a chair in his house, he assumes that it is the same chair. If he sees two brown cows a mile apart when he is out for a walk or drive, his first conclusion will be that they are the same cow.

But I am still oversimplifying when I imply that the same or similar objects can look the same on different occasions; this is just not the case. In fact we rarely see an object in the same way twice. Depending on the distance, angle and illumination at which most objects are presented to the eyes, these objects' size, shape and color change—at least as far as the retina is concerned. If we "see" the same object on two occasions, it is primarily because we can ignore the immediate evidence of our eyes. We do not believe that a plate has changed shape just because we view it from a different angle; nor do we believe that a person has become only half the size he used to be just because he has moved across a room. We do not believe that an object that we see from only one angle is not solid or that there could be a hole in the table top hidden by the book that is lying upon it or that the wall changes color as its appearance changes from white at noon to grey at dusk. In fact we are so used to seeing objects in a world constructed from our prior knowledge and expectations that we find it almost impossible to imagine how they are represented on the retina of the eye.

But how does a child know all this? How can he ever find out about objects and their permanence when the evidence of his eyes (and mouth and hands) is that there is nothing about their size or shape or structure that can be relied upon to remain constant from one moment to another. A baby is capable of far more complex perceptual and intellectual feats, without any direction from adults, than we ever give him credit for. I shall review some of the evidence about what an infant can do when he begins to make sense of visual noise.

Mastering the visual world

A child demonstrates visual skills at birth or a few hours after. Provided his mother has not been anaesthetized, a newborn baby is immediately responsive to his visual environment. His eyes do not move randomly, but converge and fixate upon objects and follow their contours or movement. He can *look* long before his arms and legs are capable of any kind of orderly activity and before his head can move in support of the eyes. He prefers patterned surfaces to plain ones, and is especially attracted by quite small differences in shape or texture (the aspects of the viusal world which will be the main clues for object recognition). He looks for *change*—for movement or contrast—and will focus on the points where change is greatest, for example, along contours.[10]

A baby looks for complexity, but not disorder. His attention is held by shapes and stripes and regular patterns, particularly circles. A most attractive visual lure is a bull's-eye. From his earliest weeks a baby is interested in faces. The amount of interest he shows can be measured, for example, by the time he will spend attending to a particular object. There are more direct indicators of his degree of involvement with the visual world. He will stop sucking when he is interested; his rate of heartbeats will increase when he is surprised and fall when he is thinking; and he will smile at moments of recognition—all within the first few weeks after birth.

As an infant becomes more familiar with objects in his environment, he pays less attention to them. At two months he will spend less time looking at objects he has seen before. He is also not interested in objects that are completely different from anything he has seen before; he can make no sense of them. An infant looks for relative novelty, which he can relate to what he already knows about the world. He is looking to learn.

Initially a child's attention seems independent of his will, his visual system can be "captured" by events in his surroundings. He may try to look away, but his eyes will be unable to unlock themselves from an object, or a movement, which has caught his attention.[11] Eventually, however, his distractability leads to an attention switch from one event in his environment to another. This persistent distractability of children may be frustrating to teachers; but as an adaptive mechanism in the development of the species this tendency not to devote too much attention to any one event must have considerable survival value.

By two months of age an infant begins to get his eyes under voluntary control; he uses them to examine what *he* wants to look at. At three months he begins to look where objects are *not*, anticipating their arrival. This ability to anticipate is a sign that he is developing an internal model of how events occur in the world, a predictive system based on past experience. This process of anticipation is so advanced by the end of the first year that a child uses his eyes to test hypotheses, looking not just because an event is taking place, or because he expects it to take place, but to see whether it will take place. In other words, the child is asking questions about the world.

No one has to tell a child how to use his eyes, or how to explore his visual environment. He knows how to set about making sense of the world he is in—how to develop cognitive structure—by exercising the basic learning strategy of constructing and testing hypotheses about the nature of the world. To this end, even a child of a few days of age is quick to demonstrate boredom with familiar events by shifting attention in a constant search for the new and unknown. He seeks noise to make sense of.

But initially an infant appears to have (from an adult point of view at least) a very odd notion of how the world is organized. It is not until he reaches the age of four or five months that he begins to get more than a very hazy idea about how anything in the world can have any stability or permanence. For example, recent research[12] has shown that an infant has no idea about the constancy of objects, including persons, in his environment; nor does he care if they appear to change their color or shape or size. In fact he is scarcely interested in stable objects. But he is interested in movement, and he is worried by an unexpected change in direction or speed. This means that he makes his first predictions about the motion of objects, not about the objects themselves. Objects do not exist in the world of the newborn child.

If a two-week-old baby is propped up to watch a moving object like a ball or model railway engine disappear behind a screen, he will look at where the object should come out and be surprised if it reappears too soon or too late. Many parents will assert that it is impossible for a two-week-old child to respond in this informative way to anything, because infants act as if they were half-asleep most of the time. In fact when infants are flat on their backs they are half-asleep. It is only when propped up into a semi-sitting position that they are alert enough to have their attention grabbed by objects moving across their line of sight.

If the ball or the engine reappears from behind the screen in the wrong position or at the wrong time the infant is surprised. But he is not surprised if the engine goes in and the ball comes out, provided the changed object appears at the right moment and speed. He has not been attending to the object itself, but only to its movement.

It would be easy to speculate about the adaptive advantage nature might confer upon animals that attend to moving aspects of their environment, rather than to stationary aspects. For example, babies (like most lower animals) instinctively avoid any object moving rapidly towards them.[13] If an object moves towards their eyes from any direction, they flinch. But how can a child know that an object is moving towards him? Unless he is actually hit, the only cue he gets is that the object seems to grow progressively larger. It can be demonstrated experimentally that the cue to duck is indeed the steady enlargement of the image of an object, because a baby will flinch when he sees a circular shadow growing larger on a screen. We do not know why or how a baby interprets movement in one direction (the expansion of the shadow) as movement towards him. But his innate concern with movement is apparent.

There may be a profound significance in the fact that an infant first finds his way in the world in terms of movement and space. All humans seem to like to organize, and even talk about, their world in spatial terms. We move from "peaks" of excitement to "depths" of despair. We prefer maps and graphs, which are approximate, to coordinates and tables, which may be precise. Plane geometry is generally easier to comprehend than algebra. We tend to remember places rather than faces—which is why teachers prefer children to keep the same desks—and to remember where a book is located in the library rather than what it looks like. We are creatures of space, and we organinze our cognitive structures accordingly.[14]

From multiplicity to identity

Movement teaches a child that the world is more than unpredictable visual noise on a two-dimensional backdrop; it has depth. And the knowledge that the world has three-dimensional depth tells him that solid objects can exist. But the fact that an infant has decided that there are objects still does not tell him that they are permanent. He could decide that the ball you retrieve from beneath a blanket is not the ball you put there.

How would you prove that an object you can no longer see still exists, especially if you are not permitted to ask somebody else? How would you find out that an object does not go away when you are not looking at it? A baby seems to decide that objects are permanent because this is the least complicated explanation. It is easier to make a theory of the world if we assume that objects tend to stay where we put them. The world makes "more sense" from this point of view.

But even when an infant has made the decision that objects have permanence and that they do not change their size and shape and color arbitrarily, he is still confronted by the fact that similar objects can turn up in more than one place. Some objects, an infant will eventually discover, can do this because there are many of them. It is quite possible that a chair in his own house will look like a chair in someone else's house without being the same chair, just as a spoon in the kitchen may not be the same as one in the dining room. But other objects are unique. How does he find this out?

A child's first assumption seems to be that there is a multiplicity of all the objects in his life—even of mothers.[15] Until he is five months of age, a child is not at all surprised to see two or three mothers at the same time. He can be shown them in full-length mirrors. He apparently concludes that the mother of the kitchen and the mother of the bedroom and the mother of the bathroom have gotten together. At five months, however, he begins to be suspicious; he has developed a hypothesis that there is only one mother—or, more accurately, that he should not be confronted by three people all looking the same as the person we call his mother.

A disillusioning blow for a fond mother! She may believe that her baby is unique, but to her child she is just one of a crowd. This tendency to predict multiplicity rather than uniqueness persists. When a child learns the name "Daddy" he does not bestow it upon one person, but upon many men and perhaps even women, standard lamps and other objects over five feet tall. Similarly he will call all dogs "Fido", and even cats, cows and other four-legged objects, possibly including inanimate ones. The process of learning about the world is one of progressive differentiation,[16] and this is reflected in the way names are allocated. Children do not establish narrow categories which they then expand, or "generalize", to use a common psychological and educational term. Rather, they start with very broad categories, with the "abstract" rather than the "concrete", and refine the category or restrict the use of the name only as a result of further learning.

Once again one might speculate that there is a basic evolutionary advantage in constructing a theory of the world in general rather than specific terms. A child who can allocate an object or event to a category is making sense of the world; he may be overgeneralizing by adult standards, but he is not confused. Humans are bewildered or confused only when something happens that they cannot place in any category. For adults these days this would probably have to be the sudden manifestation of a bug-eyed monster from outer space. Similarly we are surprised only when confronted by an object or event that runs counter to our expectations. It is instructive to consider how rarely we see a baby who is bewildered or surprised. This lack of bewilderment is a clear indication that he has a system of broad categories into which he can place almost all of the events in his life, and which can he can use as a basis for expectations about the future.

Developing the theory in the brain

An infant constantly tries to make sense of the world through the development of a theory about it, his cognitive structure. Not until a child establishes that the world is furnished with objects can he begin to make a category system. And not until he develops the notion that objects have permanence can he proceed to the insight that an object can move from one position to another. To grasp the idea that objects can sometimes be stationary and at other times in motion is an important advance, and is followed by the even greater insight that people can cause objects to move. Yet a greater discovery remains to be made: The child himself can cause people to move objects from one position to another, which is mastery over the world indeed. The latter discovery of course becomes a prime factor in motivating the use of language.

Concurrent with an infant's conceptual progression from a world in constant flux to a world in which individuals can control objects and even other people is the development of the child's understanding that he can change the world himself. Not only can he cause sustenance or entertainment to be provided, but he can intentionally acquire information that he needs, a huge intellectual leap.

Once again there appear to be definite stages through which an infant must progress as he develops intellectual control of his world. At first he is limited to a spectator's role, watching and drawing conclusions about the nature of the world which become the basis of his cognitive structure. But passively waiting for events to occur is not a satifying occupation for an infant. As soon as he develops some basic relationships within his cognitive structure, he starts to make predictions about what may occur. He is still very dependent upon the environment for his experiences, but he can anticipate how events should succeed each other.

And once an infant can begin to predict events he can go one stage further. Rather than wait for the environment to test his predictions, he can set about obtaining some feedback for himself. He can reach for an object to see how long his arms are, or drop a cup to see if it breaks. Even then a child's growing mastery of the informative properties of his experience has not been exhausted. He can test hypotheses in his imagination, in the cognitive privacy of his mental life. He can imagine what the consequence might be if his mother found him engaged in the actual experiment of dropping a cup, and decide whether he wishes to undertake it.

In other words, as a child develops cognitive structure he uses it not only to interact with the world but to examine possibilities and test outcomes in the seclusion of his mind. Experience becomes vicarious. This complete development, from the initial discovery that the world contains objects to the ultimate insight that the world can be modelled in the mind, is accomplished in all its basic essentials within a child's first year of life, and without the use of language. This progress is a demonstration of a very powerful capacity for learning indeed. Yet it can be described in terms of the relatively simple model I have proposed—a constantly developing cognitive structure that is the basis of all perception, and a learning mechanism that operates by hypothesizing and testing modifications to cognitive structure. This is the fundamental learning skill every child brings with him to school, and on which he must depend for learning throughout the rest of his life. None of this is to say that adults have no active role to play, or no influence, in how a child will learn. What he learns, and how early he learns, will depend to a large extent on people around him, especially his parents and teachers. Teachers should not feel helpless in their efforts to instruct children; they need not be subservient to a child's whim. But unless they understand what each child is like, teachers may achieve little but damage.

CHAPTER 5

Meaningfulness
and Memorization

In the preceding chapter I discussed in general terms the elaboration or modification of cognitive structure through learning. I asserted that hypothesis testing is at the core of human learning for the simple reason that much of the knowledge of the world embedded in cognitive structure is implicit, and therefore cannot be communicated and taught. Children must rely largely on their own resources in order to learn about the world. This responsibility is no handicap for children, however, if the conditions in which they endeavor to learn are meaningful, because the basic learning process of hypothesis generation and testing is closely related to the fundamental process of comprehension by which every human individual strives to make sense of the world.

However, children are not left to discover and learn everything for themselves. In fact a large part of the activity at schools is directed toward the communication of "facts" that are intended to be preselected packages of knowledge. The emphasis on "imparting information to children" in the educational literature—together with the bulk of psychological research and theorization on the topic of learning—might lead one to think that rote memorization is at the heart of learning. But not even rote learning can be independent of hypothesis testing. Children must strive to make sense of new information, even when it has been prepackaged for them. Twice two is four, a molecule of water consists of one oxygen atom and two hydrogen atoms, and Paris is the capital of France: these are all "facts" which can be communicated through language. But these facts can make no sense to a child until they have been integrated into other knowledge that the child has already acquired and tested—not simply memorized as a meaningless sequence of sounds. In the present chapter I propose to examine hypothesis testing and rote learning in a little more detail, especially with respect to their relevance in classrooms and to the manner in which learning is often discussed in educational psychology texts and reports. I shall not be concerned with how specific subjects should be taught—a broad and complex issue that demands analysis of the material to be learned as well as of the manner in which learning takes place. I shall focus instead on aspects of learning that are often thought to be critical at school, for example, discrimination learning, concept learning, rote memorization and problem solving, with a brief reference to the learning of motor skills.

My aim is not simply to outline what is involved in these different manifestations of learning but to show how the basic "hypothesis-testing" urge to make sense of the world by relating the new to the known underlies them all. In fact I have been careful to use terms like *aspects of learning* rather than *different kinds of learning*. I am reluctant to conclude that there are a number of different, independent, *kinds* of learning, just as I do not think it necessary to postulate a variety of different processes of comprehension. I see one basic process by which every individual tries to make sense of the world. Everyone tries to develop a theory he can use to summarize his experiences, interpret his environment and predict his future —although this process naturally manifests itself differently in different circumstances. Theorists who propose the existence of multiple processes of learning have difficulty in explaining how both the processes and the products of these different kinds of learning are integrated in one mind. Moreover, there is a further risk of making the assertion (which I believe to be unjustified) that learning sometimes may not take place because children have not reached the "stage" of development at which a particular kind of learning has matured.[1] The basic learning process outlined in Chapter 4 can be identified in children at least from their first year.

Discrimination Learning

Discrimination learning is frequently regarded as a topic of central concern in the early years of a child's life, especially when it is employed as a scapegoat for the child's failure to learn. For example, the difficulties of some beginning readers are often attributed to "inability to discriminate" or "inadequate visual (or auditory) discrimination". Yet the majority of studies of discrimination learning are conducted on rats and other animals somewhat lower on the phylogenetic scale than children because—disconcerting though it may be to some educators—human subjects, including children, always find the tasks too easy. All children have been learning to "discriminate" among familiar objects since birth. What schools call discrimination learning, like learning to tell the difference between the letters *A* and *B*, often involves very little discrimination and a good deal of concept learning, which will be the next topic on our list.

Studying "discrimination"

Discrimination learning studies are concerned with how two "stimuli", two distinctive environmental events, come to be perceived as different. For a reason that will become apparent, such studies are generally conducted with animals. In a typical discrimination learning experiment, a hungry rat faces two doors on hinged flaps. One door provides access to food; the other door is locked. Whichever door happens to conceal the food is always decorated with a triangle, and the other with a circle. The question is whether the rat can learn to "discriminate" between the two doors. To further motivate the rat to make the choice, the entire experiment is conducted above the rat's ground level, the rat leaping to second-storey doors from a raised jumping stand which it is encouraged to leave by an electric shock. If the rat makes a mistake, it collides with a locked door and falls into a net. All of this experimental ingenuity and rodent discomfiture is aimed at discovering whether a rat can distinguish between a triangle and a circle. By such means do psychologists contrive to communicate with animals.[2]

It may seem reasonably clear that the subject in a discrimination learning experiment is not learning to discriminate, in the sense of acquiring an ability to distinguish between triangles and circles. It must be taken for granted at the beginning of the study that the animal can "see" that triangles and circles are not the same. No one can teach a rat, or any other creature, to distinguish a difference that it is not capable of seeing. Instead, the initial purpose of the experiment would appear to be to train the rat to pay attention to a difference that it might initially ignore, and to learn a rule about how the difference is related to alternative consequences. In other words, the experimental task is primarily cognitive, not visual.

The capacity to detect differences in the first place—the physical ability that enables one to say that two objects or sounds or smells or tastes or textures and so on are different—is usually called *acuity*. For example, whether or not you can perceive any difference between the lengths of the following two lines ——————— is a question of acuity, not of discrimination. Acuity varies with physical conditions, such as the lighting, the state of your vision, the distance of your eyes from the page, and can be modified by physical devices such as spectacles or a microscope. Neither instruction nor maturation will improve school children's acuity. On the other hand, spectacles will not guarantee that a child can learn to discriminate *A* from *B*. The ability to *detect* a difference does not ensure that attention will be paid to the difference.

Attending to significant differences

The discrimination experiment works. The rat very quickly learns to jump only to the triangle, whether it appears on the door to the right or left of the cage. The experiment also shows that discrimination learning occurs in two stages. In the first stage, which usually requires the most time, the rat learns that there is a significant difference between the two doors to which it must pay attention. In the second stage, the rat learns *how* the difference is relevant; that is, it discovers which shape is related to which outcome. The "response attachment" part of discrimination learning is very quickly accomplished.

Experimenters sometimes attempt to fool their subjects after a particular discrimination has been learned by suddenly reversing the clue. For the rat, the door with the triangle will suddenly be locked every time, while the door with the circle will be open. One might expect such a switch to throw the rat into some confusion, or at least require as much relearning as the initial learning situation. But not at all; in very little time the rat changes its responses and starts jumping to the door with the circle rather than to the door with the triangle. If the experimenter persists in changing the situation as soon as the rat has settled on one habitual response, the rat quickly learns how the rules of the game have changed, and switches to the opposite response as soon as it gets one clue (one "mistake") that the situation has changed.

Some psychologists are profoundly impressed by the preceding phenomenon, since it is not easily compatible with theories that learning is simply habit formation. They call the experiment a demonstration of "learning to learn". But it might be regarded more simply as an illustration that the complicated part of discrimination learning is discovering and learning to pay attention to the difference that is significant. Once the relevant clue is discovered—once the rat learns to attend to the pattern on the open door, rather than to the side the open door is on, or was on the last time—the rest is easy. The difficult part of discrimination learning, in other words, is cognitive rather than visual. Until it has some reason to attend to a difference, the animal will not pay attention.

The world is full of differences, but most of them are not significant.

Most differences are irrelevant because they do not play a part in determining whether two objects or events should be treated as the same or different. The tendency of rats, and children, is to ignore differences until these differences become relevant in their theory of the world. The question is not whether the differences are discriminable, but whether they convey information the individual wants to use. Ignoring irrelevant differences is by no means an insensitive or careless way of going through life. Because of the limitations of memory and of visual information processing, everyone must disregard the noise in his environment, and attend only to what is relevant.

As I said earlier, discrimination experiments are usually conducted on animals such as rats, partly because humans, even infants, tend to find the tasks too easy. Very young infants in their cribs will spend a good deal of time looking at patterns and then lose interest, presumably because they have learned all they want to know. Six-month-old babies quickly learn to reach for triangular blocks to suck and to ignore circles if the triangles are coated with saccharine. A more difficult task—and one a good deal closer to real life situations—is discovering the significant difference when it is complex, or when it is just one among a number of otherwise irrelevant differences. Discriminating a triangle from a circle is one thing; but how do we learn to distinguish *A* from *B*, or one person from another, when many of the differences involved may be not only irrelevant but also confusing? This is the problem that has been studied in a multitude of experiments variously labelled *concept formation, concept attainment* or *concept learning,* the topic to which we now turn.

Concept Learning

A large part of school activity may seem to be directed toward the conceptualization of new knowledge; and a frequent observation on the adverse report cards of children is that they have difficulty in learning new concepts. Yet the notion of a concept is very poorly defined, both within education and outside. The dictionary defines a concept as "a thought", which is probably as much as the word means to most teachers. The dictionary also defines a concept as "a generalized idea of a class of objects", which is almost certainly not the way teachers would perceive it, but is closer to a typical psychological definition. Psychologists sometimes talk as if a concept is a *category* of objects or events; sometimes as if it is a common *property*—a "feature" or "attribute"—of all the objects or events in a category; sometimes as if it is an internal *representation* (a little like the "idea" the dictionary mentions). Concept learning is sometimes seen as a *process* of abstracting common features or attributes that specify a category, and at other times as primarily a matter of understanding word meanings. In fact the topic of concept learning is often covered in the portion of textbooks dealing with language.

In keeping with my earlier observation that few words or expressions in our language are used in only one sense, I shall not attempt to find a unique answer to the question, What is concept learning? Instead I shall outline a very simple "concept learning" situation to serve as a summary or paradigm for some more complex studies that we shall examine, or that you might meet in the future.[3]

A concept learning experiment

For our experiment you must imagine that I have put nine wooden blocks in front of you, which for convenience I shall identify with numbers. The nine blocks look like this:

The task I shall ask you to perform will always be the same. I shall indicate two or more of the blocks, and ask you to show me another that is "like them", or that "goes with them". For example, I might ask you to nominate a block that goes with blocks 1 and 2, and I would expect you to say block 3, making a set like this:

Alternatively I might show you blocks 1 and 4, in which case you would probably select block 7:

If I asked you at this point what the experiment is about, your answer might be close to one of the psychological definitions of concept learning—abstracting common features or attributes of a set of objects. I was in effect asking you to identify the characteristic that each pair of blocks I selected had in common, and that distinguished them from certain other blocks—"triangularity" for blocks 1 and 2, and "whiteness" for blocks 1 and 4. This common characteristic is sometimes called a *criterial attribute* or *distinguishing feature* (or even *significant difference*). The common characteristic is also sometimes referred to as a *rule,* which specifies the concept, or even as the concept itself. Each attribute (triangularity, whiteness) may be referred to as a *value* on a *dimension.* Thus our nine blocks were distinguished from each other along two dimensions (shape, color), each of which had three values.

CONCEPTS AND CATEGORIES   The earlier terminology of this book could also be employed to state that the experimental problem was to discover the category rule (or distinctive features) that I had established to determine how the set of nine blocks should be subdivided, or grouped. In the first experiment I established a category to which blocks 1 and 2 belonged; and your problem was to discover that the distinctive feature of the set of blocks I wanted treated as the same was "triangularity". In the process you had to ignore a number of irrelevant features, either because they were features of all the blocks (they were all made of wood, or all the same thickness) or because they did not make a difference (like color in my first example).

It will be noted how arbitrary was my decision about the category rule that determined which blocks should be regarded as "the same". In the first instance I decided that blocks 1 and 2 should go together, that the concept or rule was "all triangular blocks" and that the whiteness of block 1 was irrelevant. In the second instance I decided that the concept or rule was "all white blocks", and that the triangularity of block 1 was irrelevant. Your problem was to decide what was relevant.

I could have tried to fool you and said that blocks 1 and 2 should go with blocks 4, 5 or 6 because my concept was "anything not a square". But in that case I would have given you insufficient information. Moreover, human nature seems to be such that when we are shown two objects that "go together" in some way and asked to find another to go with them, we tend to look for something that has a property that the other two have in common. If I had made my question ambiguous, for example, by selecting blocks 1 and 5, would you have chosen block 9 on the assumption that my concept was "all different"?

Or would you have considered that the concept was "either triangular or circular" or "either white or shaded" or "anything neither square nor black"? As you can see, there can be many reasonable alternatives that even the experimenter may not consider.

In one sense, performing concept learning tasks might be considered the equivalent of tackling several discrimination learning tasks simultaneously, or handling a discrimination task complicated by the presence of a number of irrelevant cues. Such is the general looseness of this area of study that tasks involving irrelevant differences are sometimes called discrimination learning (for example, identifying letters or faces) while tasks having no irrelevant differences are called concept learning. For example, the study of the rat learning to jump to the door with a triangle could be interpreted as "learning the concept of triangularity". I make this point because it would be a mistake to assume that experiments with a similar label are necessarily studying the same thing. What an experimenter thinks he is studying sometimes has little bearing on what is actually going on.

The ultimate test in any concept learning task is not whether the subject is able to point to other "instances" of the concept from the array in front of him, but whether he can demonstrate that he has learned a rule by applying it to instances he has never met before. For example, which of the following would belong with blocks 1 and 2, and which with blocks 1 and 4?

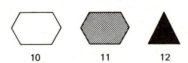

COMPLICATING CONCEPT LEARNING   An obvious step we could take to make the concept learning experiment more complicated would be to increase the number of irrelevant dimensions. We could make the blocks different from each other in size (so that there would be small, medium and large white circles), thickness, weight, surface texture and so forth. We could increase not only the number of dimensions but also the number of "values" along each dimension; we could make the blocks a dozen different colors or a dozen different shapes or a multitude of different sizes.

Furthermore, with a larger number of alternatives we could also complicate the category rules. Instead of making just one value of one dimension criterial, such as "white" or "triangular", we could establish criterial values on two or more dimensions, such as "all large white" blocks. Such concepts are *conjunctive* because the category rules involve a conjunction of two or more attributes. They are also more difficult to learn because, although all instances of the concept are white, whiteness is not sufficient to allocate a block to the category. Our concepts of dogs and cats are conjunctive. It is necessary to have four legs to be a dog or a cat, but the animal must possess some other distinguishing attributes as well.

Even more difficult to learn are *disjunctive* concepts, which are "either or". For example, a block might have to be a triangle or a circle in order to belong to a category. There could be even more complex rules, both conjunctive and disjunctive, such as "all white and triangular, or black and circular, blocks". This last kind of rule can also be put into propositional form—"if white then triangular, if black then circular". Many of our everyday concepts are disjunctive. There is no simple set of rules for defining what constitutes a game or candy or crime or justice.

PREFERRED DIFFERENCES   The experiment I have described so far might be referred to as a matching task. You are shown a couple of instances of the concept, and must match these instances with another. The task requires you to discover a category rule that has already been determined in advance. In this sense the experimental situation is not different from that a child is in when he is shown a few examples of dogs, cats, apples or houses, and is expected to discover the rules by which he should recognize other members of these categories in the future.

Another common experimental technique is to present a subject with an entire collection of objects, and to ask him to sort them into piles in any way he likes. He could organize our original set of nine blocks into white, shaded and black, for example, or into triangles, circles and squares. Such a sorting task puts the subject into a choice situation, provided he sees that alternative solutions are available. Of course he might legitimately put the blocks into nine categories of one, on the very logical premise that they are all different in one way or another; or into one heap of nine, on the equally logical basis that they are all wooden. However, it is usually not difficult to get subjects down to the youngest children to organize in some way—supporting the assumption that one of the principles of human thought is to organize and to learn rules for organizing.

The sorting experiment can be used to investigate the basis on which individuals do categorize. Children, for example, if shown a group of objects different in kind (toy cars and toy airplanes), color and size will ignore the color and size differences and group according to kind.[4] Such a result should not be surprising in the light of what we already know about children and the world they live in. A car or a plane or a toothbrush is still a car or plane or toothbrush, no matter what its color or size. In other words, even the youngest children organize objects in terms of whether they are treated in the same way rather than in terms of superficial characteristics.

NAMING   A second variant of our basic experiment would be to give the blocks names. For example, the experimenter might decide in advance that all white blocks are to be called TAV, all black blocks ROP and so forth. The experimenter would begin the experiment by showing the subject a white triangle and a white circle and saying, "These are two TAVS, can you show me another?"

You can see that this variant is hardly different from our original matching task, except that it has now somehow become a language experiment. In fact some theorists have argued that language is basically learned in this way; one hears a word that is essentially a nonsense syllable, and learns its *meaning* by associating it with the objects or events to which it refers. But learning a vocabulary to attach names to concepts or categories is a relatively trivial part of language learning compared with learning a grammar. And, in any case, the major problem in learning names is not to remember the name, but to discover the rules or features defining the category to which the name applies.

POSITIVE AND NEGATIVE INFORMATION   Yet another variation can be played upon our original experimental theme. This variation might be called "Guess what the experimenter has in mind". The experimenter might show just one block, perhaps the white triangle, and say "Here is one instance of a concept; find the concept rule". He is not interested in whether you can deduce the concept rule from the evidence he gives you; in fact he deliberately gives you insufficient information. He wants to study your strategies for learning—how you go about selecting evidence for yourself.

Under the rules of the game there is only one way in which you can acquire additional evidence about the concept the experimenter has in mind, and that is by pointing to another block and asking "Is this an instance of the concept?" The only answer the experimenter will give is yes or no. In effect, your questions represent tests of hypotheses about the concept, unless you choose to act quite randomly. For example, if you think the concept might be "all white blocks regardless of shape", you could test the hypothesis by pointing to a white circle and asking "Is this one?" in which case you would expect a yes answer. Or you could point to a black circle or a black triangle, in which case you would expect a no answer. When you think you know the concept rule, you say so. Obviously both yes and no answers can be informative; both positive and negative information helps to reduce uncertainty.

The "concept guessing" situation is perhaps closer to life than any of the other variants of the experiment. An adult does not usually tell a child "This is a dog" every time a child sees a dog. The child would never learn what a dog is this way. Instead the adult identifies just one or two examples of "dog"—in effect saying little more than that the category exists—and leaves the child to discover the rule by using the basic learning strategy of hypothesis construction and testing. As I have already noted, the child tests his hypothesis by saying "There's a dog", or words to that effect, whenever he can point to an object that fulfils his hypothesized rules for the category. He can also point to an object that does not conform to his hypothesized rules, and say "That's a cat", or anything else that means "That's not a dog". Either way the child will find out whether to stay with his hypothesis or change it.

Which kind of information is worth more—positive or negative, a yes or a no answer—is a complicated question, and depends on the number of relevant and irrelevant attributes, the complexity of the concept rules and on other factors besides. For example, a negative answer may constitute a heavier memory load. Moreover, many people tend to react emotionally to negative answers, to being "wrong", even when they may be just as informative as positive answers, and society is not always willing to give as much credit for a question that draws a no response as one that gets a yes. As I have said before, you cannot learn unless you risk being wrong, but you must often pay a price for taking such a chance.

Let me summarize the kind of information about human learning that can be derived from a concept-guessing experiment. The experimenter can not only assess how accurate you are in such a task; he can examine your caution, how much information you require before you will make a decision, your relative preference for positive and negative information and your ability to use it, the nature of the hypotheses you choose to test and your preferred strategies for acquiring information and testing hypotheses. Obviously this is one kind of experiment from which a good deal of information can be gained.

STRATEGIES FOR LEARNING[5]   I have used the word *strategy* a number of times without going into detail about what I mean. There is usually more than one way to go about solving a problem; and not only do the various alternatives have different probabilities of success, but they tend to reflect the different personality characteristics of the problem solver. Once again we can use our "Guess what is in the experimenter's mind" concept learning situation to illustrate different kinds of learning strategies. But now I want to make the set of alternatives larger and the concept slightly more complicated. Let us assume that we have blocks that can differ from each other on four dimensions—size (large, medium, small) thickness (thin, thick), color (black, white) and shape (triangle, circle, square)—and that the concept is conjunctive ("all large circles"). As his example of a positive instance, the experimenter indicates a large thin white circle. What you must discover is that large and circular are criterial attributes, or significant differences, and that thin and white are irrelevant.

What strategies can you use in such a situation? One possibility is to select a number of other blocks at random and ask whether they are examples of the concept, trying to see what all the positive instances have in common. As you can imagine, such a strategy puts an enormous burden on memory, since you must try to remember the outcome of every test and the exact nature of every hypothesis tested. An alternative is to select hypotheses at random and test each in turn until you find one that works. Once again this strategy places quite a burden on memory, since you must remember every hypothesis that has been tried and found wanting so that you do not try it again. Moreover, a positive instance does not necessarily indicate which parts of the hypothesis are criterial. A guess of "all large thin circles" may lead you to make correct positive identifications; but it will not show that the dimension of thickness is irrelevant.

The previous two strategies have been called *scanning* because they try to take a wide field into account at one time. More systematic methods reduce the load on memory. For example, one could take as the initial hypothesis the value of every attribute of the positive instance the experimenter first indicates (such a hypothesis would be that the concept is "all large thin white circles") and then vary and test each attribute in turn. Size might be varied first, for example. If the *small* thin white circle proves not to be an instance, then it is obvious that size is criterial, and the concept must include large. If a large *thick* white circle proves to be a positive instance, it will be clear that thickness does not matter, since both thick and thin large white circles conform to the concept rule. Just two more tests will indicate that the white color of the original positive instance is not criterial (since the large thin *black* circle will be positive) and that shape is criterial (since the large thin white *square* will be negative). Ergo the concept is any large circle.

The beauty of the previous strategy, which has been given the label *conservative focussing*, is that you never have to remember more than one hypothesis, which is always there in front of you (the original positive instance). All you have to do is test each feature of the hypothesis in turn, a strategy that considerably reduces the load on memory. The method is effective, though it may be time consuming because every attribute must be checked out separately. Such a painstaking approach does not really allow for the brilliant hunch; nor is it particularly effective for disjunctive concepts. In other words, this slow but sure strategy is not necessarily the best.

Another alternative strategy that does not involve remembering more than one hypothesis at a time is called *focus gambling;* this follows the conservative focussing technique of using the original positive instance as the basic hypothesis, but varies more than one element at a time. Such a strategy is a good time saver if the modified hypothesis turns out to be correct; but it runs into trouble with negative instances because these do not indicate which of the changed attributes may be criterial. In short, a variety of strategies can be employed in any concept learning situation, and in many other learning situations too. These strategies may be systematic or random, involve a high memory load or a low one, be conservative or involve a greater element of chance.

When the topic of learning strategies arises in education, one question almost inevitably follows: What is the best way to teach the most efficient learning strategies to children? This is an enormously complicated question, and its answer would probably give some advantage to teachers. But one answer is not known. Obviously the best strategy will depend on the particular situation, and probably on the particular individual as well. Only rarely will a "pure" strategy be entirely appropriate. In the many cases when an individual has some prior expectation of what is likely to be a right answer, a reasonable combined strategy might be to gamble an inspired guess or two followed by a relatively conservative focussing procedure.

But if there is no simple answer to the question about efficient learning strategies, I think there is an effective and even comforting alternative: if they are given sufficient opportunity to employ their innate learning capacities, children on their own initiative can master individual concepts such as cats, dogs and tables, and even systems of knowledge as complex as language. Children employ inadequate learning strategies, such as the wild guess or the slow unnecessary grind, only when they do not understand what they are doing. The solution may be not to try to inculcate different learning strategies in a struggling child, but to make the situation more meaningful to him by providing more relevant information.

Reversal and nonreversal shifts

One aspect of concept learning shows an interesting difference between younger and older children. You will remember that in the discussion of discrimination learning we looked at the situation in which the experimenter played a trick on his experimental rat by changing the rules halfway. Access to food and freedom was no longer through the door marked with the triangle, but through the door marked with the circle. Such a change in the rules is termed a *reversal shift* because it involves a complete reversal of the situation—the positive becomes negative and the negative positive. As we saw, a rat has little difficulty in adjusting to a change of this kind.

However, in a concept learning task that has at least one irrelevant dimension there is a second way in which a rule can be changed. Instead of being *reversed*, the rule can be *changed completely*, so that shape is no longer the criterial attribute. Such a complete change of rule is called a *nonreversal shift*. Let me give an example.

Suppose there are just four blocks varying on two dimensions—color (white or black) and shape (triangle or circle)—and that the original concept was "any triangle", so that the white and black triangle were positive instances and the white and black circles negative instances. Now the rule is changed. If the change is a reversal shift, then shape remains the criterial attribute; but the white and black triangles now become negative instances and the white and black circles positive. If the change is a nonreversal shift, however, color becomes the criterial attribute, so that the white circle and white triangle become positive instances and the black circle and black triangle negative. The question is which kind of shift is easiest for humans to learn—the reversal, which turns a rule around, or the nonreversal, which results in a completely different rule?

The answer seems to depend on the age of the learner. If you are imagining doing the task yourself, then the answer is that the reversal shift would be easier. Once you have discovered the relevant dimension, you would find it less difficult to do a complete switch in that dimension than to change to a different dimension. However, children under four, and other animals, find the nonreversal shift easier. Apparently, once the old rule does not work, these subjects like to discard it completely.

You might care to speculate upon the reason for this very distinct difference between older and younger children. One interesting suggestion is that the difference has something to do with language. The reversal shift—switching from "circle yes, triangle no" to "circle no, triangle yes"—is facilitated by implicit speech. Without the benefit of language, the nonreversal switch is easier. You might also care to speculate on what analogies all this may have to normal classroom practice. I must confess that while I think it important to understand what concept and discrimination learning involve, it is not easy to think of many situations outside the experimental laboratory in which children will be called upon to master either reversal or nonreversal shifts. However, the results raise an interesting practical question if they do in fact demonstrate that the ability to put problems into language facilitates certain learning in certain situations.[6]

Rote Learning

In a few aspects of learning the learner has no problem to solve; the information is provided for him and he has little alternative but to commit it to memory. This type of learning is called *rote*, in which memorization is achieved primarily by repetition, and there is little possibility of prior knowledge being brought to bear. Learning the *names* of letters of the alphabet is one example (as opposed to learning how to distinguish one letter from another). There is no way for a child to hypothesize or predict what the names of the twenty-six letters might be; he is dependent on being told. In fact critical examples of learning that rely on direct external sources of information include the names of persons or objects, addresses, telephone numbers, multiplication tables, mathematical formulae. All these are fundamentally instances of *sensory memory representations,* the "storage" of sequences of sounds, just as we might memorize a particular visual configuration, such as a face or the layout of a room.[7]

Now I am aware that aspects of many names or numbers are predictable; they are not completely nonsense. It is predictable, for example, that certain sequences of sounds should be proper names in English; we have either heard them as names before or they are sequences of sounds that could be names—for example, *Smith, Jones, Brown* or *Blenkinsop,* as compared with *Nk* or *Krsplhhf.* (I would have preferred the latter examples to consist of sounds that cannot even be represented by letters of the alphabet, but of course that would be impossible in print.) To the extent that the sounds of names of persons and objects appear familiar to us, and can be related to what we know, they are meaningful and predictable. It is not by chance that *telephone* and *television* begin with the same sounds. Similarly the seven digits of a telephone number may not be completely unpredictable. Not only are they taken from a familiar number system, but if we are aware of how the first three digits of a number are related to a particular geographical area, we might have a prior idea about the probability of at least some of the digits in a phone number. Nevertheless, despite some degree of relationship to prior knowledge, names and numbers must be committed to memory.

There are few occasions at school where learning is, or should be, completely rote. Mathematics has aspects of rote learning—from multiplication tables to such formulae as $(a + b)^2 = a^2 + b^2 + 2ab$ and *the circumference of a circle* $= \pi r^2$. But since these formulations are parts of complex knowledge systems, they can be computed in principle and roughly checked in practise. A mathematics teacher would be likely to know instantly, for example, that $(a + b)^2$ generally cannot equal $a^2 \times b^2 \times 2ab$, though many of his students might have difficulty in perceiving why not.

Similarly, a certain logic is contained in chemical formulae, the names of geographical features, historical dates and economic and demographic statistics in that these elements are subject to internal checks of consistency. Anyone with a smattering of history, for example, realizes that Napoleon could not have died before 1805, the date of the Battle of Trafalgar—a check that completely escapes a child who is trying blindly to memorize a list of dates, and is unfamiliar with the Battle of Trafalgar or its relation to Napoleon. For a variety of reasons a geography instructor knows that it is impossible for Moscow to be the capital of France or for pineapples to be exported from Labrador, although his knowledge of capital cities and of pineapples was originally based on rote learning. Foreign language learning is a special case of rote learning. We learn that *été* is the present participle of *être* by rote; but rote learning is not sufficient to teach that *être* is the French for *to be*, since there are occasions too numerous and complex to be specified by any teacher when *être* does not mean *to be*, to *to be* should not be translated as *être*. Eventually a foreign language must be learned by the same process of hypothesis testing the individual uses in learning a native language; we learn language by using it, not by being told about it.

Despite its limited importance at school—a topic upon which I intend to elaborate—rote learning is the aspect of human learning and forgetting that has received by far the greatest attention from experimental and educational psychologists. It is far easier to exercise the required scientific control when the material to be learned in a psychological experiment has no meaning. And the outcome of such experiments is always predictable to a large extent, with the result that "laws of learning" can be formulated. Unfortunately for theorists and experimenters, these laws of learning break down as soon as the material becomes meaningful, when either the task or the material can be related to something the learner already knows.[8] Meaningful learning is invariably easier—so much so that it frequently appears to be instantaneous—and forgetting is markedly reduced. As a consequence, the best advice for any teacher about to engage in a rote learning exercise is, Do not. The teacher should try instead to make the learning as meaningful as possible, even if this effort appears on the surface to make the task more complex. An explanation of why having more to learn may result in less to memorize invites a brief look backwards into the history of experimental psychology.

Learning nonsense

The fact that anything is easier to learn if it is meaningful may simplify life for the student, but it plays havoc with psychological experimentation. Experiments become "contaminated" when subjects can use prior knowledge to help them with the task. As a result, psychologists developed a way to look at learning that is "pure", in the sense that it is completely independent of meaning. They invented the nonsense syllable, usually a pronounceable three-letter consonant-vowel-consonant sequence such as TAV, ROP or ZIT. And since that invention a large part of psychological theorizing about human learning has been immersed in nonsense—looking at how nonsense syllables are learned, retained and forgotten—even though the intention is to make both the task and the content as different as possible from anything that anyone in his right mind would otherwise endeavor to learn.[9] But there has been a constant war between experimenters struggling to find syllables that are more and more meaningless and experimental subjects trying to confound them by making sense out of the nonsense. There is nothing malicious in this subversive activity on the part of experimental subjects: it seems a natural tendency of human beings to make as much sense as they can out of anything they are asked to do. It is remarkably easier to remember anything if you can associate it with something sensible—which means something you know already—no matter how bizarre or outrageous the association might appear.

The nonsense syllables TAV, ROP, ZIT, for example, are much easier to remember if they are imagined as a perverse instruction by a drunken ship's petty officer on shore leave: "Tavern ropes, sit!" Imposing sense or order on a sequence of unrelated items makes them much easier to learn, even if there seems to be much more to learn.

One of the principal techniques for studying the learning of nonsense syllables is known as the method of anticipation. The subject is shown ten or a dozen syllables on slips of paper, which are turned face up one at a time, and he is allowed just one glance at each. At the end of the first "trial" the subject goes through the list again, this time trying to say what each syllable will be before he is permitted to see it. In other words, he must try to remember and anticipate both the syllables and their order. After every trial the experimenter notes how many of the syllables have been identified correctly, and the subject continues until he gets all the syllables correct according to some criterion of achievement, such as two faultless repetitions of the entire list. At that point the list is regarded as "learned", although the subject may be allowed more trials in order to "overlearn" the material. Once he has learned the syllables to the experimenter's satisfaction, the second part of the experiment begins. The subject is tested to see how long it takes him to forget the syllables. This information is gained by seeing how many syllables he can remember after varying intervals of time.

There are many other variants of such studies concerned, for example, with the effect of spending more or less time studying each syllable, the effect of longer and shorter intervals between trials, the degree of over-

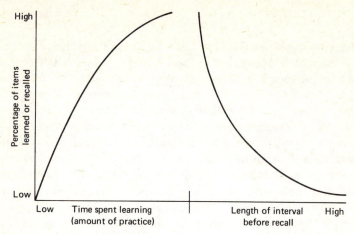

Figure 5.1 A learning and a forgetting curve

learning and the length of time and nature of activity between the final learning trial and recall. However, from the thousands of experiments conducted with nonsense syllables, it is perhaps not unfair to say that only two basic rules have emerged. The rules can be summarized in a single sentence: *Ease of learning is a function of list length, and ease of recall a function of the number of repetitions.* To be more precise, the fewer the items to be learned, the. faster they will be learned. And the more they are overlearned, or repeated, the less likely they are to be forgotten. These laws may be represented graphically in what is known as a "learning curve". If you examine the learning curve in Figure 5.1, you will see that the first few items are learned fairly rapidly but that the rate of learning soon drops off. It takes more and more time to learn each additional item on the list. On the other hand, the forgetting curve in Figure 5.1 shows that most forgetting takes place immediately after learning has been completed. The longer an item stays in memory, the less likely it is to be forgotten.

PAIRED ASSOCIATES LEARNING   The memorization of lists is not the only way in which nonsense syllable learning has been studied. In "paired associates learing", the subject is given a list of pairs of nonsense syllables to learn, such as TAV–ROP, ZIT–VUG, KOV–DEK. To demonstrate learning, he must be able to say the second member of a pair when the experimenter says the first, to give the "response" DEK to the "stimulus" KOV.[10]

Paired associate learning is widely regarded as more similar to real life than merely learning lists of nonsense syllables. For example, learning to say VUG when the experimenter says ZIT is considered highly analogous to learning to say *dog* when you are confronted by a real one. There are, however, differences that we have already noted between the paired associates situation and learning the name of the dog. The most difficult part of learning names is not to associate a name with a concept, but to find out what defines the concept in the first place. In the paired associates situation, there is no doubt that the stimulus is TAV or ZIT or KOV.

CONDITIONS OF LEARNING   Although the kind of experiments just characterized intentionally deal with nonsense, there has been little reluctance in extrapolating their results into educational dogma. Part of the folklore of the classroom, for example, is that practise makes perfect, even though no amount of drill seems to guarantee learning for an unmotivated child or for incomprehensible material. Nor does frequent repetition seem to be required for a child who is interested in a topic that he can make sense of. Two other venerable psychological laws are that learning is a function of recency and reinforcement. Yet the most casual observation of an actual classroom discloses that there is absolutely no guarantee that the most recently imparted information will be remembered or that habits or attitudes learned early will be forgotten. Similarly, no material or spiritual reward appears sufficient to ensure learning; nor does its absence necessarily prevent learning.

One insight from studies of "list learning"—whether the material is a dozen nonsense syllables, a chunk of foreign language vocabulary, the names of parts of flowers or a catalog of a country's major exports—is that not all items in a list are equally difficult to learn. List learning tends to reflect what are called *serial order effects*, especially effects of primacy and recency. The primary and recency effects are that items at the beginning or end of a list tend to be remembered better than those in the middle. A plausible explanation for this phenomenon is that at the time of testing the last items are still in short-term memory and the first items succeeded in getting into long-term memory, but the remainder found themselves evicted from short-term memory with nowhere to go.[11]

If serial order effects are likely to occur in a particular classroom situation, then it should not be difficult for a teacher to overcome them, for example, by changing the order of items occasionally. However, it is probably more important for a teacher to remember that serial order effects occur only with lists of unrelated items, and that the rote memorization of such lists is not an efficient mode of learning in any case. On the other hand, the memorization of simple words, such as names, liberally spaced in time and embedded in a meaningful context, seems to present no problem to children.

The preceding assertion is supported by another well-established principle from studies of rote learning, that "distributed practice" is more efficient than "massed practice". It is better to try to learn a little at frequent intervals than a lot all at once. But once again common sense must be exercised in interpreting this principle, since the best duration for the practice periods, and for the intervals between them, depends very much on individual circumstances and on the material to be learned. It may be reasonable to attempt to learn a list of spellings in six ten-minute periods during a day rather than in a single one-hour cram, but it would be foolish to make the practice periods too short—say, only a few seconds at a time—or the rest intervals too long. The distributed practice rule also contradicts to some extent a principle which applies to material that has any degree of meaningfulness, namely, that "whole learning" is better than "part learning". According to this principle, it is better to learn a poem a stanza at a time, or in even larger chunks, rather than a line at a time.

Another aspect of learning relevant to the question of massed and distributed practice is *interference,* a matter which will come up when we consider forgetting. Many experiments have shown that one of the greatest factors in whether material once learned is retained or forgotten is not the passage of time, but what transpires during the interval.[12] Learning is best consolidated if you switch to some completely different activity after the practice period, or better still if you have your night's sleep. There is a concise and fundamentally irrefutable psychological rule about interference which is impossible to put into practise except on the basis of common sense. The rule is that highly similar or highly dissimilar tasks tend to facilitate learning, while moderately similar tasks interfere.[13] The catch of course is to define what is meant by *similar.* If you must learn two lists of nonsense syllables and many of the items are common to both lists, then the two learning tasks will facilitate each other. On the other hand, a completely different task, such as some simple arithmetic problems, will not interfere unduly with any prior learning of a list of words. But the learning of a potentially confusing set of items, such as RAV, ZOP, RIT, after one has learned a sequence like TAV, ROP, ZIT, will be highly interfering because basically the same elements are involved in the different combinations. In learning foreign language vocabularies, the problem is not so much with words that are almost the same in both languages (such as *cat* and *chat*), or with words that are quite different (such as *dog* and *chien*), as with words that look the same but have different meanings (such as *poison* and *poisson*).

It is difficult to conceive of any actual learning situation outside of the experimental laboratory—with the unfortunate exception of some classrooms—in which the subject of learning is completely devoid of sense and totally unfamiliar. "Pure" learning is in fact the most impure you could get. Even when a real life learning task looks like list or paired associates learning, it is never as nonsensical or as unpredictable as the laboratory task, and always has an element of meaningfulness.

Meaningful Learning

Like many other aspects of educational psychology, meaningful learning is frequently considered and sometimes confused from more than one point of view. The first viewpoint might be called theoretical, since it is concerned with the nature of the learning *process* when the learning task involves meaningful material or activities. The second is essentially practical, since it is concerned with actual teaching techniques. In fact terms such as *reading readiness, problem solving, discovery learning* and *meaningful learning* are often used in schools to refer to a particular instructional strategy, or to something a *teacher* does.[14]

Meaningful learning in the instructional jargon denotes a range of activities from the provision of prior "organizers" intended to give the learner cognitive pegs, or mediators, on which to hang new information, to going through the "proof" of mathematical statements step by step so that the learner can see for himself why the statements hold.

The assumptions underlying meaningful learning ·strategies in the classroom are worth considering, since they help to exemplify some differences between meaningful and rote learning (or what might better be called learning meaningfully and memorizing nonsense). In a meaningful learning situation the learner is able to relate new information to what he already knows—a contingency that experimenters so often and so painstakingly try to avoid—and is also able to impose interrelationships or structure upon the new information and consequently reduce the memorization demands of the task.

It is possible to be more specific about the factors that tend to make learning tasks more meaningful. Meaningfulness is increased when

(a) The elements of the material to be learned are already familiar—for example, the sounds or letters of a name or nonsense syllable or the individual digits of a telephone number

(b) the sequence of elements is a sequence with which we are familiar—for example, HIJ rather than HPM, 3456 rather than 3465

(c) the new material can be related to something already known that is easily remembered—for example, *Tavern ropes sit* rather than TAV ROP ZIT

(d) the new material can be assimilated into a network of existing knowledge, when it is supplementary to something we already know—for example, a discussion of Mars with a child familiar with the notion of a planetary system

I shall illustrate with a number of examples in the remainder of this chapter how these four factors can make learning easier by making the task more meaningful.

Assessing meaningfulness

You may still wonder how it is possible to assert that one word is "more meaningful" than another, or that nonsense syllables can be meaningful at all. Here we find psychologists adopting what may appear to be quite arbitrary and even exotic strategies in order to measure meaningfulness. For example—to answer the second question first—nonsense syllables are regarded as meaningful to the extent that they resemble sequences of sounds or letters in real English. Thus, STR would be considered more meaningful than TSR because the former is part of many English words while the latter is not. And such a working definition can be considered reasonable because the closer a sequence of letters is to actual English sequences, the better a learner can relate it to what he knows already. It is more predictable and more easily retrievable.

This notion that the more familiar is more meaningful is applicable also to individual words, where one definition of meaningfulness has been related to frequency in the language. By this yardstick the words *table* and *chair* are in general more meaningful than *samovar* and *mitosis*. An alternative method for measuring meaningfulness has simply been to count the number of "associations" people can make to a word in a given period. If I asked you to write down all the words that *table* makes you think of in one minute, you would almost certainly write many more words than if the key word had been *samovar*.[15]

However one looks at meaningfulness, it is clearly not an all-or-none affair. Learning tasks, or learning materials, are not either meaningful or rote. There are differing degrees of meaningfulness, depending on the extent to which the material to be learned can be related to what the learner knows already, with rote right at the bottom of the range. The fact that one cannot make a clear distinction between the rote and the meaningful may be an indication that there are not two kinds of learning, but differing extents to which a basic learning process can be effective. It would also be misleading to suggest that meaningfulness is inherent in either learning tasks or the material to be learned. Meaningfulness depends on what the learner knows already. In other words, it would be more accurate to say that what the learner knows, or what he does, makes learning meaningful or rote.

As material to be learned becomes more congruent with what a learner knows already, the "laws of learning" we examined earlier and the neat learning curve in Figure 5.1 go completely by the board. There is nothing like the steady climb to mastery of a list of nonsense syllables. Instead the learning appears to take place all at once—perhaps after a long period when no learning seems to have occurred—or it manifests itself as a series of unpredictable bursts of improvement. Neither the sudden insight into the meaning (and thus the application) of $(a + b)^2 = a^2 + b^2 + 2ab$ nor the seemingly spontaneous increments in skill in reading or foreign language learning shown by many learners fit the "laws of learning" paradigm.

Problem solving

In books and in classrooms problem solving and meaningful learning are frequently treated as if they were different kinds of learning. Once again I think the distinction is primarily due to the different kinds of situation in which the learning takes place rather than to a difference in the learning processes themselves. In fact, as we shall see, the type of learning called "meaningful" and that called "problem solving" appear to have a good deal in common.

The range of situations examined in psychological studies of problem solving is wide and varied.[16] On the one hand, the attempts of cats to escape from cages have been referred to as problem solving. Some classical problem-solving experiments have involved constructing a pendulum out of sticks and pieces of string, or sticking candles on walls without props. Others have been quite discursive, for example, imagining how to gain access to a locked house. Some kinds of concept learning task appear to involve problem solving, and are occasionally so called. All, it seems to me, involve cognitive restructuring.

One characteristic of problem-solving situations is that the solution should be apparent to the learner the moment he has achieved it. In some sense the answer to the problem is already known; the task is to find a route between problem and solution. The learner is not dependent on anyone else for feedback; he knows if he has succeeded or failed. The "specific information" required to test hypotheses is already available in the learning situation or the learner's head. The problem of opening a locked box, for example, is solved when the box opens. The square root of 289 is discovered when a number is found which multiplied by itself equals 289. Problems are usually not solved by recollection or by working out a single solution, but by testing possible alternative solutions, perhaps only one of which will be "correct".

Skill in problem solving therefore depends on two factors that are both part of the basic learning process. The first is the ability to think of alternative solutions, or alternative routes between a known initial state (the "problem") and a known or recognizable final state (the "solution"). In more common terminology, this factor would be called the ability to get ideas, or "creativity". This factor clearly involves the generation of hypotheses. The second factor in problem solving is separating the desired or "correct" solution from all the others, a process of evaluation that may require what is often known as "reasoning" or "judgment", and which involves implicit tests of hypotheses.

Both meaningful learning and problem solving require a reorganization of cognitive structure. Meaningful learning situations generally demand relatively permanent changes in cognitive structure—one is *learning* something—while problem solving is more likely to require provisional changes which are tested vicariously. Usually we do not want to remember incorrect solutions.

INSIGHT AND INCUBATION   A prominent part of many problem-solving situations is often called *insight*, the sudden flash of intuition that brings not just a solution to a problem but also the knowledge that the solution is correct. This satisfying and even thrilling moment of realization—sometimes known as the "a-ha" or "eureka" phenomenon—may be experienced when we crack a difficult crossword puzzle clue, or solve an anagram such as the school subject that is "a garble" (the answer begins with *a*_____). The fact that a correct solution may come as something of a surprise demonstrates how much of the underlying thought process in learning is independent of conscious control. In fact the first state of problem solving, when nothing much seems to be happening, has been termed *incubation*.[17] We put problems into our heads and wait like broody hens for solutions to hatch. The remarkable thing is that they often do. The conscious (and trainable) part of problem solving or any other creative activity often seems less concerned with generating alternative ideas as with evaluating them. There is little evidence that people can be *taught* to have good ideas; ideas grow out of encouragement and improve with experience. Skill comes from being able to examine one's own ideas critically, to distinguish the good ideas from the bad.

Manufacturing meaningfulness

Here is a remarkable phenomenon: If you want to make nonsense easier to learn, embed it in something that makes sense, even though this leaves the original nonsense unchanged and presents you with more to commit to memory. The syllable TAV is nonsense until it is related to something we know about, perhaps as the brand name of a drink or a detergent. The very fact that a sound is attached to a particular concept makes both easier to remember: "When you think of beer, think of TAV". "Pure" nonsense syllables are difficult to recall because there is no cognitive structure through which we can reach them. Making a nonsense syllable part of a fictitious name, such as *Mr. T. A. V. Smith*, is another example of what might be called the paradoxical rule of that learning more is often less. Just as it is easier to memorize an entire poem than a few unrelated words of that poem, so it is easier to remember a name than a few letters of the name.

To repeat an example already given, if you must learn a list of nonsense syllables such as TAV, ROP, ZIT, associate each nonsense syllable with a word such as *tavern, rope,* and *sit.* You have now complicated the learning task, since instead of committing TAV to memory you must remember something like "the first three letters of *tavern*"; instead of ZIT you must remember "*sit* with the *s* changed to *z*". Nevertheless the mnemonic (memory aid) usually works, because it is easier to retrieve words from long-term memory than nonsense. Associating nonsense syllables with words improves the probability of retrieval, and performance on a learning task is therefore facilitated.

The more structure can be imposed on the material to be learned, the higher the probability of subsequent recall will be. For example, making nonsense syllables into a sentence, or associating them with a sentence, improves learning even more than relating the syllables to separate unrelated words. The fact that a sentence, however nonsensical, has grammatical structure, provides an additional cue, as in the *Tavern ropes sit* example. If you are able to remember just the first word of the sequence now, you are likely to get all the items back, and in the right order too. Grammatical structure also improves the chances of recall, even if the nonsense syllables are not associated with real words; *The tav rops zit* is easier to remember than TAV ROP ZIT. Many other structure cues such as rhyme and meter facilitate recall, and thus make learning easier.

BIZARRENESS MAY BE BETTER   The fact that some of the associations among nonsense syllables or words may be bizarre is not a handicap; in fact bizarreness often seems to facilitate recall. A well-known example involves associating a list of words that must be learned with words previously learned easily because they rhyme with the numbers up to ten. One trial is usually sufficient to memorize and subsequently recall the following rhymes: *One is a bun, two is a shoe, three is a tree, four is a door, five is a hive, six is sticks, seven is heaven, eight is a gate, nine is a line, ten is a hen.*[18]

Suppose now you had to memorize a list of ten words beginning: *horse, cheering, justice, water, apples* and so on. Your strategy would be to make a bizarre visual association between the word in the list and the already-learned word that rhymes with its position in the list. For example, *horse* is the first word to be learned and *one is a bun* might lead you to imagine a horse eating a bun. *Cheering* is the second word and *two is a shoe* might have you visualize a shoe cheering. For *justice,* which is three, you might imagine a tree wearing the robes of a justice; for four, a door with a tap pouring out water; for five, a beehive full of apples.

The principle of the previous mnemonic is very simple. While there is no easy way to associate a number with an arbitrarily selected word, it is not at all difficult to associate a number with a word that rhymes with it or to associate two words which have been combined in a single image. To be more precise, it is not difficult to *recall* such pairs if the associations can be established. The rhyme gives the clue and provides access to both the numbers and the list of words.

It is not necessary for the superimposed associative structure to be verbal for mnemonic intermediaries to work. A familiar spatial organization, a "cognitive map", can also be employed as a memory crutch. For example, a useful trick if you are playing "Kim's game", where the task is to remember a dozen or so different objects briefly displayed on a tray, is to imagine putting each object in a different location on your person. You might "put" one object in each shoe (make sure you can *"feel"* the objects there in your imagination), two more in your socks or stockings, one in each pocket and so forth. To recall what the objects are, take a tour around your person. Alternatively, you could have associated the twelve words of the previous unrhymed list with objects around your room: The horse is at the door, the picture next to it is cheering, while a justice looks through the window. To recall you would simply have looked around the room, with your eyes or in your imagination.

Two psychologists in Australia[19] tested a venerable variant of this mnemonic called the "philosopher's walk", because it is reputed to have been invented by Simonedes. First the investigators memorized a familiar walk through their campus, giving every prominent feature a number—one for the main gate, two for a large tree, three for the clock tower and so forth—until they had fifty features. Back in their laboratory they gave themselves a few minutes to memorize a list of fifty words by associating each word with a feature of their walk—a horse at the main gate, the tree cheering, a justice peering from the clock tower and so on. The psychologists found that out of the fifty they could recall an average of forty-eight items and their number in the list, simply by taking the walk in their minds and "reading off" each word as they came to its location. Could anything be easier?

CHUNKING   The mnemonics so far discussed have been primarily concerned with facilitating retrieval from memory, with the utilization of prior knowledge to provide a structure within which "unrelated" information can be placed. The mnemonic in effect provides a relationship that makes the new information meaningful, and therefore easier to retrieve. There is another highly efficient way to facilitate learning and subsequent recall that enables you to reduce the dimensions of the learning task from the start. *Chunking* is a technique that gives you less to remember.

You will remember from the discussion of short-term and long-term memory in Chapter 2 that the input problem is a matter not of the *kind* of information being stored away, but of its *amount,* the number of unrelated items. Short-term memory can hold half a dozen letters or half a dozen words or several chunks of "meaning" taken from a dozen or more words. To try to remember TAV as three unrelated letters will occupy about half of short-term memory, far more than is required to remember the first three letters of *tavern.* The sequence of letters PRZYJEZDZAC will more than overload short-term memory and require a good minute of concentration to be put into long-term memory (from whence it will be very difficult to retrieve) unless you happen to read Polish, in which case it will be just one easily remembered word for you.

It is important to understand exactly what chunking involves. Although the *effect* of chunking is to reduce the quantity or extent of the material to be learned, the process itself is one of making the material to be learned more meaningful by relating it to whatever makes the most sense to the learner. A word makes more sense than a random sequence of letters, and a sentence makes more sense than random words.[20]

My purpose in describing these mnemonic tricks has not been to instruct you how to "improve your memory"—though they are the basis of many commercial courses claiming to do just this—nor even to suggest that the mnemonics should be taught in classrooms. They constitute both illustrations and explanations of the fact that learning becomes easier as it becomes more meaningful. It is not necessary to change the child to enable him to learn meaningfully; that is already the way his brain is constructed to function. What is usually required is to change the learning task or situation so that a child can make sense of it.

Cognitive Structure and Motor Skills

Psychologists often distinguish motor skills, which involve the integration of physical movements, from cognitive skills, such as concept formation and language. But the fact that skills may be nonverbal does not mean that they are not cognitive, that thinking does not play a part in them. And, unfortunately, it is as difficult to study motor learning when thought is involved as it is to study meaningful verbal learning. The consequence has been that psychologists have tended to concentrate on motor learning that is essentially deprived of meaningfulness, for example, the rate at which subjects can learn to run their fingers through the pathway of a maze or to pursue an errratically moving spot with a pointer. When the task is as meaningless as in these two examples, all the classical "laws of learning" noted earlier in this chapter seem to apply—for example, that ability improves with practice.

With a few exceptions,[21] psychologists have not concerned themselves with more common complex skills, such as dancing or skiing, model building or sewing, car driving or the assembly of stereo systems, partly perhaps because such meaningful learning once again defies the "laws of learning" and introduces variability and unpredictability into experiments. What many people learn to do quite easily, psychologists find very difficult to explain. And the problem, as always, is that it is practically impossible to find any form of human behavior that does not involve a large component of cognitive activity.

Even so-called tasks of eye-hand coordination, such as catching a ball, should more properly be termed *eye-hand-brain coordination,* because very few balls would be caught without the brain controlling the tracking movements of the eyes, predicting where and when the ball will fall and monitoring the position of the hands so that they can be brought together at just the right time and place to intercept the ball's flight. So little direct coordination of eye and hand is involved that catching is easily accomplished with the eyes closed, once the brain has had an opportunity to gauge the speed and trajectory of the ball. The skill is basically one of accurate prediction.

Ability to drive a car is also much less a matter of knowing which pedals to push, or of how far to spin the steering wheel, than of acquiring and integrating information from a variety of sources about the traffic outside the car, the performance of the car itself, and the map in one's mind of the route to be taken, together with a host of other considerations concerning where the vehicle should be placed preparatory to maneuvers like turning and stopping.

The car-driving example illustrates that there must be much more to feedback than simple "knowledge of results". Such knowledge is useless unless it can be matched against some expectation of what the feedback ought to be. Feedback about the sound of the car's engine, for example, must be checked against some prediction of how the engine ought to sound. Feedback concerning the position of the car relative to the car ahead must be evaluated in the light of some prior expectation or hypothesis of where the car *ought to be* in relation to the car ahead. The problem with inexperienced drivers often is their concern with where the car is now rather than where it should be in a few moments later.

The serial ordering of behavior[22]

Most everyday human activities, such as talking or writing or driving a car, are performed so fast and involve so many different muscle movements simultaneously that it would be impossible for the brain to organize them if it looked after movements one at a time. Consider typewriting or piano playing. The brain must not only move two sets of fingers—complicated enough though this must be—but also hands, wrists, elbows, shoulders and eyes. Such complex movements require a good deal of prior planning because none of them begin at the same time, although all depend on each other. Before the brain can determine how to move a finger, for example, it must know where the finger should go and also where it is in relation to the keyboard and to the hand, arm and shoulder.

To orchestrate such complicated sequences of activity, the brain must send neural information to all the muscles involved in a very precisely organized sequence. Although a finger may have to wait until the elbow has been moved, the brain may have to send the neural message to the finger first, because nerve impulses need more time to travel to finger muscles than to arm muscles. Furthermore, feedback is clearly critical to the organization of successive movements. Yet there is no time for the feedback from one movement to· get to the brain before the neural messages controlling the next movement are sent out. (Neural impulses do not travel as fast as we generally think. While light rays travel to the eye at 186,000 miles a second, the fastest neural impulses, down the long thick nerve fibres of the spinal cord and legs, scarcely reach 200 miles an hour, while those in the short fine fibres of the brain travel at only a tenth of that speed.)

All of this means that piano playing and typewriting would be impossible if the brain were directing one note or letter at a time. Instead the brain organizes entire sequences of behavior in advance. Such sequences, examples of the *plans* or *programs* referred to in Chapter 1, are so overlearned that it is practically impossible to break them into components or to stop them once their execution has been started. It is just about impossible to get a skilled typist to type words incorrectly deliberately—to spell *the* as *teh*, for example—without slowing down considerably. More than mere "motor skill" is involved in the typing of words and phrases, and the playing of arpeggios.

Complex skills cannot be taught by simply having the learner watch someone else perform, or by merely giving the learner critical information. The learning comes only through doing. The learner instructs himself, and the teacher is primarily responsible for providing feedback indicating whether the desired result is being reached or not.

Motor learning is basically a matter of *fluency*, acquired only through practice. Alternative patterns of behavior must be preorganized so that they can be produced with a minimum of attention and effort. Just as infants learn to use prior knowledge in their perception of the world in order to circumvent the brain's bottlenecks of information processing and memory, so they learn to overcome in advance the difficulties of producing complex patterns of behavior.

CHAPTER 6

Learning To Speak and To Read

Next to the facility with which an infant organizes himself in a three-dimensional world of predictable events and objects, the ease with which he goes on to master language is perhaps the most underrated intellectual accomplishment of childhood. Everybody learns to talk, save for the patently abnormal, so what is so special about language? Since the development of speech seems to be part of the birthright of almost every human child, why should the transmission of language from one generation to another require our attention—even if the torch of this supreme cultural tool changes hands when the recipient is only a few years old?

A child receives remarkably little credit for his mastery of language. Because he is given no formal instruction by adults, the magnitude of his achievement is grossly underestimated. Adults tend to assume that they have a monopoly on intelligence, and rarely imagine that substantial learning might take place in the absence of their direction and guidance. The present chapter sets out to redress the balance by exploring the impressive manner in which infants learn to understand and speak their mother tongue. This examination will serve as an example of the powerful and independent learning facility young children can bring with them to school, and a demonstration of the basic learning process in operation. Since the topic is the learning of language, we can then turn conveniently to a subject of central concern in school, learning to read.

The Language of Children

Most children can utter only a few isolated words on their first birthday, yet three years later they have mastered almost all of the rules of adult language.[1] They have developed an adult grammar. Of course four-year-old children do not talk like adults—which is one reason their achievement does not get the credit it deserves. They have neither the general experience nor the specific interests of adults; they have smaller vocabularies, and to some extent use language for different purposes. They just do not talk about the same things as adults. Nevertheless children seem to have very little left to learn about the fundamentals of their native language by the time they come to school.

Learning without imitation

Children gain their basic competence in language without formal instruction; and the common adult effort to salvage some of the credit by claiming that children learn language by imitating them is a gross exaggeration. There are two good reasons for asserting that children learn very little language by imitating adults. The first reason is very practical: Language could not be learned in this way. As we saw in Chapter 3, the surface structure of language does not directly represent meaning, nor does it provide unambiguous cues for the grammar that relates sound and meaning. In other words, the sounds of adults' language are meaningless until a child understands them; and there is no reason for a child to imitate meaningless sounds.

The second objection to the imitation theory is a matter of observation: Children learning to talk show very little imitation of adults. The language that children first produce is primarily a language of their own. The vast majority of their early utterances of the *Want wugwug* or *Daddy goes walkies* variety are part of a language every child makes up for himself. Babies speak baby talk, a language parents never use unless they are themselves imitating their offspring.

The assertion that children learn very little by imitation does not mean that they pay no attention to the language of adults. On the contrary, children rapidly modify their unique language, so that by the age of four most of them are recognizably talking the language of the people around them. But this is not because children start out by mimicking adult language. Instead adult language is the *target* towards which children address their language-learning efforts. Children use adult language both as a source of information about the rules of language and as a model. The closer that children can approximate adult speech, the closer they have come to acquiring the appropriate rules. But this use of adult language as a model is far different from imitating the sounds of language in the same way in which a child might ape the actions of a parent smoking a pipe or reading a book.

A painstaking recent study[2] has shown that children are extremely selective in the manner in which they imitate adult words—*copy* might be a more appropriate term—in order to modify and develop their own vocabularies. For a start, they will not imitate something they know already. If a mother says "See the big plane" to a child who knows very well that he is looking at a big plane, he will not repeat what she has said. Nor will a child imitate something that is completely meaningless to him. If the mother says "See the big plane" and the child has no idea what she is talking about, he will not repeat her sentence. But if the name is new *and he knows what it means*—if he knows the plane is being referred to but has not yet learned its name—then he will indeed "imitate" the word. At this stage of learning I think that *adopt* might be a better description of what he does. When a child imitates in this way, he is taking exactly what he wants from adult language. He is copying in order to test a hypothesis.

The first words

By the time he is a year old the average child is starting to produce language sounds meaningfully.[3] (I should point out here that I am talking about a mythical "average" child and about behaviours whose onset varies over a period of months and is difficult to determine with precision. Girls are usually a couple of months ahead of boys, and first children speak sooner than their brothers and sisters—two interesting topics for speculation. But a variation of several months on either side of the "norm" is cause for neither dismay nor jubilation.)

Already the child is inventing. The first words a baby utters are frequently not words that he has heard used by his parents; and, in any case, he uses words differently from adults. When a child begins to produce his first words, his main concern is that they have meaning. And in order to express meaning, he will use any combination of sounds that serves his purposes. Sometimes he will borrow an adult word, such as *mama* or *drink*. Sometimes he will use an approximation of that word, such as *dwink* or *dink*. And sometimes he will use a construction like *googum* or *nashnash* that bears little or no apparent relation to adult language.

The child of one year looks for words that will communicate meanings he wants to express. He begins with meaning, at the level of deep structure, and generates a surface structure of sound that he hopes will express it.[4] He never waits for an adult to utter a word that he wants to use. If necessary he invents a word to express his meaning, although if an adult word is available he will borrow it (whether or not the word has the same meaning for adults) or produce an approximation. The child's main concern is that the word he uses—whether invented, adapted or taken directly from adult language—will convey the meaning that he wishes to express. If he wishes to refer to a drink, and gets a response that makes sense to him when he uses an invented word such as *googum*, then *googum* becomes his word. He has generated a hypothesis that the meaning he wants to convey can be expressed by this word; and if his hypothesis is supported, he stays with *googum*. But if his hypothesis fails, if saying *googum* does not have the consequence he desires, he looks for an alternative. He asks in effect, "What is the word in adult language that expresses the meaning I wanted to convey when I said *googum?*"

It is at this point that most adults give a child precisely the information he needs in order to develop language. When the child says *googum*, the mother says "You mean *drink*, don't you?" or "Do you want a glass of milk?" In other words, by "expanding" the child's utterance, the mother offers information about adult surface structure for a deep structure she has intuited from the child's utterance and situational clues. Thus the first language exchanges between adults and babies are conducted primarily at the level of deep structure, or meaning. The child generates a surface structure he hopes will express a particular meaning; and with appropriate feedback from an adult he compares his surface structure with that of adult language.

Of course the "reasoning" that I put into the minds of mother and child is completely metaphorical. The majority of parents do not know what they are doing for a child when they repeat his utterances in their own language, but they tend to do it instinctively. Children who grow up with limited or distorted language have generally been deprived of opportunities to converse with adults. Similarly, it should not be thought that an infant is aware of what he is doing in developing and testing new words; children also play the language game instinctively. It is as if a child never makes a statement on only a single level. When he asks for a drink, he is also making the linguistic inquiry "Is this the way you ask for a drink in adult language?" It is reasonable to regard every statement made by a child learning to talk as an experiment in language, just as every look since he was born can be regarded as an attempt to add to his knowledge about the visual world.

ONE-WORD SENTENCES   The first words uttered by children are never mere imitations of adult language. Even when a child uses the same words as adults, he uses them in a different way. A child does not imitate adult words; he borrows them for his own purposes.

Adults never use isolated words to express meaning unless other words are clearly understood and can be supplied. For example, the adult one-word statement "Drink" is elliptical for the question "Would you like to have a drink?" or the demand "Drink this"—it is a noun or a verb. By itself, out of context, the word *drink* would be so ambiguous as to be meaningless.

When an infant says *drink* or *dwink* or *googum*, however, a meaning underlies the single word that adults could express only with a complete sentence, such as "I would like a drink" or "Take away my drink" or "Is this a drink?" or "I have just thrown my drink all over the floor". The infant's one-word utterance *is* a complete sentence. It is a statement, not a part of speech. The child in effect has a language rule that a particular meaning, sometimes quite complex, can be expressed in surface structure by the single word *drink*. And since there is no such rule in adult language, a child's first words cannot be said to be an imitation of adult usage.

This practice of using single words to express what adults would call complete sentences appears to be a universal feature of language; all children on their way to becoming fluent talkers produce one-word sentences as they leave the babbling stage. However, not all children produce the same word first. That would hardly be likely, since each child is largely inventing his first words for himself. And the meaning of the words he will first produce is also dependent upon the individual child and his particular surroundings. Drinking does not necessarily dominate a child's first attempts at conversation. But while the particular words any child will utter are completely unpredictable, nothing is more certain than that he will begin his talking career with such one-word sentences.

These unique first words of children's language have earned a special name in technical jargon. They are called *holophrases*, indicating that they are single units expressing a complete thought. A child moves out of the holophrastic stage of his career about six months after he enters it. At roughly the age of eighteen months, when he has a dozen or so holophrases in his repertoire, a child begins to put two or three words together to make sentences.

The first sentences

Once again the first sentences that a child produces are nothing like the language he hears around him. When an infant begins to produce his first very short sentences, he does not repeat utterances that he has heard older members of his family produce. Instead he starts to use his own holophrases as words, combining them into sentences so that their meanings in isolation are submerged into richer and more precise sentence meanings. In order to produce his first sentences, a child does not put words together randomly. Instead he constructs his first sentences according to a rule, his first grammatical rule. And once again we find that this rule is not one that adults employ, but is unique to the earliest stages of children's language development. The child invents the rule for himself—it is his first grammatical hypothesis—and he persists in using it until he learns from adults' responses that its modification would bring him to a closer approximation of adult language.

As soon as a child begins to put two or three words together into sentences, it becomes apparent that he has done something very interesting to his vocabulary. Words that were grammatically indistinguishable, and could each suffice as a single-word utterance, now assume a grammatical distinctiveness. The words in his vocabulary become segregated into different "parts of speech", although not the parts of speech that can be distinguished in adult language.

For example, a small proportion of the words a child can use will appear only at the beginning of a sentence, and never alone. A variety of grammatical names have been used to label this group of words so privileged that they occur only in front of other words; one example is *pivot class*. The remainder of the words in the child's vocabulary are left in a larger class which also attracts most of the new words that a child acquires, and is therefore often called an *open class*. Open class words may never appear before a pivot word, although one or two open class words may occur alone or following a pivot class word. So for example, if *see, allgone,* and *my* are pivot class words, and *truck, red* and *drink* are in the open class, then the child may say "Drink" or "See truck" or "Allgone red truck," but not "Truck allgone".

This first sentence rule is not found in adult language. We do not divide all our words into two basic classes; nor do we have words that can appear only at the beginning of a sentence. The first sentence rule is invented by babies, used for a while, then discarded when they find it does not produce sentences such as are produced by adult language.

I must repeat my earlier qualification with respect to holophrases. While all children seem to start their grammar with the same kind of sentence rule, they do not necessarily employ the same words; nor do identical words necessarily perform the same grammatical function for different children. Grammatical or semantic function is not determined by the actual word, but by the way in which the child uses it.[5]

AFTER THE FIRST SENTENCES   An infant does not stay with his first sentence rule for very long. Barely three months after he says his first sentences, the basic rule is being modified. There follows an elaboration of rules and classes, which is part of the development of grammar, and a constant development and reorganization of words within classes, which is the development of vocabulary.

I shall not go deeply into the process of language development, a topic of great complexity and considerable controversy. I have tried to show that a basic learning process of hypothesis generation and testing underlies the development of the child's first utterances. All that remains is to show with the broadest of brush strokes how the same learning mechanism enables the child to bring his earliest and primitive language into a closer approximation to the language spoken around him.

The development of the first rule proceeds very rapidly. For example, the pivot class of one child[6] was elaborated in two and a half months from a single undifferentiated set of words to a group of articles (*a, the*), a group of demonstratives (*this, that*) and a further undifferentiated cluster which within another two and a half months had been sorted out into adjectives and possessive pronouns. Thus adult word classes have their roots in the child's earliest language. But who tells an infant about word classes?

Concurrent with the development of more defined classes of words are additional rules of grammar which determine very precisely how words in the various classes may be ordered into sentences. In other words, a child does not begin by learning parts of speech, or even by learning the particular grammatical function a word may have in adult language. A child begins by using words in the way he wants to; and only gradually as his grammar grows does his vocabulary develop the grammatical class characteristics of adult language. He seems to be asking himself constantly and implicitly "Can I use my rules to construct the kinds of sentences I hear adults speak?" and "Are the sentences I construct using my rules similar to the sentences adults construct using their rules?" Using this kind of comparison and feedback, the ever-flexible, ever-responsive, child acquires mastery over adult rules of grammar without any direct instruction about what these rules are. Without even being aware of what he is doing, a child teaches himself to talk.

Two basic rules

The development of children's competence in spoken language can, I think, best be characterized by two simple rules. The first rule is that meaning always precedes grammar; or, in the terminology of Chapter 3, deep structure comes first. A number of recent theorists have pointed out how children's semantic, or deep structure, capabilities always exceed their linguistic capacity to express these underlying conceptual structures.[7] Before a child puts together or comprehends sentences that have an actor and an action, or an action and an object, the underlying propositional structure must be represented in his cognitive interrelations. Before he can handle assertions about spatial (locative) or temporal (tense) relations, he must comprehend the nature of these relations at the cognitive levels. All this may sound obvious, yet the fact that the most important aspects of language learning lie *beyond* language has been widely overlooked—possibly because superficial aspects of language are observable while thought is largely hidden.[8]

The second rule is that language development, both semantic and grammatical, proceeds from the simple to the complex.[9] Semantically, development must follow the general course of cognitive elaboration and differentiation, from the broad strokes with which an infant paints his world to the finer detail that is a consequence of his efforts to make sense of his experience. A child may be eight or nine before he can use the word *brother* in exactly the same sense as adults; at first all boys may be brothers, or the family pet dog may be a brother. The notion that an uncle must be someone's brother is difficult to grasp, and the abstract reciprocal nature of the brother-sister relationships comprehended last.[10] Children's grammar is also not complete by the time they reach school.[11] One rule that invariably arrives late is the passive; not until the age of six or later can a child differentiate *John chases Mary* from *John is chased by Mary*. But once again we can see how meaning precedes grammatical mastery. Not even a five-year-old would believe that *The ball is chased by Mary* means *The ball chases Mary*. These two characteristics—the priority of semantics over grammar, and the development from simplicity to complexity—seem to apply to all languages,[12] and to all children. All children develop basic processes of thought and language in roughly the same progression, although they may differ widely in rate.[13]

The development of comprehension

I have so far discussed the development of language from the point of view of talking—an emphasis that is conventional and convenient, but also somewhat misleading. The view that a child learns language by speaking and that his skill as a talker represents his language ability is misguided. A child learns to talk both by speaking and by comprehending; and his ability to comprehend sentences is always greater than his ability to produce them. In other words, a child's skill in talking does not represent the full extent of his language ability.

Children use speech—their own and that of adults—to test their hypotheses about adult language; but their hypotheses come originally from their efforts to comprehend adult speech (as in the "See the big plane" example given at the beginning of this chapter). The best cues to language available to a child are the meanings he is able to associate with the noise he hears around him. It is because he looks for sense in the noise of his environment that a child develops speech rather than imitate, say, the sound of the air conditioner.[14]

The initiative to make sense of language must come from within the child. When an infant hears his mother mouth a sequence of noises, there is no way in which he can decipher a meaning from these noises alone. For this reason, blind children face a particular difficulty in learning to speak. In order for an infant to make sense of what an adult is saying, he must first decipher the adult's meaning nonverbally. He is then in a position to associate a meaning with an utterance, and to begin to inquire into the nature of the grammatical rules that enable someone to produce the surface structure utterance for a particular meaning.[15]

A baby whose mother says "Would you like your juice now?" or "Here is your juice" as she offers him a beaker of juice does not *hear* his mother say the sentences I have just quoted. To a child the utterances are an intrinsically meaningless sequences of noise, not even differentiated into words. The intuition an infant brings to bear is that the noises his mother makes are related to something meaningful—to the juice that she holds—and are not random and unpredictable.

This search for meaning, the process of making sense of the world, is central to a child's development of language. A child begins with the hypothesis that language is meaningful—that the noise he hears produced by people around him is not arbitrary and meaningless, but can be related to what he knows or can discover about the world. When he hears an adult talking, he does not try to "decode", or extract meaning directly from the utterance. Instead he takes note of what is going on around him and tries to relate it to the adult utterance. In effect he tries to hypothesize the rules by which adults might generate a particular sequence of noises on a particular occasion. He tries to hypothesize a grammar.

On the other hand, grammatical analysis alone will not enable parents to make sense of a child's first efforts at speech. The surface structure of infant speech, even more than that of adult language, conveys insufficient information about meaning. What the adult literally attempts is to understand what the child is *trying to say*. In other words, the adult looks for the meaning underlying the child's utterances, just as the child looks for the meaning underlying adult speech.

From both sides parent and child make use of their expectation of meaning in order to make sense of utterances that they do not have the grammatical rules to comprehend. There is a difference, however. The adult is satisfied simply to understand the child's meaning; he is not usually concerned with trying to go further and master the grammar of the child's language so that he could produce this language himself. A child, on the other hand, must not content himself simply with understanding adult meaning; very often he could achieve this without paying much attention to the actual utterances. A child is confronted with the problem of working out the complex rules by which adults represent a particular meaning in a particular sequence of sounds. The process of trying to discover the rules that produce meaningful utterances in a particular situation is what eventually leads a child to learn not simply a vocabulary of words but also a complex set of grammatical rules. In the face of such evidence, statements that adults teach children language, or that children imitate adults, are obviously considerable oversimplifications.

THE ROLE OF ADULTS   Parents, however, do make two significant contributions to a child's development of language. Their first contribution is that they actually talk in the presence of the child, either directly to him, or in conversations that he can hear. The mere fact that mothers will chat with their babies while feeding or cleaning them plays a considerable part in their infants' subsequent language development. Yet I know of no research into what motivates a mother to spend so much time conversing with an infant who cannot understand her, let alone reply. This constant exposure to adult language is precisely analogous to the "general information" that a child requires to differentiate between cats and dogs as he elaborates his cognitive structure. The noise of adult language confronts a child with the problem he has to solve and stimulates his basic motivation for understanding so that he attempts the learning of language.

The second parental contribution to language learning is the feedback parents provide for a child when he is hypothesis testing. This feedback is the same "specific information" that a child requires in developing his cognitive structure in regard to any other aspect of his experience. The feedback that adults provide for a child's language learning, however, has an interesting peculiarity. Adults do not usually try to correct an infant's speech development by telling him whether he is "right" or "wrong" (in contrast to the way in which reading instruction is often carried out in school). Adults are usually much more tolerant of baby talk than they are of other rudimentary aspects of children's behavior. For example, they may repeat back to a child what they think he has said in adult language. They translate from his surface structure into their own. This process by which an adult translates "Want dwink" into "You want a drink, do you?" is called *expansion*.[16] Parents who talk to children in baby talk deprive them of one kind of opportunity to test their infantile utterances against corresponding adult formulations. Parents who encourage their child to talk in his own language, and then expand his utterances into the corresponding adult form, give him opportunities to test his hypotheses about language rules and to gain fluency. They permit a child to learn not through blind imitation, but through the discovery of the complex relationships underlying sound and meaning.

The motivation for language learning

Obviously a child does not learn to comprehend language by working out the meaning of every new sentence he hears and then memorizing that particular sentence and its meaning, in case he might want to comprehend it again on a future occasion. Nor does he discover and memorize a particular sequence of words for every meaning that he wants to express. Instead a child hypothesizes and tests a relatively small number of rules that will enable him to speak and understand a very large number of sentences.

You may recall the discussion in Chapter 1 of a child's motivation for constructing a theory of the world in his head. Discovering underlying regularities is a far more economical and efficient method of organizing knowledge than trying to remember every individual incident. A mechanism that leads a child to interpret and predict events in terms of underlying relationships is precisely the kind of mechanism that will motivate and enable him to discover the underlying rules of language.

Infants themselves provide irrefutable evidence that they set about learning language in terms of rules rather than specific words. Some of the first adult words that children learn to use are common verbs with an irregular past tense, such as *ate, went, took.* After a period in which these verbs have been used correctly (by adult standards), children often slip into an "incorrect" usage of the past tense, with such constructions as *eated, goed, taked.* A child is not imitating adults when he uses these invented forms; they are not words that he hears spoken around him. Where then has he gotten them from? The answer must be that the child is not trying blindly to learn many hundreds of words, but is testing rules. One rule that children discover early is that the past tense of verbs is often formed by adding the suffix *-ed* to the present tense stem, so that *talk* becomes *talked, push* becomes *pushed,* and by analogy *eat, go* and *take* should become *eated, goed* and *taked.* It is only by testing hypothesized rules, and by modifying them in the light of feedback, that a child will discover which words follow a rule and which words are exceptions.

MAKING SENSE OF LANGUAGE   I have questioned the common assertion that children learn to talk in order to satisfy physical needs, or because they have a drive to communicate. Children practise language in order to master language, rather than to meet immediate needs, and they can communicate quite well without language. Obviously if parents expand their children's language by deciphering a child's meaning from what is going on, rather than from what he says, then a child is not initially communicating through language.

An alternative possibility is that children learn language simply because language is there, and that they talk primarily to test the rules that will help them comprehend. To a child, language is noise until he can understand it; therefore language constitutes a challenge to be understood. A child learns language because he wants to make sense of it, and because it becomes meaningful to him, just as he develops all of his cognitive structure by trying

to make sense of the world. And in order to learn language he uses the powerful and systematic learning process which is part of his birthright, and
which he does not need to be taught. It is this powerful, systematic—and
by the time he gets to school *experienced*—learning process that a child
must bring to bear if he is to solve what is probably his next great intellectual challenge, learning to read.

Reading

Reading is the only subject on the curriculum that I shall examine
specifically in this book; but I shall not examine it as a subject. In other
words, I shall not try to give any principles by which reading should be taught,
a topic that I have written about fairly extensively, and rather critically,
elsewhere.[17] Instead I propose to look briefly at what is involved in learning
to read—at the *problem* of learning to read—and the manner in which a
child must seek its solution. I want to relate the basic skills that a child has
employed long before he comes to school—in order to master spoken language and to make sense of the world in general—to the particular task of
learning to read.

I have already discussed two of the most important aspects of reading.
In Chapter 2 I pointed out that reading is only partially a visual activity,
that the reader must rely far more on *nonvisual information* that he already
has behind his eyeballs than on the *visual information* that comes to him
from the printed page. There are two reasons for this necessity to rely upon
the already known—the limited amount of visual information processing
that the brain can accomplish, and the "bottlenecks of memory" through
which new information has to pass. The consequence of overloading the
brain with incoming visual information I characterized as "tunnel vision";
the more a reader depends upon the print on the page, the less he is likely
to see.

In Chapter 3 I discussed the comprehension of language in very general
terms, particularly the gulf between surface structure and deep structure in
both spoken and written language. Comprehension, I argued, is a matter of
sampling surface structure—the "visual information" of written language—
in order to test predictions and resolve uncertainty about underlying meaning. I claimed that the manner in which written language is comprehended
is no different from the way speech is comprehended. You may therefore
have wondered why I did not claim that all a reader need do is translate
the written symbols into sounds, which seems to be the conventional picture
of what reading is all about. But direct translation of symbols into sound is
not only unnecessary (and would constitute a crippling demand on the information-processing capacity of the brain) but fundamentally impossible.

Despite widespread belief, it can be argued that written language does not *primarily* represent the sounds of speech, but provides clues to meaning. It is self-evidently possible to convert writing into speech. We can read aloud, —or "decode into sound", to use the popular jargon—but this conversion is possible only through the intermediary of meaning. In other words, it is only by understanding what you read that you can read aloud, or to yourself. Reading cannot be a matter of translating to sound and listening to one's own voice to get meaning. The sound must come last and can be dispensed with altogether. It is this point that I shall examine first.

Written and spoken language

Writing is not spoken language written down. I am not stating the obvious fact that the language one would use for a talk would be quite inappropriate for a written paper. Instead I am asserting that writing and speech are parallel and independent aspects of language; we have no more need to transform writing into speech in order to understand writing than to write spoken language on paper in order to understand speech. Writing does not require speech in order to be understood.

I am not claiming that written and spoken English have nothing to do with each other. To a large extent they share the same syntax and lexicon. Similarly, spoken language is of tremendous utility in learning to read, since it helps a child to understand what his teacher is saying to him. But the sole reason auditory acuity is so often regarded as critical for reading is not that reading requires good hearing, but that the method of instruction puts a premium on distinguishing fine differences of sound the teacher believes he is making.

THE TWO LEVELS OF WRITING   To grasp the complete independence of spoken and written language as far as comprehension is concerned, it is necessary to return to the original discussion of the nature of language in Chapter 3. You will remember that two aspects, or levels, of language can be distinguished; the physical manifestation, or *surface structure* (which in the case of speech is the sound waves passing through the air) and the meaning, or *deep structure*. The bridge between the two levels is *grammar*, a lexicon and a syntax defined as a set of rules for language developed by every individual in the recesses of his mind, and largely inaccessible to examination. The distinction between surface structure and deep structure applies to written language as much as to speech. For written languages, surface structure is the ink marks or the chalk marks on a contrasting surface. Until interpreted or comprehended in some way, the surface structure of written language is simply visual noise.

There are distinct differences between spoken and written language at the surface level, which is the level at which "decoding" would have to take place if reading were in fact a matter of waiting until sounds were produced at least "subvocally" before meaning could be ascertained. For example, we differentiate many words in writing that we do not differentiate in speech, and this helps to clarify their meaning. Most of the words in the following sentence are "wrong" when written but not when spoken: *The none tolled hymn she had scene a pare of bear feat inn hour rheum.* It is easy to detect the improperly spelled words in this sentence, an indication that we can get clues to the *meaning* of written words from their visual properties and from syntax, not their sound. If we attached meaning to words only through their sound, there would be no basis for asserting that any of the written words are spelled wrong.

Less often we differentiate words in speech that we do not differentiate in writing. Compare *He winds his watch while the children read* with *I read yesterday that the winds would be strong.* In each of these two sentences the words *winds* and *read* are pronounced differently but spelled the same. How could we read these sentences aloud correctly unless we articulate the words on the basis of meaning?

Furthermore, much of the meaning of spoken language is conveyed by intonation, which is not directly represented in writing. It is a fallacy to assume that punctuation indicates intonation. Most punctuation comes too late to signal anything about how a sentence should be read. Instead intonation is signalled by meaning. Once you know the meaning of a sentence you know how to articulate it.

Written language is not a reliable representation of the sounds of spoken language, even at the word level. The principle of relating spelling to sound is dropped in two quite frequent circumstances, when it would interfere with the principles that (a) words related in meaning should look alike, and (b) words not related should look different, as in *The none tolled hymn* example. The latter principle explains why relatively few words with totally different meanings (such as *lead* and *wound*) look alike, although a large number of different words sound alike in our language. The former principle explains the similarity in spelling and dissimilarity in pronunciation of such word pairs as *medicine-medical, nation-national, bombing-bombard, sign-signature, extreme-extremity,*[18] or the varied pronunciations of the past tense marker *-ed* at the end of *kissed, hugged* and *patted.*

The frequent suggestion that our written language should be easier to read simply because it is alphabetic is fallacious. We identify everything else in our visual world directly, without the mediation of naming. We immediately recognize a cow, or a picture of a cow, without having to first associate the object or picture with the name *cow*. We do not have to utter the name aloud or subvocally in order to hear ourselves say the word and identify the referent. Such a suggestion would indeed be absurd, because we obviously must identify the object or picture before we can utter its name. How then can it be possible to utter the name in order to get the meaning?

It is not true that we need the alphabet to help us remember the names or meanings of all the written words we can recognize. We can all recognize and recall many thousands of words in our spoken language vocabulary, and many thousands of different faces and animals and plants and objects in our visual world, without any such clues. Why should this fantastic memorizing capacity suddenly fail in the case of reading? It is no more difficult for a

person to remember that 家   or the printed word *house* is called "house"

than that 🏠 or an actual house is called "house". Unfortunately, it is

often believed that the alphabetic form *house* is read in an exclusive manner simply because that form is composed of letters.

In some languages the relation between written and spoken forms is far more tenuous than in English, and children still manage quite comfortably to learn to read. In Chinese, for example, the written language is largely logographic (the written symbols represent entire words) and can be read quite independently of the reader's spoken language. In fact reader and writer may speak quite different spoken languages, but because Chinese writing is logographic they can communicate through writing when they cannot communicate through sound. The situation is precisely analogous to the way in which monolingual speakers of English or French may share a common understanding of such numerical and mathematical ideographs as $2 + 2 = 4$, but not of "Two and two are four" or "Deux et deux font quatre".

WORDS LACK INFORMATION   The importance of individual words in reading is often grossly exaggerated. A competent reader is expected to be able to read aloud word-perfectly—at least at his "grade level"—partly because of a belief that to read with comprehension it is essential to identify every word. But experimental evidence supports the common observation that it is much easier to comprehend a passage than to read it word-perfectly.[19] In fact it is generally not possible to read word for word without prior understanding of what is being read; that is why professional readers, such as broadcasters and actors, invariably try to acquire the meaning of what they are to read before they attempt to articulate the actual words.

To understand why the apprehension of meaning must often take priority over the identification of words, a rather unfamiliar notion must be grasped: There is not enough visual information in the spelling of words to permit their being read aloud meaningfully in sentences. At first glance such a statement may appear absurd. Surely, for example, it is the letters in the written word *dog* that tell us it is the animal that buries bones and chases cats? But at best all that the letters in the written word *dog* do is suggest a certain combination of sounds—and we shall see shortly how unreliable letters are as guides to the sounds of spoken language. But the sound of a word is not its meaning; we do not know what the word *dog* is just by looking at it or hearing it, as the following sentence shows: *The stranger began to dog my footsteps.* I have not deliberately selected a trick example to make a trivial case; almost every word in the English language is many times as ambiguous—particularly the commonest ones, which often have as many as fifty meanings.[20] The sentence *Man catches fish* probably appears to be unambiguous, and so does the following elaboration of the same theme: *The villagers man their boats at dawn, fish through the day and sell their catches in the evening.* But the three words *man, catches, fish,* occur with quite different meanings in each of the sentences, and do not even represent the same parts of speech. (Incidentally, I have just given one example —quite a different one will follow shortly—that reading is *not* a matter of going from left to right in English. The meaning of the word *man* is determined in both sentences by the words that come after it.)

In addition to carrying relatively little information about their meaning or syntactic function, individual words also tell the reader little about how they should be pronounced. A "list" of words such as *minute on permit print read should the the we* cannot be read with anything but what is called "list intonation", which is quite different from the intonation the same words get when put together in the sequence *We should read the minute print on the permit.* Only the meaning of the entire sequence will tell you the syntactic role of the individual words. The pronunciation of *permit* depends on whether it was perceived as a noun (*PER*mit) or verb (per*MIT*). *Read* has two quite different pronunciations (/reed/or/red/) depending on tense, and so has *minute* depending on its meaning and syntactic form—none of which can be determined until the meaning of the sentence as a whole is worked out. How could meaning ever be comprehended if words had to be correctly articulated first?

The relevance of phonics

I make an issue of the decoding aspect of reading because of the number of people, many of whom are involved in producing reading programs, who think a child could never learn to recognize a word unless he could use phonic rules to unlock its sound. But we all know that the first words a child reads are learned by the "whole word" method. He recognizes his own name and *Mummy* and *Shell* and *Texaco* and *cornflakes* long before he learns that *m* is pronounced /m/ and *p* /p/ (except when joined with *h*, when it may be /f/). In fact children generally learn that *m* stands for /m/

because they know that /m/ is the sound at the beginning of words such as *Mummy* that start with *m*. Children learn phonics through reading, they do not learn to read through phonics. That is why the best readers are always good at phonics—they keep ahead of the teacher.

A group of investigators at an educational research laboratory in California have published the results of a study in which they calculated how many "spelling-to-sound correspondence" rules would be required to account for the pronunciation of 6000 one- and two-syllable words in the spoken language vocabulary of six- to nine-year-old children.[21] A rule is required for each of the different sounds with which a particular letter or group of letters may be associated. One rule, for example, is required to account for the pronunciation of the letter *p* standing alone, while another is required for *p* in company with *h*. If a particular correspondence occurred relatively infrequently in their 6000 words, such as the /v/ sound in the word *of*, the researchers called it an exception rather than a rule.

Even so, when they surveyed the fruits of their labors, the researchers found no less than 166 rules for spelling-to-sound correspondences—106 for vowels and 60 for consonants—although more than 600 of the most common words were still not completely accounted for. In addition the researchers found no rules which would help the learner select among the alternative rules that were applicable on many occasions; nor were rules found that would tell when a word was to be regarded as an exception. Some rules could not be applied unless the appropriate intonation of the word had already been determined or a decision had been made about its syntactic role (for example, whether *permit* was a noun or verb) or its morpheme structure (for example, the *th* in *father* and *fathead*). In other words, it is easy enough to apply phonic rules, provided you know what the word is in the first place.

I might add that most of the rules these researchers found apply only if the word is decoded backwards. You cannot even decide whether *p*, *g* or *k* should be pronounced, for example, unless you first determine if they are followed by an *n* (*pneumonia*, *gnash*, *knot*), and we all know how a silent *e* at the end of words affects what comes before.

Learning to read

I have been making the point that reading cannot be considered a process of "decoding" written symbols into speech; it is neither necessary nor possible for writing to be comprehended in this way. Instead written language must be directly attacked for meaning—a process not usually "taught", at least not consciously to any significant extent—but learned by many children anyway. We will be better able to ask how children manage to learn to read, if we consider briefly what they must learn to do.

It seems to me that fluent reading entails two basic skills, neither of which is unfamiliar to a child coming into the learning situation. The first skill is the prediction of meaning and the sampling of surface structure to eliminate uncertainty, a process that I discussed at some length in Chapter 3, and that is fundamentally the same for both reading and the comprehension of spoken language. The second skill is the ability to make the most economical use possible of visual information. Every child is also quite familiar with this need and skill because he has been making sense of other visual aspects of his world in this way since birth—as I outlined with examples from reading in Chapter 2. Neither of these skills, the prediction of meaning and the parsimonious use of visual information, is explicitly taught in school. But it is not necessary that these skills be taught. If he is put into an appropriate learning situation, a child will develop them—just as he has developed his skills for comprehending spoken language. And an appropriate learning situation is easily specified: A child can only learn to read by reading. Only by reading can a child test his hypotheses about the nature of the reading process, establish distinctive feature sets for words, learn to identify words and meanings with a minimum of visual information and discover how not to overload the brain's information-processing capacity and to avoid the bottlenecks of memory.

There are other advantages to reading as a method of learning to read. It is through reading, for example, that we develop the skill that enables us to identify unfamiliar words, words not in our sight vocabulary. Before a child becomes involved in a formal instructional situation at school, obliging adults usually tell him the names of unfamiliar words so that he can concentrate on the more complex task of establishing distinctive feature lists. But at school this vital assistance is precipitately removed, and the child is expected to find out the names of words for himself. In recompense he is offered a set of phonic rules which are only marginally efficient, and which would overload his memory and result in his trying to read in a most unnatural manner. But there are easier ways of discovering what a word may be than sounding it out phonically. You almost certainly cannot guess what word I have in mind when I write h _____, but you can tell if I put it in a sentence; *I stayed out of town last week in an expensive h* _____, or, to use a different word, *He jumped on his h* _____ *and galloped away.* If a child meets an unknown word in reading, he can often safely ignore it (unless he is corrected for word-perfect reading) or he can decide from context what it must be. And when experience in reading is made easy for him—either because much of the text is familiar or because difficult parts are read for him—a child is helped to acquire knowledge that will enable him to identify new words by making analogies with similar words or parts of words he already knows. A person may never have seen the word *tele-photo* in print before, but it is not difficult to identify if he can read words like *telephone* or *television* and *photo*. The more words you already know, the easier it is to identify new ones, especially when you have context to give you a clue.

In brief, learning to read, like reading, is easier if you can make sense of what you are doing. Most children realize this tacitly when they learn to read, which is why—rather than grasp at every word—they will skip difficult words and guess at the general meaning. The source of this "unconscious knowledge" which seems to guide a child's early reading efforts until we train it out of him is no mystery. The fact that his visual system and memory become so rapidly overloaded makes him realize it is impossible to read in the overprecise and mechanical way adults often expect. However, when a student is later required to read books "for information", he may find that he is expected to acquire and store far more visual information than he can cope with, or that he has developed the crippling reading habit of trying to get more information from the text than his memory can handle.

Reading and school

Rather than construct a formal list of the implications I think teachers should draw from my previous remarks, I shall make two general statements and relate them to widespread educational practises. They are general principles that should be observed intelligently, not "helpful hints" to be mindlessly applied.

My first general statement is a reiteration that reading can be learned only through reading. It is only through the experience of reading that a child can learn to make minimal use of visual information and to use redundancy to reduce the load on short- and long-term memory. It is only through reading that a child can learn to identify new words on the basis of old. Furthermore, although nobody knows enough about reading to tell a child what he should learn, children can teach themselves to read. Reading skills cannot be thrust into children's heads, yet there is ample evidence that children know how to learn to read, if given half a chance. But in the average hour of reading instruction, the amount of time children spend actually reading is four minutes.[23] The problem with formal instruction is that it deprives a child of critical learning opportunities.

My second general statement follows directly from the first. Obviously, if reading is essential for learning to read, then reading should be made as easy as possible for children. Instead reading instruction often becomes a veritable obstacle course. Children are subjected to decoding drills and word identification exercises, although these are the most difficult tasks for any reader. Children are often presented with words in sentences devoid of interest or of anything that could reasonably be called meaning, although meaning provides both the clues *and* the confirmation for the nonvisual process of prediction which reading basically is. Although reading is directed towards comprehension, and comprehension is essential if words are to be identified, children are often corrected on the basis of individual words rather than meaning; the cart is put before the horse. Besides, word-perfect reading aloud is something that most adults find difficult, especially with material low in meaning. The process of reading is often confused with that of speech, in which dialects and styles vary greatly. Children are "corrected" when reading aloud because they do the sensible thing and translate the meaning of the written text into the language that they speak. A child who says "The boy ain't got no candy" when the text reads "The boy has no candy" may understand the sentence far better than another child who gives a word-perfect reading. Children having difficulty are told to slow down and be careful, although reading is typically impossible unless the reader reads fast and takes a few chances.

As a student grows older he is expected to assimilate a good deal of new information through reading. Many students in high school and beyond are accused of functional illiteracy, which often means that they are expected to read material that is fundamentally incomprehensible to them. Yet it is obvious that many of these students can read: They read articles that interest them in newspapers and magazines; they read correspondence, advertisements, programs, menus. But they do not read schoolbooks.

Whether a schoolbook is easy or difficult to read does not depend simply on the student's basic ability, or even on his motivation. Reading becomes difficult when the visual information it requires is too much for the reader because he has insufficient prior knowledge or nonvisual information. For example, a student confused by a math or history text often does not need more reading ability, but a better understanding of math or history. A book is not the same to an instructor who has read it many times and knows the topic backwards as it is to a student unavoidably afflicted with tunnel vision. Moreover, some texts are so poorly written that even experienced instructors find them practically impossible to read. Reading is made difficult whenever a book makes too many demands.

An instructor can also make too many demands. Fluent reading normally does not place a great requirement on the reader's long-term memory. Popular novels and newspaper reports are easily readable because much of what they say we know already. We go through a novel in much the same way that we go through an average day, experiencing events, interpreting what is going on in terms of what we already know and putting only a few highlights into long-term memory. Trying to put too much information into long-term memory—for example, the complex cast of characters with unfamiliar names and obscure interrelations at the beginning of Russian novels —cripples reading. It is only when we skip the detail that such novels become readible. But usually the student cannot skip detail; he is forced to try to assimilate large amounts of new information. Not only does this forced feeding clog memory systems and slow the reader down to a rate that precludes comprehension, but the emphasis on information on the page overloads the visual system with visual information. In short, emphasis on acquiring and retaining new information interferes with comprehension.

In any situation where an individual is anxious or unsure of himself or has experienced an unhappy succession of "failures", his behaviour exhibits an inevitable consequence: he demands far more information before he makes a decision. His very hesitancy aggravates his difficulties. A similar dilemma confronts anyone trying to read in a condition of anxiety, regardless of the material he is reading or his underlying reading ability. The more anxious he is, the less likely he will be to rely on nonvisual information. The ironic consequence is that such demanding behaviour increases rather than lessens the probability of error and of misunderstanding. Where the relaxed individual sees order, the tense individual sees visual confusion.

Remedial action with older students who are diagnosed as "reading problems" may magnify difficulties rather than facilitate fluency. The main need of a student inexperienced in reading is to engage in reading that is both easy and interesting. Instead he is likely to get less reading and more exercise and drill and texts. Material that is challenging (a euphemism for difficult) rather than easy raises the anxiety level so that reading is neither meaningful nor pleasant. The problem of a fifteen-year-old who has difficulty reading may not be insufficiency of instruction, but the fact that his previous years of instruction have made learning to read more difficult. Otherwise such a student could learn to read as fast as one who has had no reading instruction, who typically learns to read in a few weeks. After ten years of instructional bruising a student may be far more in need of a couple of years' educational convalescence than an aggravation of his injuries.

Writing

Attempting to understand the process of writing can unfortunately be as complicated as attempting to understand reading. I shall briefly examine the relation of writing to reading, and then the physical process of writing, that is, of getting words, once composed, on to paper. Of the complex process of composition I shall have least to say, and say it last.

Writing and reading

There are quite radical differences between the skills and effort employed in reading and writing, and our writing system might be regarded as a compromise between the interest of the reader and the interests of the writer, each of whom benefits—at the expense of the other—from one aspect or another of written language. In particular I want to suggest that the fact that there is any relationship between the written form of language and its sound may be one of the major concessions made by readers to writers.[24]

The notion that the form of language represents a compromise between the transmitter of information and the receiver is not limited to writing. Slurred speech is easier to produce but harder to understand than speech in which every difference is clearly articulated. In written language, ease of production seems similarly antagonistic to ease of discrimination. As a very obvious example, compare a scrawl of rapid writing with any script in which every letter is carefully and precisely represented—and consider the relative costs in terms of time and effort for writer and reader. Clearly, the gain for the rapid writer is made at the expense of the reader. I suspect that several gains for writers were made at the expense of readers when the alphabetic principle was developed, partly because so many other things are easier for the reader.

To begin with, recognition is easier than reproduction; it is easier to recognize a face than to draw one. And recognition memory is generally more efficient than recall; it is easier to recognize words or objects that have been seen before than to recall in their absence what they were. The form of a written word—even a Chinese one—is more easily recognized by the reader than it is recalled by the writer.

Reading is also easier on an individual's information-processing system than writing. The reader need not identify every word, nor even every phrase, in order to comprehend, but the writer is committed to producing every letter. The reader is able to proceed much faster than the writer and can skip over items that he is not sure about or that he regards as relatively unimportant. But the writer is forced to put into the text a good deal of visual information that the reader probably will not look at. It does not matter if the reader is unfamiliar with the spelling or meaning of a particular word; for a writer such failure may be quite disabling. There are severe conventional sanctions against a writer using rough and ready spelling, even in such trivial matters as writing *recieve* or *disimilar*, but I doubt whether this is because such spellings constitute grave difficulties for readers. We may notice that a word is misspelled, but we generally know what the word is. In contrast, the writer seems to have only one basic advantage over the reader, and that is that he is assumed to know what he has said and what he will say. This means that the writer should have much less of a working memory load than the reader, unless he is writing so slowly that he must remember what he wants to say.

By and large, then, written communication would appear to be intrinsically more demanding for the writer than for the reader—which may be the reason most of us prefer reading to writing (although our preference is often the other way around for listening and talking). It might seem reasonable therefore that compromises would be made on precisely the points that are intrinsically more difficult for the writer, namely, the simplification of distinctive forms used in written language and the reduction of their number. It is easier for writers to use a system in which only a couple of dozen different symbols can be combined in a variety of ways to produce many thousands of unique configurations, than to produce thousands of distinctive symbols. But writers have also demanded some convenient ways of learning and remembering how the elements of written language—the alphabetic characters—are combined, by relating the spelling of words to sound.

The alphabetic system of relating written language to sound in theory at least makes prediction of the written form possible. But even this advantage has been largely offset from the writer's point of view because of the necessity (a self-inflicted injury) to make spelling consistent despite historical and individual differences in the pronunciation of words.

Word representation

Just as a reader comes to identify words as words, without reference to individual letters, so the practiced writer commands a large repertoire of written word forms that he can put on paper, even by typewriter, without worrying about how they are spelled. The word is written as a unit, as an integrated sequence of movements. Such words are written much faster than if their letters were spelled out one at a time.[25] Once again, however, this is a skill that comes only through experience. You learn to write by writing.

It is not difficult to demonstrate that such integrated sequences of movement exist for writing; very often we cannot be sure of how a word is spelled until we write it down and see how it looks. In addition, experience also gives a writer a lengthy list of "spelling" for words (not all of which need be correct, however). These are the words whose spellings we can vocalize immediately, letter by letter, when asked. We know that *receive* is spelled r-e-c-e-i-v-e, that *woman* is spelled w-o-m-a-n and so forth. An internalized spelling list has nothing to do with either spelling rules or sound; in fact the words we remember on a letter-by-letter basis tend to be those whose spelling is relatively unpredictable by any spelling rule. Familiar words, even when irregularly spelled, are usually spelled better than unfamiliar but regularly spelled words; in other words, we tend to learn and use specific spellings, or integrated movement sequences for spellings, not rules.[26]

There are also several strategies available to the writer for dealing with words for which neither an integrated movement sequence nor a remembered spelling is available. One strategy is based upon a set of taught or induced "sound-to-spelling rules" which are used extensively, and with quite indifferent success, by children. A more efficient strategy than spelling from sound is constructing or remembering words by analogy—*telegraph* is spelled with a *ph* because that is the way *photograph* is spelled. Somewhere between and overlapping the sound-to-spelling and analogic strategies are purely orthographic rules that dictate whether certain letter combinations are applicable, for example, the change of *ie* to *y* before *ing* as in *lying* and *dying*.

Is the alphabetic principle useful for writers? There is no doubt that the physical act of reproducing a word is easier and faster when the word is constructed from a set of just twenty-six alternative forms (excluding variants of the same letter) than from thousands of distinctive pictograms or ideograms. It is also far easier to maintain consistency across writers when a spelling can be conventionalized. A word is easier to copy, and thus to learn, when it can be broken into easily recognizable elements like letters. None of these advantages, however, seems to have anything to do with the reader, except that they probably make his discrimination of words more difficult.

The fact that the letters of the alphabet are related to the sounds of spoken language may be a mixed blessing, however, even for the writer. The predictive power of the alphabetic principle would play a much greater part in both writing and reading if spelling were allowed to vary as much as pronunciation. However, the desire to maintain consistency over time and space, and the general rule that words with shared meanings should look alike, reduce the overall usefulness of the alphabet to the writer.

Composition

Two main topics require consideration under the heading of composition. Unfortunately, a great deal cannot be said about either topic, although much is waiting to be understood. The first topic is concerned with how thoughts are generated, and the second with getting these thoughts down on paper.

THINKING WHAT TO WRITE   Though it is far from clear what transpires in the head when we think of something to say, there can be no doubt that the skills of saying something efficiently, and of having something to say in the first place, are best developed by being put to use. In fact we cannot examine the nature of our own thought processes, or of anyone else's, except by making them manifest in some way. We cannot directly examine the process of composition, only its product. Unless we put something into words that we can look at, there is nothing we can say or do about writing. It is not unreasonable to assert that we are rarely aware of what we think until we say something or write it down. I am not saying that language *is* thought (see Chapter 3), but that language certainly helps the thought process. When we believe we can hear ourselves thinking, we are talking silently to ourselves. And silent speech is poorly adapted for critical evaluation, since no one else is around to react to it, and the message fades too soon for us to give it much examination ourselves. The best way to examine our own thoughts, and to organize new ideas into productive parts of our knowledge of the world, is often to put them down on paper. Perhaps the only defensible justification for the term papers and other written assignments to which students of all ages are subjected is that the act of composition provides the victims with an opportunity to confront the state of their own thoughts.

Since the practice of writing therefore appears to be so desirable, not merely for communication or for learning how to write but also for examining and developing our powers of creative thought, it must be considered little short of tragic that so many people have such a tremendous resistance to writing. I do not intend to distribute blame for the extent to which this resistance to writing is due to experiences at school, but an examination of its likely causes suggests that one factor is deeply involved—a fundamental misconception that something is wrong with a person who does not write easily.

Part of the resistance to writing is frequently emotional, though a precise reason for such a reaction is not easily provided without a careful analysis of an individual's history. There is often an apprehension that anything one writes will not be worthwhile, that the individual has nothing interesting to say, although such a reluctance is not always reflected in the same person's readiness to talk. Very few people are ready to believe that they write well. This disbelief—when not attributable to a past history of "failure"— is often due to an unrealistic conception of the practical difficulties of writing, and a perverse idea that good writing should spring fully formed out of a writer's head. Many people are highly intolerant of clumsy writing, even when it is their own, and even when it is a first draft that no one else will read.

Writing is a laborious process physically, because of the manual effort involved, and mentally, because it tends to be slow. These handicaps can be overcome to some extent by such devices as typewriters and dictaphones, although these aids are typically reserved for individuals who have achieved some competence in writing, not for those who need them most. Many people who write only occasionally would be less critical of their own efforts if they understood that an essential part of writing is editing, a skill rarely promoted or taught at school.

The best way to encourage writing, like the best way to develop reading, is to make the task easy. Expecting a child to write about something he would not be likely to talk about, or to write as fluently as he might talk, is not a reasonable attitude. It is more important to ensure that any writing task is meaningful, which means embedded in a situation and focussed on a topic both of which make sense to a child.

MAKING WRITING DIFFICULT   Writing and reading may be relatively different in their component skills, but the manner in which these skills must be developed is remarkably similar. Practise is the means by which all language skills are developed and tested, and practise must be on tasks that are easy. Writing fluency will not flourish if the writer cannot think of anything to say.

A final example may suffice to illustrate how reading, writing and comprehending another subject may be inextricably complicated. A student confronted with the task of writing an examination on an historical novel must first read the novel. In reading, he may suffer from a shortage of topic-relevant nonvisual information, and overload his memory as he tries to second-guess the exam questions he knows he will be asked. Having tried to comprehend a difficult book under conditions that make comprehension almost impossible, he must then try to read and interpret a set of questions while in a state of high anxiety, perhaps unsure even of the meaning of examination jargon like "Contrast and compare". Doubtful now about whether he has understood either the question or the book, he must begin to "compose", bearing in mind that he will get no credit for his fleeting thoughts unless he gets them down on paper. But he must not only conceptualize and communicate, he must conform. Grammar, style, spelling, punctuation, layout and neatness must all be attended to, in one fell swoop, with scarcely a chance for revision or even reflection. Feedback will come three weeks later in the form of a letter grade. I exaggerate of course, I hope; but do you see how concerns which individually might be meaningful and worthwhile in conjunction become a futile exercise in confused exasperation?

CHAPTER 7

Differences

The assertion that people are all the same and the counterproposition that everyone is different are probably heard equally often, and even stated with the same tone of despair when the topic is some imperfection of the human race. The truth of course is that we are all alike in some ways and different in others. Our basic elements are the same, but they tend to go together in different combinations and proportions.

So far in this book we have been concerned with the attributes of the human brain, the mechanisms of comprehension and learning, that are universal. All children (except the very small minority with obvious functional defects), whatever their social, cultural and economic background, are born with precisely the same basic learning process for comprehending and predicting the world, just as all children tend to have the same complements of heads, arms and legs. Despite this sameness in fundamental equipment, however, the diversity of human beings is enormous. All people seem to have different interests, different funds of knowledge, different skills, different attitudes and different motivations towards different goals for different reasons. They learn different things at different times with different degrees of facility and different personal involvement in the different outcomes. They make sense of the world in characteristically individual ways.

This chapter is about differences which in themselves are often assumed to have an intimate relation to comprehension and learning. The chapter will be especially concerned with what is often regarded in education as the biggest difference of all, intelligence. However, intelligence as a topic is so complex, confused and theoretically and emotionally overloaded that it will be well to flank it with a couple of related issues that can be discussed more dispassionately. The first issue concerns cognitive styles, or the characteristic ways in which people seem to think, perceive and learn about the world; and the second, which will be left until the end of the chapter, concerns language and the different attitudes it seems to reflect towards comprehension and learning.

It may be objected that my treatment of these important topics is cursory, unfair and even biased; and I must acknowledge that I make no claim to being exhaustive or even comprehensive. But within the limits of a reasonably brief survey I want to indicate how topics related to individual differences can be perceived from the perspective of the earlier chapters of this book. Cognitive structure is not just part of the way we interact with the world; it is the basis of all our interactions. And whether we appear quick or slow, keen or apathetic, fulfilled or frustrated, the general outline I have provided would be inadequate if it could not suggest some manner in which these differences might be related to an underlying consistency.

Cognitive Styles

All individuals differ along a number of dimensions—some are happy and others sad, some cheerful and others morbid, some gregarious and others reclusive. I term these differences *dimensions* because they are normally "more-or-less" characteristics rather than "either-or". You and I are both optimistic, but I may be more optimistic than you. A person who is not boastful may be far from modest. There is a whole range of positions at which a person might be located between the extremes of each pair of alternatives. And while a few people might be located towards one end of a dimension or the other, most of us tend to cluster and vacillate somewhere around the middle. Unremitting optimism is probably as maladaptive as perpetual pessimism, total frankness as intolerable as impenetrable reticence.

Individuals differ also in the characteristic manner in which they approach problems and make decisions, including decisions of a purely perceptual nature. We do not all learn or make perceptual judgments in the same way, even though we employ the same basic processes. We have distinctive *cognitive styles*.[1] The best way to explain a cognitive style, and to indicate how it describes individuals in comparative rather than absolute terms, is to talk about the kind of experiment in which a cognitive style is examined. The illustrative cognitive style I have selected is called field dependence-independence (the hyphen is because it is a dimension) and the description requires you to imagine that you are participating in another psychological experiment.

Field dependence–field independence[2]

You are alone, comfortably seated on a rather plain chair facing an illuminated rectangle which might be an empty picture frame hanging on the opposite wall, except for the fact that the room is completely darkened and you cannot see any wall—any more than you can see a floor, ceiling, corner or intersection to reassure you that you are sitting the right way up in the world.

Your mission, according to the unseen experimenter, is to watch as he adjusts the position of the rectangle by means of some invisible mechanism, and to tell him when it is properly aligned with the walls and the floor. The task is not as difficult as it might sound because you still have a couple of ways of orienting yourself in order to tell which direction is up, and these would normally be sufficient for you to determine the correct placement of the frame. One clue is wholly within your body; the vestibular system in the inner ear will relate the orientation of your body to gravity and tell if you are off balance. The second clue is external to your person, perceived through a part of your body not normally regarded as a sense organ. The clue is based on the position of your body relative to the seat of the chair which is assumed to be parallel to the ground, and is transmitted to the brain from your area of contact with the chair.

At this point, however, the experimenter manifests the diabolical ingenuity that makes psychology so exasperating for subjects. He has rigged the chair so that its seat is not parallel to the ground. When you are sitting on the chair, you view the world with a decided bias.

You will probably realize that something is odd as soon as you sit in the chair. The information from within your vestibular system tells you that you are unbalanced, and contradicts the external information from the chair that your orientation is normal. The question is, Which source of information will you believe? Different individuals attach different weights to the different sources of information.

Those who tend to believe the chair characterized as more *field dependent*; they are influenced by information from the world outside. Subjects who tend to believe their vestibular system, on the other hand, are characterized as more *field independent*; they are not completely swayed by external evidence.

Most people fall somewhere between the two extremes. A completely field-dependent individual would have no volition and be completely at the mercy of his environment. A completely field-independent person might be dissociated from reality and live entirely in a world of fantasy. Nevertheless the tendency of individuals to be more or less influenced by external evidence seems to be stable over time, and related to a number of other characteristics of behaviour. The person who is field independent in the experimental situation is likely to be independent in his attitudes towards other people generally, higher in self-esteem and less conforming, while the field-dependent individual inclines to passivity and is responsive to people and events around him.[3]

OTHER COGNITIVE STYLES   There have been more than a score of claims of discovery of independent cognitive styles, some closely related to particular modes of thinking, such as "analysing and synthesizing" and "broad and narrow categorizing"; some related to interpersonal behaviour, such as introversion and extraversion; and some related to the way individuals prefer their world to be, such as their tolerance or intolerance for ambiguity.

Some people appear to go through life looking for differences and even emphasizing them; they are the sharp-eared, sharp-eyed individuals who quickly note if something is unusual or discrepant in their world. In psychological experiments they tend to exaggerate when asked to estimate differences. These "sharpeners" are contrasted with "levellers"[4], who prefer a predictable environment, minimal novelty and limited change.

Many individuals are inclined to be precipitate, leaping to conclusions and undertaking enterprises with a minimum of forethought and information. They prefer almost any decision to uncertainty. Others are more tentative, collecting and weighing evidence as long as possible, and preferring indecision to the risk of error. Although a person's relative position on the scale of the cognitive style called *impulsivity-reflectivity*[5] is supposed to remain rather constant throughout life, children tend to begin life impulsively and to become more reflective with age.

All learning involves *risk taking*, another cognitive style that has been claimed to distinguish individuals fairly consistently.[6] Low risk takers are unlikely to learn very efficiently because of their reluctance to take the chance of being wrong. High risk takers, on the other hand, may take insufficient account of the odds. Perception is a decision-making process, and therefore also involves risk; and again some people seem to demand more evidence than others before making up their minds. As we saw in the discussion of signal detection theory in Chapter 2, the amount of information required to make an identification will vary with the observer's willingness to risk a mistake.

Cognitive styles and cognitive structure

Many correlational studies have been conducted to assess the extent to which these various cognitive styles are related to each other, or even identical, and to explore whether more general personality or intellectual characteristics might underlie them. The evidence is highly equivocal. The way that individuals handle similar situations does not seem to change very much over time, but their cognitive style on other, different, occasions is very hard to predict. A man who would hesitate to lay a bet at the races might be prepared to gamble on an examination question, and a cautious accountant might be a reckless driver. In other words, what the investigator discovers depends less on the individuals he examines than on the experimental situation he puts them in. Nevertheless a general statement can be made about all cognitive styles: they are a reflection of every individual's solution to the problem of handling complex information in a noisy world.

Many cognitive styles seem to involve the amount of information an individual requires before he will make a decision, and the kinds of decisions he prefers to make. The amount of information required by any individual will depend on how sure he wants to be that his decision will be correct, and at what point he thinks that degree of certainty will be achieved. The risk of error he is prepared to accept is itself a function of a number of other cognitive factors such as his perception of the relative costs of being wrong and of acquiring further information to reduce the chance of error. Another factor is often the control that an individual perceives he has over the situation he is in, or his confidence in others whom he perceives as controlling the situation. You may have noticed my careful overuse of the verb *perceive*. All of these complex factors depend not so much on actual probabilities in the real world—on whether an error is truly likely and whether the individual will in fact be highly penalized for a mistake—but on what he expects or believes to be the case. Once again we find that most of the explanation for behaviour lies in the mind, in cognitive structure.

Cognitive styles do not "explain" individuals, nor do they act as mysterious forces that direct our brains from within. They are observable and relatively consistent characteristics of thought and behaviour which reflect an intricate pattern of beliefs, expectations and rules that are all about interaction with the world. They are a consequence of experience and learning.

Cognitive styles and learning

Cognitive differences are obviously reflected in the manner in which children learn, or at least in the circumstances in which children are happier and more efficient learning. Cognitive styles have two important educational implications, which may in fact be related. The first implication concerns the amount of "structure" that a child prefers in any learning situation, and the second his tolerance of uncertainty.

A child who is characterized as a "poor thinker"[7] often behaves in class as if he has no time to consider alternatives; he may plunge blindly into solutions—as if anxiety over the possibility of error makes the continuation of doubt insupportable. On the other hand, children who fare better academically seem to have much more time; they proceed with a calm

assurance that must be based in part on an expectation that they will succeed, or that the penalty for failure will not be high. There are similar
variations in the amount of direction and reassurance that a child needs to
learn.[8] Whether these differences are attributable solely to cognitive styles
or depend also on the situation in which the learner feels most comfortable
is not clear.

There is even evidence that individuals matched for cognitive styles
are more productive in a variety of settings.[9] Teachers and students, therapists and patients, even roommates, prefer to be in each other's company,
tend to work better together and to achieve more if they are at roughly the
same location on the field dependence–field independence continuum.

The question of what should be done about such findings of cognitive
difference and their consequences itself provides an interesting illustration
of how the amount of uncertainty and lack of structure individuals can tolerate will vary. Some theorists and teachers feel that everything discovered
about individual differences should be translated immediately into classroom
practice and materials. They want to eradicate if not the differences at least
their consequences, for example, by segregating all children of one "type"
into one kind of instructional situation and all other "types" of children into
others. But an alternative point of view holds that homogeneity is undesirable, that teachers and materials should be flexible and adaptive rather
than that children should be sorted into narrow categories. Why should it be
undesirable that all children in the same group will not want to learn the
same things in the same way at the same rate? A more appropriate response
to the growing acknowledgement of individual differences may be to develop
procedures and materials that recognize that children will not comprehend
or learn in exactly the same way, and that make sympathetic and constructive allowance for their individuality.

Intelligence

Of all the ambiguous and misleading words in the language, *intelligence* probably causes the most uncertainty, alarm and even damage in
schools. The word is used in a variety of contexts, and it is often not clear
whether people who raise pointed questions about intelligence, or even
argue about it, are talking about theoretical issues or trying to lay down the
law about how the word should be used. For example, is someone who
asserts that "Intelligence is being able to cope with your environment"
making a statement about the nature of intelligence or about what should
be called intelligence?

My limited aim in this section—and it is nonetheless an overly ambitious aim—is to explore what individuals might be talking about when

intelligence is the topic, and how this topic might be related to the analysis of human comprehension and learning outlined in this book. If we can distinguish the semantic from the psychological, we shall still be confronted by problems. But we may have a clearer idea of what the problems are.

Defining intelligence

There will probably never be unanimity on what *intelligence* is, because people are frequently talking about different things when they use the word. And there will certainly never be agreement about how the word should be used. But if people could be persuaded to make it clear what they think they are talking about, then we might be able to begin answering some very important questions about whether the tests we use to measure intelligence are fair, and if they have a point, in any case. Instead we have a variety of opinions—almost all of a controversial and socially inflammable nature—about what constitutes intelligence (or how the word should be used), where intelligence comes from, how it should be measured, who has most of it and what, if anything, should be done about it.

The situation is basically absurd—rather as if we had several alternative methods of measuring height, none of which gave quite the same result; and no one could agree upon what height was in the first place; and many people thought we should not be distinguishing individuals on the basis of height at all. Absurd, but not laughable, since large groups of people feel they are discriminated against educationally, socially and economically on the basis of measures of intelligence; and the progress of a child through his education and into his working career is frequently influenced by the scores he obtains on intelligence "tests".

Paradoxically, when we use the word *intelligence* informally, in our everyday language, it usually makes sense to us. We know what we mean. It is only when the word is used technically or "scientifically" that it becomes meaningless. I propose to examine why this is so.

"Intelligence" in and out of context

The noun *intelligence* is probably not used in our everyday language as much as its adjectival or adverbial forms; we assert or deny that a person is *intelligent*, that he behaves *intelligently* or that a particular behaviour is *intelligent*. In other words, we use these terms descriptively, to characterize individuals or their behaviour.[10]

Not only are these terms descriptive, they are also relative. What is intelligent depends on the situation. It may or may not be intelligent to take a large amount of luggage with you on vacation, depending on whether you will be in a ocean liner or a canoe. It may or may not be intelligent to light candles during a power failure, depending on whether you suspect the pilot light in the gas furnace has also gone out. In some circumstances unintelligent behaviour might be inability to operate an elevator, in other circumstances ignorance of how to ride a camel or gut a fish. Teachers usually have no trouble understanding a colleague who says in conversation that a particular student is intelligent; this statement means that the student is easy to teach, and can grasp what is going on.

In short, words like *intelligent* and *intelligently* are generally used in situation-specific contexts, explicit or understood, and imply behaviour that is adequate for, or appropriate to, that particular situation. Statements containing the word *intelligent* would in fact be meaningless unless a listener could use the context and his prior knowledge and understanding of the situation to give a reasonably accurate characterization of the specific behaviour to which the term applies. The question of whether intelligent is a fair or culturally biassed label to apply to an individual should never arise, although of course one might doubt the judgment or motivation of the person making the evaluation.

In some contexts of our culture, the connotation of terms like "intelligent" has come to focus rather exclusively on reasoning ability or the capacity to grasp and manipulate certain kinds of facts. This narrowed emphasis is a reflection of the particular situation in which the evaluation is often made. The definition does not tell us what an intelligent person is; it only reveals how we tend more and more to use the term.

There is a complication to be considered, however. In addition to employing *intelligent* to describe an individual or his behaviour, we can exercise the metaphorical properties of language and place *intelligence* inside him. We can say that individuals *have* intelligence, and that one may have more than another. But still, I want to suggest, we have not made the term meaningless. In our everyday language, statements about a person's intelligence continue to be made in reference to a particular situation. If we are talking about someone's intelligence with respect to school, we mean one thing. If we talk about his intelligence on a fishing expedition, we mean another. There is no ambiguity. To use the terminology of this book, the prior knowledge of a listener—his understanding of both the language habits of the speaker and of the context in which the statement is made—eliminates all uncertainty about the word *intelligence*. The word is meaningful.

Now psychologists enter the picture, anxious as ever to be both relevant and scientifically objective, to organize our use of the word *intelligent* for us. First they decide to *measure* intelligence, which means they have to interpret the word in a literal rather than a metaphorical or elliptical sense. They attempt to put a number, or "quotient", on everyone's share of intelligence and to use these numbers to perform all kinds of mathematical tricks. For example, they try to calculate the "average amount of intelligence" everyone should have, and to arbitrate the extent to which an individual's portion of intelligence should be above or below the average before we are entitled to call him a genius or an idiot. It might look as if psychologists have done a magnificent job in tidying up one corner of our language, except for the fact that no one knows quite what they are talking about. Since there is no context to indicate what all these different amounts of intelligence are supposed to represent, the numbers remain largely meaningless. It is as if a decision were made to sell food by weight alone, to save the consumer the trouble of having to interpret weight in terms of the actual product involved. You would not know whether the packages contained sugar or salt, but you would know that you would be getting more if you choose six ounces rather than four.

Now it is almost as if we have one word with two distinct meanings: one *intelligence* that is always relative to fairly specific situations, explicit or implied, in which certain behaviours are more or less adequate or appropriate; and another "intelligence" that is a mysterious and practically immutable mental quality every individual has in different amounts. An unfortunate kind of Gresham's law of language has even begun to operate, with the debased form of the word driving the "purer" and more meaningful form out of general circulation. Many people have stopped thinking about intelligence as the way you behave, and have been persuaded that it is a quantity, something like your weight or height.

Psychologists have in fact introduced an alternative way of talking about the mysterious intelligence that they measure but cannot define. They refer to an individual's *intelligence quotient*, or IQ for short. And oddly enough the abbreviation IQ has to some extent acquired a reasonable meaningfulness in our everyday language, even though there is no agreement about what is the *I* that everyone has a *Q* of. Most people in education at least know that a person's IQ score is primarily an indication of academic ability. When they hear that someone has a low IQ they assume that he should not be expected to perform well on academic tasks in school.

It is time to look at what psychologists thought they were measuring.

The aims of intelligence tests

I shall not attempt to list all the different kinds of questions or tasks involved in intelligence tests, or even to give specific examples. Any student who has graduated from grade school, let alone reached the portals of the teaching profession, has had more than one personal encounter with the WISC, the WAIS, the Stanford-Binet, the Scholastic Aptitude Test, the Miller Analogies Test, or the Graduate Record Examination. Everybody knows that all these tests seem to favor verbal fluency, mental speed and agility and a broad base of general knowledge of an academic kind. What else could intelligence tests be for?

Intelligence tests were originally intended to make statements about people as they happened to be at the time of testing.[11] The tests were *diagnostic*, designed to indicate whether a child would be most appropriately placed in a particular kind of school, or whether a recruit had the right aptitude for a particular service occupation. In other words, the tests made specific statements about individuals.

The basis of these early intelligence tests was largely pragmatic. The subject was confronted by a sample of the kinds of levels of tasks involved in the particular schools or occupations for which he was being assessed. The idea was reasonable: instead of taking on the expense and risk of putting an individual to certain tasks in the real world, you would examine his performance on a few representative tasks in a test situation. No question of criterion or validation or fairness was involved; the tasks involved in the test were samples of, or close analogies to, the kind of task involved in the situation for which the individual was being tested.

This close and eminently sensible correspondence between test and objective is to a large extent reflected in the tests children take at school. A student who scores high on an intelligence test is likely to be a high achiever academically because the test involves precisely the kinds of academic tasks encountered in school. There is nothing unreasonable about such a test if its objective is to see how well a certain type of task is currently performed, and to use this current knowledge as a basis for estimating future performance. Of course the test could become unreasonable if the school's expectations are unreasonable.

A more complex function of intelligence tests is to make predictions about a person's achievement in the future. Tests are not interpreted so much with respect to a subject's present ability as with respect to the level of performance he might demonstrate in the future. And, on the whole, people who do well in a test now are likely to do well in a similar test in a few years' time. There is nothing surprising or mysterious or even remarkable about the fact that IQ scores reflect academic potential or appear stable over time. The tests are constructed with academic-type items, which are themselves tested. Items that do not turn out to predict academic performance, that are not stable over time, are thrown out by the test constructors. Therefore people who score high today are more likely to succeed academically in the future.

However, a qualification has now entered the discussion; I am no longer talking about an individual but about "people", and my last statements were prefaced by "on the whole". Most people who perform at a certain level on a test now will perform at a similar level in the future; but there will be exceptions. The exceptions present no problem as long as it is realized that statements made about *groups* and future probabilities make no sense when applied to *individuals* and the present. It is not possible to predict who the exceptions will be.

The fact that only 20 percent of grade 9 students who score 37 or less on a certain test (my figures are quite arbitrary) will graduate into college in four years' time is a respectable datum for statisticians and a useful guide for educational planners. It tells administrators that for every 100 students now entering grade 9 and scoring 37 or less on the test, only 20 places should be reserved at college in four years' time. However, the score does not make a useful statement about whether a particular individual who has scored 37 should have the advantage of a particular academic program now. His "chances" of going to college if he joins the special program may be 20 percent, but when it comes to the point either he will or he will not. Twenty percent of students who score 37 will succeed; and on the basis of the one test score there is no way of distinguishing among them. If only 20 students out of 100 who get a particular score are likely to succeed, do you reject all of them in advance (including the 20 who presumably would succeed) or do you select 20, and on what grounds? In deciding this question, you are no longer saying what a person can do, but what he is to be allowed to do. For the administrator the question may involve a gamble on the future; but for the individual the die will be cast now, and the stakes will be all or nothing.

Thus another aspect of the use of intelligence tests becomes apparent. Tests are employed to segregate people, to put them into one category rather than another. This function may appear fairly innocuous when it involves current abilities only, and distinguishes cooks from combat troops; but it raises all kinds of questions when applied to matters of probability. Who should get the chance to enter the most exclusive schools, the better paying jobs? Do we want to discriminate among our children on the basis of which individuals will be the better bets?

What do intelligence tests measure?

There has long been a debate in psychology about the fundamental nature of whatever it is that confers the ability to score high on intelligence tests. The issue is whether there is one general underlying ability—which would probably be what most people would call intelligence—or a number of separate abilities, all unrelated to each other.[12] At first glance something might be said for both points of view. The fact that a person is a skilled mathematician does not necessarily mean that he will be a good reader and writer. But, "on the average", people who score high on one kind of intelligence subtest tend to score high on others. Because the evidence is equivocal, some psychologists have concluded that both points of view are correct —that intelligence consists of a general factor and a number of specific abilities. This view may seem to be close to saying that in some circumstances you may be intelligent, and in others not. One psychologist, however, has gone so far as to suggest that there are no fewer than 120 different aspects of intelligence, of which about 100—statistically speaking—have been successfully isolated.[13]

The issue would seem to be a standoff, until one realizes that there may be other factors that intelligence tests do not take properly into account, for example, interest. Suppose that a mathematician just happened not to be interested in literature; would that not account for a discrepancy among his abilities? And suppose that some people were interested in just about everything; would that not explain why they might do well on a variety of tests?

It could also be argued that intelligence tests do not take into account other idiosyncratic aspects of individuals, such as their preferred cognitive styles. Test takers almost always do better if they are willing to take a chance, for example. Even when the scoring method contains a "correction for guessing", fear of being wrong may prevent an individual from making a response that would certainly be correct, not to mention other guesses that he might get right by chance.

There is a common assertion that intelligence is what intelligence tests measure. As we have seen, intelligence tests are reasonably good predictors of academic success, so it would look as if a number of people might argue that intelligence is the ability to perform well on academic tasks, or at least that the ability to perform well on academic tasks is a reliable indicator of intelligence. By such a yardstick, children who do not perform well academically are not very intelligent. It is here that a good deal of the controversy begins over the concept of intelligence and how it is measured. Not everyone is convinced that the academic values treasured in so many of our schools are either "culture free" or an appropriate basis upon which to distinguish among or even discriminate against individuals.

However hard test constructors try to find items that will not penalize individuals because of their experience rather than their "intelligence", assumptions are still made about the kind of content that is most appropriate for test items and about the language in which this content should be expressed. Tests still basically assess individuals on the basis of what they know; and different cultures, different levels of society, even different age groups, differ on the kind of knowledge they believe is important.

Although conclusions are often drawn about an individual's learning ability on the basis of his IQ, intelligence tests do not in fact measure learning; they mainly measure what an individual happens to know and is able to demonstrate at one particular point in time. There is no test to see how fast or efficiently new information may be acquired and utilized. Nor do existing tests measure the use to which an individual can put his existing knowledge, his creativity.

In short, all that can be said about intelligence tests is that they provide a score, a rank, which predicts well but not with certainty what an individual will score on the same kind of test in the future, and his likely grade levels in school. They indicate whether an individual is "school oriented".

ALTERNATIVES   Some psychologists have argued for alternative approaches to the whole question of learning at school. It has been asserted, for example, that any subject can be taught to any child, provided it is explained in terms the child can understand.[14] In other words, all children can attain the same objectives, provided it is realized that they start from different positions and therefore must follow different routes.

It has also been asserted that all children can learn anything, but that it takes some children longer to learn some things than others. In other words, intelligence may be a matter of time.[15] Others have argued that individual differences are a consequence of our methods of teaching.[16] Because all children in a class tend to be taught in the same way, differences among these children tend to be amplified with the passage of time. The children who are able to learn fast learn very fast, but those least likely to learn fast learn very slowly. When they have finished, the difference between the fast learners and the slow learners is greater than ever. Paradoxically, if children were treated as individuals, individual differences should vanish.

Age differences

There are evident differences among children as their ages vary. Young children make sense of the world differently from their older brothers and sisters, and why not? They have had less experience.

Some theorists attach great significance to changes that they perceive to take place in the actual *processes* of thought as children grow older.[17] They may chart a course of mental development beginning with a primitive *sensori-motor stage*, when all a child knows is based on his own actions or the consequences of these actions, and leading to a *formal operational stage*, which starts at about age twelve as the child's thought moves progressively away from direct perception and action, and towards logical and scientific reasoning. When children come to school they are at an *intuitive*, transitional stage. They have begun to construct an active and independent world in the mind, but their thought is still *prelogical* rather than rational. To such psychologists, intelligence is the *process* of adapting to the environment, and interpreting new experience in the light of previous experience.

The conceptualization of mental growth as a series of transitions or changes from one stage to another has not gone unchallenged.[18] Other psychologists see a much smoother continuity in mental development, and reject any notion of sudden qualitative changes in the nature of thought. For example, it has been attested that there are three trends behind the development of children's intellectual growth: (a) an increasing specificity of discrimination, (b) an optimization of attention and (c) an increasing economy in the use of information for search and selection.[19] In other words, as they grow older, children know better what to look for and how to look for it.

Many observers have been particularly struck by the apparent distractibility of children between the ages of five and seven; some interpret this as a time when a child is changing mental gears between different modes of thought. But it is by no means clear whether the difficulty, or reluctance, of children to exhibit sustained attention during their early school years is a matter of ability, interest or even the simple experience of knowing where attention should be directed at particular times. Evidence for the allegedly limited and sporadic learning capacity of children at five or six must be counterbalanced by the same children's dramatic learning feats in their earlier years of life; making sense of the world around them and mastering language.

Few psychologists would assert that children pass into any developmental stage automatically. Yet experience—the opportunity to build skills and knowledge as a basis for further skills and knowledge—is so often overlooked or underrated that a few words should be said about the alleged process sometimes thought to be a complete substitute for experience, namely, maturation.

EFFECTS OF TIME   The words *maturation* and *maturity* are often employed in arguments that are resoundingly circular. Why hasn't Johnny learned to read? Because he is not mature enough (or he is not ready). How will you tell when he is ready? He will learn to read. Why does a preschooler believe there is more fluid in a tall thin glass than a short fat one? Because he has not reached a more mature stage of development. What will happen when he has reached a more mature stage? He will know the volume of fluid does not change with the shape of the vessel it is placed in.

But there is nothing magical about maturation. The mere passage of time is not sufficient to improve any aspect of a child's knowledge or intellectual ability. If time were of the essence, one might just as well shut a first-grader in a closet for a couple of years and wait for all his arithmetic and language skills to develop. The reason a child of eighteen months does not usually learn to read is because he does not know enough; it is as simple as that. Time alone will do nothing to remedy this situation. What matters is the child's experience during the passage of time.

A child cannot test hypotheses about the world until he has hypotheses, or expectations, to test. And he cannot have expectations until he has established a prior base of knowledge. In other words, a child's mental development is just as progressive and predictable as his physical growth. In fact intellectual and physical development tend to be coordinated. Some intellectual achievements, such as the first articulation of words, tend to occur around the same time as certain motor achievements, such as standing unsupported.[20] But this does not mean that either mental or physical development is dependent upon the other. Helping a child to stand will not accelerate his speech, nor will verbal drills help his posture.

Some of the most distinct and predictable "stages" of development are demonstrated when adults are taught typewriting or telegraphy.[21] After a slow start the student shows rapid improvement when he learns where the individual keys are; and he stays at that "plateau" for some time. Suddenly there is a spurt, a marked increase in speed, when he moves to the next plateau of typing words. Finally there is a third period of rapid improvement when he begins typing entire phrases. These "stages" of development in typewriting are orderly and universal. But would it make any sense to attribute them to physical growth on the part of the student—even if he happened to grow an inch or two during training—or to say that they are a consequence of his increased maturity?

The discussions of reading readiness in many guides for teachers exemplify how vague the concept of maturation can be. Anything that superficially appears to be related to reading is listed as a contributory factor, whether inadequate visual acuity, inadequate auditory acuity or physical, social or emotional "maturity". Yet children without obvious physical defect must have extremely sharp visual, auditory and intellectual acuity; otherwise they would never have made sense of the visual world and of spoken language. As far as vision and hearing are concerned, acuity is at its peak at the age of four. After that, senility begins. Of course children of five may not know what a teacher wants them to look or listen for, but this difficulty is not overcome by growth, by "maturity", but by learning. Similarly, a child with obvious visual or auditory defects will not be cured by maturation. The passage of time alone will only see these deficiencies grow worse.

Differences in Language

Variation in language is one of the most obvious differences among people. No two people speak exactly the same language; how could they when so many chance and idiosyncratic factors enter into the learning of language and into what individuals actually say? All of us have had different language experience to some extent, even if we are as close as identical twins (who often develop differences in their modes of using language simply to distinguish themselves from each other). These language differences from one person to another are recognized by the technical term *idiolect,* which is the language spoken by an individual. Obviously the more similar the backgrounds and interests of two individuals, the closer their idiolects are likely to be. Nevertheless there will be some differences; our language is as personal as our fingerprints.

Groups of individuals whose idiolects are all very similar speak the same *dialect.* Usually the same dialect is spoken by people who live in the same geographical region, and who share a common background and the same interests. All of this is simply to say that people who tend to communicate a good deal with each other tend to speak the same dialect. It is very unsurprising.

Some dialects are more similar to each other than to other dialects. To some extent these differences depend on geographical and cultural and economic proximity, but not entirely. Two children may live on the same street but speak different dialects if the father of one is a farmer and the father of the other an insurance agent. Two teachers may have exactly the same educational and economic background but one will still retain his New England accent, while the other will keep his New Jersey one. A variety of factors determine the exact dialect an individual speaks, not the least of which is the dialect a person wants to speak. We try to incorporate into our idiolect the speech characteristics of those with whom we feel an affinity, and reject the speech characteristics of people on whom we want to turn our backs.

A dialect then is simply a particular form of the language spoken and understood by a particular group of people. And a language is a group of mutually intelligible dialects. If the teacher from New England understands the dialect of the teacher from New Jersey, then we say that they speak the same language.

Every speaker of a language therefore speaks a dialect, since it is through dialect that language is manifested. There are dialects of British English and dialects of American English and dialects of English spoken in other parts of the world as well, but there is no pure and simple *English* even in England.

Are some dialects better than others?

There can be no dispute that certain dialects are rated more desirable than others in certain situations and to certain people. This follows from the fact that language is an emblem of the particular group to which a person perceives himself as belonging. Dialect can be used—with varying degrees of accuracy of course—as the basis for a snap decision about a person's social, economic and educational standing, as well as his geographical origin. Consequently some dialects acquire more prestige than others, especially in the minds of people who happen to speak the dialects associated with more elevated social, economic or educational status.

An alternative term sometimes used to designate a prestige dialect is *standard dialect*. The use of this term reflects the not uncommon assumption that the prestige dialect of a language is the "standard" of which all other dialects are a more-or-less inferior imitation. It is assumed that anyone who speaks a different dialect is really trying to speak the standard, but is failing to do so for one reason or another; he lacks something. The higher you rank in the hierarchy of power and prestige, the more likely it is that the variety of language you speak will be regarded as the standard to which all reasonable mortals aspire, but few achieve. To the extent that vertical social structures are eradicated, the notion of a prestige dialect tends to disappear. You cannot have a top dialect where you do not have top people. Among equals, all dialects are equal.

However, in many institutional settings where tradition is strong and social distinctions clearly marked, differences in dialect tend to be classified in terms of greater or lesser desirability. Such an institutional setting in which inequalities are clearly marked is of course the traditional classroom. If teacher and students all speak the same dialect, there is a very high probability that mutual understanding and respect will result because of what might appropriately be called class solidarity. But if teacher and students speak different dialects—or even if the teacher thinks his students speak a different dialect—there is no doubt about the prestige dialect of the group. The prestige dialect is the one spoken by the teacher. All other dialects may be regarded as impoverished or distorted, and therefore as inadequate tools for communication and for learning.

We have therefore one answer to the question of whether some dialects are better than others. Some dialects confer greater advantages on those who speak them simply because people believe that these dialects are superior, although this belief is based on egocentric and pragmatic rather than linguistic grounds. We can now turn to the rather more specific question of whether some dialects are better than others for communicating, thinking and learning.[22]

DIALECT AND THOUGHT   It is necessary to break free from the everyday logic that asserts that because individuals who are relatively poor in communicating or learning at school tend to be speakers of particular dialects, their deficiencies are attributable to their dialect. By and large the members of our population who tend to be the most articulate and best educated have better teeth, but it would be misleading to assume that their better teeth make them more articulate and informed.

Endless testing and statistics have demonstrated that children who speak particular dialects perform less well in a variety of academic settings, but none of the statistics can prove a causal connection. Correlations between dialect—or ethnic background or socio-economic status or location of residence or size of family—and educational achievement never provide an explanation, they merely highlight the problem. It is still necessary to look for reasons *why* differences in dialect, ethnic background, socio-economic status, location of residence or size of family should be related to academic achievement.

So instead of looking at the educational performance of individuals who speak particular dialects, we shall examine the dialects themselves briefly and in terms of the extent to which linguists have found one dialect to be inferior to another as a medium for communication or learning.

None of the world's languages or dialects is more primitive than the others. All spoken languages appear to be roughly at the same stage of development. No language seems to be inherently superior to another as a medium for communication. That does not mean of course that the lexicons of all the world's languages are identical. All languages lack words for some concepts that are available in other languages. But all the world's languages borrow and steal from each other. English had no word for *algebra* until it accepted the word from Arabic. It still does not have a word that combines the notions of fitness and excellence as does the common Greek word *arete*. The fact that a few concept labels are not available is not an indication that a language is inadequate, but an indication that there has been no reason for a particular word to enter the language. All languages are capable of assimilating new words when required.

Similarly, variations in syntax in different languages seem to be differences of style, or historical accidents, rather than differences in potential as a medium of expression. Two languages may not be capable of saying the same thing in exactly the same way; the French equivalent of "be good" is "be wise" (*sois sage*). But there is no statement in one language that cannot be translated into another in some way however awkward because of the underlying cultural difference.

To reiterate one of the conclusions of Chapter 3, languages reflect the underlying cognitive structures of the people who speak them. If a language does not have a direct translation for *carburetor* or *sensitivity training* or *charity* or *habeas corpus*, people who speak that language are probably going to have difficulty with these concepts. But all languages seem capable of elaboration to the point where they meet all of the requirements for communication placed upon them.

Just as no language (or cluster of dialects) seems to be inferior to other languages (or clusters of dialects) in the range of meanings it can express, so dialects do not appear to have significant differences as potential means of communication. Linguists have examined a number of dialects particularly associated with educational problems in the United States—for example, those of black children in Harlem and of Mexican-Americans in California—and found them no less rich and well-articulated than the "standard" dialects of the schools of these regions.[23] The "non-standard" dialects are still complex forms of language capable of meeting all the requirements placed on them by the people who speak them. A difference is not a deficit. These dialects can be just as expressive and communicative and elaborate as other dialects, and the fact that they may be spoken by children whose average educational performance is below a certain norm is neither a direct cause nor a consequence of inadequate intellectual functioning by the children concerned.

The same thought is expressed whether a person says "I'm going to school" or "I be goin to school" or "I goin to school", and none of the dialects that these examples roughly characterize is necessarily more ambiguous or less precise than another. After all, the "standard" English of "I'm going to school" has at least three quite different meanings—I am on my way to school at this moment, I attend school habitually or I shall go to school in the future—which are disambiguated in some less prestigious dialects.

If two individuals' idiolects are similar, there is likely to be a corresponding similarity in their cognitive structures and little confusion about either "I'm going to school" or "I goin to school". But a person who does not sufficiently understand another's dialect is usually more ready to put the blame on the other's language than on a mismatch of cognitive structures, especially if he regards his own dialect as more prestigious.

PRODUCTION AND COMPREHENSION   Production of a language is not the same as comprehension. We can all understand statements that we could not produce, or could only produce with difficulty. Children frequently understand adults, although they could not say the sentences the adults are speaking. The fact that an individual speaks like a child because he *is* a child does not mean that he can understand only childish language. Quite the reverse, children frequently understand the language of adults better than they understand the language of other children, and sometimes even better than the language they produce themselves. There can be much more information in adult language. Besides, all children seem able to comprehend the standard languages of television series. The fact that a child does not speak the same dialect as his teacher does not even mean that he could not speak it if he wanted to; although it might indicate that he is disinclined either to talk or to understand the teacher's dialect. By the same token, a teacher may be less inclined to want to understand the dialect of students if it is different from his own actual or imagined dialect.

DIALECT AND COMMUNICATION   The previous point leads to a critical question concerning dialect in school. Although all dialects may have the potential of being equally rich and productive as languages, and in themselves do not reflect or affect intellectual performance, they may play an important role in the amount of communication and learning that goes on in a classroom. A student unable or unwilling to understand or even accept the teacher's dialect will obviously suffer in his achievement. He is similarly likely to suffer if the teacher is unable or unwilling to understand or even accept the student's dialect.

If a teacher expects or demands that *his* dialect, the prestige dialect, should be the one in which communication takes place, then any student who does not speak that dialect will be in trouble. It would be misleading therefore to imply that a student's dialect will make no difference in his learning achievement. His dialect may indicate a background of experience and values not congruent with the experience or values the teacher expects. His dialect may disqualify the student from full participation in opportunities for learning in school because he will not understand what is going on, although this is not necessarily the case. His dialect may disqualify him equally as effectively if it excludes him from full participation in the school for irrelevant reasons. Furthermore, his dialect may indicate that the student himself is unwilling to participate fully because he rejects the dialect that is the working language of the school.

LANGUAGE AND LEARNING   The manner in which any language is actually used as a medium for instruction, or for enquiry and explanation, may vary tremendously. It has been claimed that these differences may be so extreme as to constitute two different kinds of language, or language code.[24] One kind of language use is characterized as *restricted*, because it excludes many possible avenues of learning, in contrast to the other kind, which is called *elaborated*. Since these "codes" are supposed to manifest themselves particularly within families, they can conveniently be illustrated and examined in two imaginary family settings. Two examples of restricted code are:

MOTHER: Don't do that.
CHILD: Why?
MOTHER: Because I tell you not to. Do as you're told.

CHILD: What does daddy do at work?
MOTHER: Never you mind. Eat your supper.

An example of elaborated code will show the difference between the two types.

MOTHER: Don't do that.
CHILD: Why?
MOTHER: Because it's dangerous. You could get an electric shock.
CHILD: Why?

MOTHER: Because that is where the electricity comes from to make the lights go on and the toaster hot.

CHILD: How?

MOTHER: The electricity comes from the power station and travels along wires that you can't see because they're under the ground or in the walls.

CHILD: How does electricity make the lights work?

MOTHER: I'm not sure, but I'll try to find out for you.

In the restricted code, language is primarily used for instruction and demands, for the here and now, to ask and to respond. It is basically concerned with what individuals may or should do. The elaborated code, on the other hand, is used more analytically, to seek and to provide reasons; the child uses it for hypothesis testing and the parents for providing feedback. Elaborated-code parents encourage questions and enjoy providing explanations, while restricted-code parents discourage questions and prefer to provide instructions.

Of course these are caricatures. No family is wholly "restricted" or "elaborated" any more than any individual is wholly field dependent or field independent. Restricted-code parents do not necessarily prefer ignorance to enlightenment. Elaborated-code parents have been heard to tell their children to shut up. I make the point because there is a tendency to associate language codes, as well as dialects, with socio-economic status and even "class". In the extreme it has been assumed that if a child's father was an unskilled manual worker, or if the child lived in one of the more depressed areas of town, then the child would inevitably be a victim of restricted code. A restricted code was viewed as the language of poor people.

But it is not only in poorer families that mothers may have little time or inclination to engage in debate with their children. And it is not only in the families of professionals that adults take pride in the verbal accomplishments of their young. One must be careful not to assume that a correlation is an inexorable natural law. A child from a poor family who speaks a nonstandard dialect has sufficient educational handicap without being stigmatized automatically as an inadequate language performer.

CHAPTER 8

Instruction
and Instructors

It has not been my concern in this book to argue about educational objectives. The principles of thinking and learning that I have discussed apply however a child is taught. My topic is what children are like now, not what schools should be like in the future (although pragmatic considerations alone would incline me to add my objection to highly structured and authoritarian environments). Everything in the book so far has tended to focus on children's efforts to make sense of the world. I have tried to show, for example, that learning is rarely a passive or meaningless phenomenon. In order to learn, a child cannot simply allow events to happen to him.

However, a child's environment is also rarely passive in the matter of learning. Few adults are content to leave a child to learn from whatever environment he happens to find himself in; they are reluctant to leave a child's learning to chance. Instead adults try constantly to organize a child's environment; they endeavor to feed him the particular kind of information and experience that they think will facilitate his learning in efficient and desirable ways. Manipulating a child's environment in order that he shall learn is called education. And in the cultures that concern themselves with a standardized education, this deliberate manipulation of a child's environment is institutionalized in schools. The aim, by and large, is not to leave a child to his own devices in learning, although it is through these devices that the majority of children gain their basic understanding of the world and mastery of language. Instead children are enclosed in controlled environments in an effort to ensure that they will learn what we want them to learn, and that they will learn in the manner we adults think best. We become instructors.

The topic of instruction, surprisingly, is not usually covered to any extent in many educational psychology texts or in the educational research literature. As far as teacher-child interaction is concerned, the usual emphasis is either on control—on how to get a child to behave in the manner in which you want him to behave—or on technique—on the materials and procedures available for manipulating a child's environment. I propose to raise some fundamental issues concerning the nature of instruction and the extent to which it conforms with the learning needs of a child. The first part of this chapter will be concerned with *instruction*, or the manipulation of a child's learning environment; the next with *media*, through which the manipulation is effected; and the final part with *teachers*, who have the awesome responsibility of being the manipulators, whether they know it or not.

Instruction

Three modes of learning[1]

If you think about it, there are only three ways in which human beings can learn anything about the world—compared with the one or two methods available to other animals. We can learn by actually doing something—the universal and evolutionary mode of development—which I shall call learning through performance or by experience. A few animals, and primarily man, can also learn by watching something being done, which I shall call learning through observation or by demonstration. Humans alone can also learn by being told. Often all three modes of learning appear to be advantageous. We can learn something about skiing by trying it ourselves, by watching other people ski and by listening to a lecture on the topic. If we wish to sing proficiently it is desirable to practise on our own, to listen to the performance of experts and to have a coach share his wisdom with us verbally. Sometimes one form of learning would seem to be more appropriate than another. The best way to discover that Paris is the capital of France, for example, is to be told, either orally or through a book. But verbal instruction is insufficient, and certainly not necessary, in learning how to swim.

An understanding of the three modes of learning is so important that I shall begin by recapitulating them in tabular form:

    (a) learning through performance, or by experience
    (b) learning through observation, or by demonstration
    (c) learning through being told, or by language

If you wonder why I have not included a fourth category, learning through thinking, the explanation is that I consider it under learning through performance. You may remember that in Chapter 1 thinking was characterized as vicarious experience. When you learn through thinking, you learn through substitute behaviour in the head.

The word *teaching*, incidentally, literally means demonstrating (in the original Middle English); while *instruction* is derived from the Latin word for communicating knowledge. Etymologically at least learning by experience has nothing to do with either teaching or instruction. And, as we shall see, in practise neither teaching nor instruction by itself is likely to facilitate the acquisition of skills.

We often hear that the function of school is to communicate knowledge. Even when it is asserted that schools are engaged in developing children's competencies, or skills, the means selected generally involve the provision of information, or instruction, through language. It seems to be widely assumed that children differ from adults only in the amount of knowledge they have acquired, and that teachers can close the gap and turn infants into adults by communicating the knowledge children lack. But if this is indeed all we attempt at school, then we have overlooked the fact that "telling" is generally far from sufficient for the development of either physical or cognitive skills. On the other hand, learning by experience is often a highly inefficient method of acquiring knowledge, and even of developing skills. Before we pursue further the question of what can and cannot be accomplished through the three modes of learning, it will be useful to examine what may be meant by two troublesome words, *knowledge* and *skill*, a topic raised in Chapter 1.

Knowledge and skill. We should first remind ourselves that *knowledge* and *skill* are words, and therefore likely to have no clearly defined psychological referents or universal definitions. Except for the matter of whether *timing* is involved in their application, I suspect that knowledge and skill are both the same in the head; they are an integrated part of cognitive structure. Nevertheless it will be convenient to examine some differences in the way the two words are generally used.

Very loosely, the word *knowledge* seems to refer to the aspects of cognitive structure that passively represent what we want to know, or believe, about the world. Knowledge, in other words, consists of *facts*, of maps and statements and labels and relations. Paris is the capital of France; $2 + 2 = 4$; water is a compound of hydrogen and oxygen; drivers should accelerate when entering a curve; the past tense of *run* is *ran*—all may be regarded as knowledge. Skill, on the other hand, might be regarded as the way in which knowledge is put to use, the ability to apply what we know or believe. Language would appear to encompass both knowledge and skill—knowledge of a lexicon and of syntax, and skill in putting them to use. One important cognitive skill must be the manner in which new knowledge is acquired.

Though it can be acquired in a variety of ways, knowledge tends to be specific. For example, you can learn about the characteristics of tennis balls by hitting and catching them, by watching others do these things, or by being told. In other words, all knowledge of an object tends to converge on that object. Skills, on the other hand, tend to diverge. They generalize. By hitting or catching a tennis ball you acquire knowledge about tennis balls, which is specific. But you also develop skills of hitting and catching which may be used for actions involving other objects such as golf balls and footballs, and which may be relevant to other complex behaviours that involve moving objects such as target shooting or driving. Often we can make a choice between acquiring knowledge or developing a skill. We usually know that $6 \times 7 = 42$, but we would rely on our skill of multiplication should we ever want to know that $63 \times 74 = 4662$. There are various ways in which we can learn the *fact* that $6 \times 7 = 42$—by working it out, being told, looking it up. But our *skill* of multiplication generalizes over many pairs of numbers.

You might want to assert that skills *are* knowledge, and in a sense you would be right, since skills are part of our theory of the world; and there is no way of making a hard and fast distinction between skills and knowledge as far as the brain is concerned. But if we permit the word *knowledge* in the present context to include skills as well, then we shall have to find a new word for the kind of knowledge we do not normally call a skill. Knowledge instead might be regarded as the only part of cognitive structure that can be communicated directly through language and that can thus be shared directly with others. A skill cannot be summed up in words, though we may be able to provide a learner with helpful hints about what to concentrate on, or about how to perform a particular sequence of operations. To repeat my earlier rough definitions, knowledge is what you know or believe about the world, and can be acquired through language at least occasionally; while skill is the way in which you use what you know or believe, and cannot be directly communicated either through language or through demonstration.

Notice that I have not said that knowledge is acquired only through communication; children would learn precious little if that were the case. Knowledge can be acquired by trying something ourselves or by thinking something out or by watching someone else; but in each case we are responsible for getting and testing the knowledge ourselves. We are not given knowledge, although we may be offered some useful advice about what to look for or to avoid doing. Someone certainly helps us to discover the difference between camels and dromedaries if he calls our attention to the number of humps the animals have. I have also not said that we can communicate *everything* we know. Much of what we seem to know about the world is not accessible to our awareness, and therefore we have no way of talking about it. We cannot tell a child how to swim or how to read, though we can help him with information about what to pay attention to. We hope he will then be able to translate the knowledge we have given him of our own skills —to the extent that we can talk about them—into skills of his own through performance.

The complementarity of modes of learning

I have already listed some disadvantages, or limitations, of each of the three modes of learning; knowledge cannot be communicated directly through performance or demonstration, and skills cannot be wholly acquired through language or by observation of someone else. Nevertheless each mode of learning offers advantages which can be employed to overcome the limitations of the other forms; the modes complement each other.

ACQUIRING SKILLS   For example, performance, or experience, is ultimately essential for the acquisition for such skills as reading, writing, bicycle riding, sailing, catching balls or doing long division; but experience alone has certain drawbacks that can be overcome only through demonstration and instruction. The proverbial wisdom that practise makes perfect is an oversimplification. Practise can only make behaviour habitual, or "automatic". Sheer blind repetition of undesirable habits has the ultimate effect of making competence more difficult to achieve. The learner who practises stepping on clutch and brake pedals simultaneously will take longer to transform into a good driver than one who has not practised that movement.

The principal disadvantage of learning through unguided experience is its wastefulness, both of the learner's time and of the accumulated knowledge of others who might help him. Use of experience alone may require the learner to reinvent techniques or procedures that a genius originally developed. Few of us would ever learn to drive a car or sail a boat if left completely to our own devices without the opportunity to watch others, or to receive specific spoken or written instruction. There is too much uncertainty in trying to acquire skills through experience alone, and always too much that can go wrong. The most critical aspects or components of a skill are rarely obvious; a learner simply does not know where to concentrate his attention, for example, in attacking a problem in algebra or geometry. In particular, experience by itself rarely gives the learner adequate warning of what might go wrong, of the maneuver to be executed when the wind suddenly changes, or a ski pole is lost. Unguided self-instruction tends to be inefficient, leading to skills and strategies that are distorted and made inflexible by their own idiosyncrasy.

Watching another person perform a skill or solve a problem can make up for many of the disadvantages of raw experience. For a start a model is provided. Demonstration of a skilled act at least illustrates what the eventual performance should look like. But it would be a mistake to believe that all a learner need do is imitate a model. Usually we cannot imitate a skilled performance until we are skilled ourselves. Showing a child how to kick a ball or hold a bat does little more than present him with a problem. He may not even know what he is supposed to be looking at. In fact a major obstacle in trying to learn from watching others is finding out exactly what is important. Children who watch their parents drive often think that turning the wheel is the most critical movement, while spectators of ball games who try to handle the ball themselves tend to keep their eyes on their hands or feet rather than on the play or the goal.

Despite such limitations, learning through observation can give the learner the important advantage of seeing what can go wrong. A skilled demonstrator will do much more than simply provide an illustration of the act to be learned; instead he will repeat and exaggerate important features, and point to errors to be avoided. In effect, the demonstrator not only provides answers to important questions that the learner should be asking; he indicates what those questions should be. Obviously the demonstrator must be aware himself of what is critical in what he does, and this awareness is not always easily attained. Before we can teach others, it is often necessary to study ourselves. (One reason many teachers experience difficulties in subject areas may be the emphasis in their training on methods rather than on the subject. When a student requires general or specific information in order to learn a point in geography or chemistry or literature, the teacher may not be able to provide it.)

Since an important part of any demonstration must be to direct the attention of the learner to significant or difficult parts of the act, language can play a major supporting role. Without a commentary—"Watch the left heel", "See how the sail is kept taut", "Observe the angle of the pencil"— a demonstration may inundate a learner with information. In effect, the accompanying verbal instruction indicates to the learner what he can ignore.

Obviously verbal instruction, in the form of spoken or written information, can make a valuable contribution to skill learning, compensating for much of the uncertainty, risk and irrelevance of learning by experience or observation alone. But verbal instruction itself must also be relevant. A focus on an unimportant or irrelevant aspect of a performance or demonstration may be misleading. And instruction that overloads the learner's limited capacity to comprehend and memorize what is going on may interfere with learning. Any instruction a learner cannot relate to what he already knows will only interfere with his acquisition of a skill.

ACQUIRING KNOWLEDGE   While verbal communication plays only a supporting role in the acquisition of skills, it is central to the transmission of knowledge. The great advantage of language—and probably the reason for good or for ill that the human race is where it is today—is that language permits knowledge to be transmitted out of context.[2] We are freed from constraints of time and place. It is not necessary to have direct experience in order to acquire many different kinds of information—to learn that coffee grows in Brazil, that the area of a rectangle is the length times the height, that hot stoves should not be touched and that certain liquids are dangerous to drink. Language permits knowledge embedded in a demonstration or a model to be made explicit to a learner. Without language many demonstrations would be virtually useless, as those involved in the education of the deaf can often testify.

But while language permits knowledge to be communicated, or at least made available, out of context, the very absence of relevant context may make the acquisition of knowledge through verbal means alone either difficult or misleading. Facts are hardest to learn, and least likely to be remembered, when their relevance is not apparent to the learner. A listener or reader must be able to relate new information to what he knows already; this is comprehension. To a teacher, a particular message (or lesson) may be clear and informative not because of the way in which the message is organized, but because of what the teacher knows already. The same message may be meaningless to a child. If the recipient cannot relate new information to prior knowledge, then the message will remain noise.

A frequent indication that instructional messages at school may remain very close to the level of noise, even though children strive diligently to learn them and to make some sense of them, is that verbal learning becomes context specific. Children are not able to generalize verbally acquired knowledge into divergent thinking skills, as they would be able to if the new information had really been assimilated meaningfully into cognitive structure. For example, children can often mouth the rules for calculating the areas of geometrical shapes without being able to compute the area of their own schoolyard; or they can recite half a dozen reasons for the rapid development of towns in the thirteenth century without being able to speculate why their own town came into existence. The acquisition and retention of knowledge in a form that children can use may be more likely to occur through a combination of language, demonstration and experience.

FROM PRECEPTS TO PRACTICE   It may seem that I have been promoting a particular classroom strategy for teachers, namely, the admixture of formal verbal instruction with practical demonstrations, or possibly some form of guided discovery. But the arguments I have employed in discussing the acquisition and use of knowledge and skills by children are relevant also to the acquisition and use of knowledge and skills by teachers. I have not intended to *instruct* teachers to do anything. A teacher's responsibility must be to *understand* the advantages and limitations of the various modes of learning, and to relate these factors to the objectives of their instruction and the prior knowledge of the children involved. Combining all three forms of learning can be as blind and inefficient as trying to teach with just one; what is important for a teacher is to know what he is doing.

Media

While there are just three fundamental ways in which a child can receive information from his environment in order to learn—experience, demonstration or language—each of these alternatives offers a wide variety of options to the teacher. All these different possibilities for conveying information from one person to another may be termed *media*.

Language, for example, may be expressed through speech or through writing; and it is not necessarily the case that speech is always direct and "live", while written language is indirect and frozen in time. Speech may be recorded and endlessly repeated, while writing can be done live on a blackboard or overhead projector.

A live demonstration may be observed in a completely naturalistic situation, as when the class visits a fisherman in his boat, a sailmaker in his loft. Or the demonstration may take place in a more structured situation, as when the fisherman comes to the school to display his nets and knots. Even more removed from reality is a demonstration by the teacher or another instructor in the classroom of some of the things a fisherman does. Each of these various kinds of live demonstration may be filmed in order to be presented and re-presented on television, in the movies or on a variety of viewing devices. In fact it is difficult to say where direct experience ends and demonstration begins; to what extent is a conducted tour of a city different from a film of a conducted tour? And does it make a difference whether the camera takes a viewer on a "conducted tour" of a city or simply records an individual talking about the same event?

There are even alternative ways of providing direct experience; for example, "dry skiing" and "dry sailing" can be experienced far from snow and water. Some surrogates for the real thing might be considered veridical in everything except risk, for example, the flight simulators for airplane and spacecraft crews.

Since my distinctions between the different modes of learning are (like all categorizations) largely arbitrary, I do not intend to try to relate them too closely to different media. Most modern technological media offer at least the possibility of simultaneous demonstration and verbal explanation. It is more important to understand the advantages and limitations of endeavoring to present information by different kinds of media. For example, we often prefer to look at a map before exploring an unfamiliar city; so presumably maps provide some information more conveniently than direct experience. But few people would regard looking at a map as a complete substitute for walking through a city.

MEDIA ARE NOT SUBSTITUTABLE   Two educational presuppositions frequently go together. The first is that the primary function of school is to distribute knowledge. The aim may be to develop skills or competencies, but the method is the dissemination of information. The second presupposition is that there is more than one way in which knowledge may be communicated. If children do not acquire knowledge through one medium, another can be substituted. A typical example is the argument that no one need bother to learn to read anymore; with television in every home and videotape in every classroom, the printed word has become redundant. According to this view, anything language can do, pictures can do better. Such an assertion is often dubious, and sometimes wrong. Different media involve and develop different skills; and the knowledge they make available is rarely comparable.

As I have noted, language is very good for disseminating facts, but only if the recipient has the necessary skill for retrieving facts from this medium. Facts themselves do not contribute appreciably to any skill development. However, there is always one skill that experience with a medium is potentially able to foster; and that is the skill of acquiring information from that medium. This explains the emphasis and relative success of traditional schools in developing language fluency, provided the children can cope with the medium in the first place. Today the major sources of information for most children are the visual media, especially film and television. Once again these media may succeed in conveying some knowledge of the world. But such knowledge tends to be specific; it will not help to solve problems, or lead to further knowledge. And the only skills that film and television can develop are skills involving film and television; they are of little help in making a child literate, or a better problem solver.

As for knowledge, it is not necessarily true that one picture is worth a thousand words. A few words may convey far more useful information than a picture. If I ask you "Please bring me my coffee mug from the staff room, its' the brown one", I have not only told you something about my own coffee mug, I have said something about all the other mugs that might be in the staff room (none are brown). But I would not have given you any information about the other mugs if I had shown you a picture of mine, and most of the information about my mug contained in the picture would be useless to you; it would be noise. So as you can see, a few words can in some circumstances be much more informative than many pictures.[3]

As I said earlier, watching someone else perform a skilled act can be completely uninformative to a learner who simply does not know what to look for. He may be inundated with information he cannot use. The same limitation obviously applies to pictures and films. The fact that visual representations or reproductions can be crammed with information is completely irrelevant if the viewer does not know what he should look for. Language may be more precise. However, the advantage is not all with language. If a child is to learn the differences between cats and dogs, we would be ill advised to try to put the difference into words. It would be much better to let the child see many different cats and dogs, or many different photographs or movies of cats and dogs.

In short, words and pictures are not interchangeable. Many different sentences might describe the same picture, and many different pictures might illustrate the same sentence. For example, a picture of a duck on a lake could be an illustration for such topics as *Canadian Scene, Threatened by Pollution, Tomorrow's Dinner, Mallard, Hunter's Target,* and *Archimedes' Principle;* while any of these topics could be illustrated by a variety of other pictures.

All media are selective; you choose whether to see an event through the eyes of a writer or of a cameraman. Each will focus on what he perceives to be most important, or on what he particularly wants you to know or to attend to. And any notion that film provides a particularly true or unadulterated image of life or experience is naive; where does the "creativity" of film come in? Nor do movies automatically enhance experience, since they may depict an event without communicating the feeling. A competent writer may give an impression of what it is like to eat a gourmet meal, suffer a napalm attack or be in love, while a movie producer might do little more than illustrate the movements involved. A certain amount of distortion is unavoidable in all media, even with the best intentions of the communicator. A television news editor with three hours of film to reduce to ten minutes may have less opportunity to be comprehensive than a writer, and face a more complex technical task.

Instructors

The role of the teacher

What is a teacher's role in a classroom? The quick answer, "To teach", in fact says nothing; nor would it be helpful to append a list of subjects a teacher is expected to teach, such as reading, writing, arithmetic. The question is more concerned with what a teacher must do in order that children will learn; and the answer will obviously be complex. In fact no one really knows what teachers ought to do so that children should learn; although there is no shortage of helpful advice. Educational psychology is far from any universal theory of what teachers do when children learn, partly because the learning process itself is so poorly understood. Instead of analysing the function teachers actually perform, we tend to offer them slogans about what they should do, and to describe their situations in very diffuse and superficial terms.

For example, a common assertion is that teachers should provide information for children; this sounds suspiciously close to the belief noted earlier that the function of schools should be to fill children with knowledge. The exact means by which teachers should fill children with desirable information is unclear. If instruction is simply a matter of delivering information to children at a certain rate and in a particular sequence, then why need instructors be human? Teachers are notoriously fallible and idiosyncratic; and many become tired and crotchety as the day, and their career, rolls on. Surely a cool, competent, predictable and unemotional computer could dispense information in a much more controlled and reliable manner?

There is no simple or universal answer. On the record to date, human instructors must be given the edge. We know that millions of individuals have been educated to some degree—some to a very high degree—without computers, while computers themselves have so far achieved very little.[4] Some teachers are so brilliant that their replacement with an electronic device would seem a waste; others are so mechanical that their replacement by a machine might not even be noticed. There is no evidence that a child who perceives a helpful and pleasingly designed computer terminal as the gift of some benign and thoughtful human basks less in the glow of interpersonal warmth and understanding than a child symbiotically linked with a cold, calculating and preprogrammed human instructor. Rather than enter further into the controversy, I propose to spend the remainder of this chapter looking at what we seem to expect the instructor—human or technological—to do, namely, to provide the kinds of information a child requires in order to learn.

Learning, according to the analysis of this book, is a process the child himself can manage—provided that the situation he tries to make sense of is potentially meaningful to him and he has access to the right kind of information at the right time. This does not mean that teachers are unnecessary, or that children will learn best if left to themselves. But the role teachers have to play in providing information is delicate as well as vital. What is the right kind of information for a child to receive? And when is the right time for him to receive it? What in fact does a child who is learning require of an instructor? To answer this question, we must again take the perspective of the child.

A CHILD'S EXPECTATIONS   I begin with two assumptions. The first is that a child arrives at school ready and willing to learn; and the second is that he arrives expecting that the noise he encounters at school will eventually make sense. In other words, his expectation is that the school environment will not differ radically from a learning point of view from the environment in which he has already been able to make sense of movement and objects and relations and, in particular, language.

For some children, unhappily, both my assumptions may prove unfounded. Some children arriving at school may not be ready and willing to learn—not because they are not old enough or mature enough or intelligent enough, but because something has happened to turn them away from learning. Every child who can distinguish a dog from a cat, or a hockey stick from a baseball bat, was obviously born capable of learning. The others are a medical rather than an educational problem; such children are relatively few and easily identifiable. More common are children who seem capable of learning anything except what we try to teach them in schools, or who obviously started life learning and then decided, or learned, that learning was a process too costly to engage in. We have already examined some of the experiences that support or reinforce learning such as success, facilitation of learning and encouragement for indulging the curiosity and making the errors that the learning process requires. But if a child finds it too costly to learn because his endeavors or errors are not appreciated, or if his attempts to learn are unrewarding because they usually fail or isolate him from the groups to which he wants to belong, then the child will turn the learning process off.

Learning, as I have pointed out a number of times, is essentially a risky business. Effective learning has little chance of taking place without the possibility of error on the part of the learner; and error frequently demands a price. There are other economic issues for any individual in learning: the initial investment of time, interest and effort, the ultimate value of the learning achievement; the probability of being successful; the rewards or disadvantages of alternative outcomes. A child might be regarded as making a cost-benefit analysis before he enters into any learning transaction, with his present and predicted emotional states as variables that are taken into account. If the costs of a particular learning task outweigh the estimated benefits, a child is unlikely to accept such a pointless bargain. Such a child is indeed an educational problem. His instructor's responsibility is to persuade him—in fact to demonstrate to him—that learning can be a possible and successful response to the school environment.

My second assumption is that a child expects all the noise in his school environment to eventually make sense. No child is a stranger to noise; he has met it from the moment he was born. Initially at least all children experience considerable success in imposing order and predictability on the noise in the world around them by relating it to a cognitive structure that is constantly being modified and rendered more complex.

Some children may arrive at school suspecting that it will fail to make sense, just as occasional events in their home life (usually unpleasant ones, such as parental ill treatment or disputes) have failed to make sense to them. Failure to make sense, you will remember, implies that there is no way in which the child can relate what is going on around him to what he knows already. Whether or not many children arrive at school with such a suspicion, there is obviously a grave danger that they will soon decide schools have no possibility of making sense.

A child may have difficulty simply in understanding the tasks imposed upon him. He may decide that what he is being asked to do does not make sense, and that the task will therefore defy learning. The tasks to which a child is required to apply himself may in fact not have any possibility of making sense to him; they may not be amenable to any kind of intelligent or meaningful attack. I do not wish to push the point too hard, but the proposition ought to be considered that the first time many children meet non-sense in their lives—in the form of pointless drills and routines—is when they arrive in school.

If my assumptions are confounded—and a child arrives at school unready or unwilling to learn, or not expecting what he meets there to make sense—then the following discussion will not apply. But a child who arrives at school without meeting my two assumptions would have no possibility of learning in any case. Children cannot be trained or disciplined into learning; nor can training take the place of learning. Learning is cognitive, and requires a cognitive involvement. Before learning at school can begin, the child must expect that he can and will learn. No special kind of treatment or preliminary training is required to bring this expectation about—it is the natural state of all children. When children lack such an expectation they have lost it; or they have decided that the world demands too high a price for its exercise. The teacher's task is then a restorative one. Tracing the antecedents of a missing desire to learn may be profoundly difficult, and effecting the necessary change may require considerable tact, skill and patience; nevertheless the teacher's basic task is simple. The task is to persuade the child once more that he is in an environment where learning is worth the trouble and risk involved, because it will pay off. And that involves finding situations in which the child wants to learn and can succeed.

LEARNING AND INFORMATION   To review the original conceptualization, a child learns, and constantly strives to learn, through modifying a cognitive structure with three components: (a) a category system for treating objects or events as the same or different, (b) sets of feature lists that specify which objects or events should be allocated to particular categories, (c) a system of interrelationships among categories. An occasion for learning arises whenever cognitive structure proves inadequate for predicting or interpreting experience, when some event in the environment is noise to the child.

Learning involves four steps: (a) the *generation of a hypothesis*, or a tentative modification or elaboration of any of the three components of cognitive structure; (b) a *test* of the hypothesis involving some direct interaction with the environment in order to obtain feedback; (c) *feedback*, which provides new information against which the predicted consequence of the original hypothesis can be compared; (d) *acceptance or rejection of the hypothesis*. If the feedback is positive—if the consequence of the tested hypothesis is compatible with the predicted consequence—the hypothesized change in cognitive structure is confirmed. If the feedback is negative—if the result of the test is contrary to the prediction—the hypothesis is rejected or modified.

For such a basic learning process to be effective, a child needs access to information under two quite different sets of conditions. For the generation of the original hypothesis a child requires *general information*, which in effect must contain both the problem and the possibility of hypothesizing a solution to the problem. To learn to employ or understand a particular grammatical rule, for example, a child must be in a position to examine the use of that rule in a situation in which the rule makes a difference. To learn to distinguish cats from dogs, he must encounter cats and dogs in situations in which a distinction between them is being made. Unless a child has this access to general information, not only does he have no basis for generating any hypothesis for making cognitive structure a more adequate theory of the world around him; he has no reason for understanding that a need for learning exists. Without exposure to a situation in which noise exists within a larger context that is essentially meaningful to him, there is no way in which the problem, nor any potential learning, will make sense to a child.

Specific information, on the other hand, must be directly relevant to the hypothesis the child decides to test. Feedback provides specific information when it answers an implicit question that the child is asking of his environment: "Does this modification of cognitive structure that I am hypothesizing result in a reduction of the noise or uncertainty of the world around me; is it a reasonable solution to my problem?"

There are but three modes by which a child can exercise this basic learning process: direct experience, observation (demonstration) and being told (language). Therefore if learning is to take place through any of these three modes, alone or in combination, general and specific information must both be available. If a child is to acquire a skill or learn to solve a problem through direct experience, for example, he must be able to see what solving the problem can be expected to accomplish. As obvious examples, he is more likely to learn how to draw a map or to multiply fractions, if the act of drawing a map or multiplying fractions makes sense to him in some wider context. Such is general information. The direct experience must also offer the child access to specific information, which is *feedback*. What are the consequences of drawing the map in a particular manner? Is the result of the calculation verifiable in some intuitively meaningful way? While direct experience may in fact be the only way in which a child can obtain the specific feedback required in order to learn or to consolidate a skill; he may initially be overwhelmed with general information, so that he has difficulty in isolating the particular dimensions of the problem to be solved. Such would be the case when the child is in a situation which he does not understand in general. If everything going on is largely noise, there is little likelihood of reasonable hypotheses being generated, and of learning taking place.

One advantage of demonstration, if skillfully done, is that it permits the learner to perceive the most relevant aspects of the problem. A demonstration has the potential advantage of eliminating unnecessary noise so that all the general information to which the learner attends is meaningful. On the other hand, a demonstration may suppress so much general information that a child cannot put the skill to be learned or problem to be solved into a meaningful context. Whether a demonstration is a help or a hindrance, then, depends on the skill of the demonstrator.

The great advantage of language, the third mode of learning, is its specificity. Language can be part of general information, either as direct experience in a naturalistic setting or as part of a demonstration; it can provide a sharp focus for the problem. The fact that a child is told "There is a dog" or "That is not a cat" or "Here is a map that will help get you there" structures the learning situation. Language can also be highly efficient and economical in providing the specific information that is feedback: "Don't do that, you'll fall off", "That's not a dog, it's a cat" or even simply "Yes" or "No", "Right" or "Wrong".

I shall not labor through specific examples in which direct experience, demonstration or language provide relatively more or less general and specific information. Nor do I plan to evaluate different media in this context. As I have said, it is misleading to suggest that general statements can be made, such as that particular modes of learning are especially suitable or undesirable for providing general or specific information. It is more important for a teacher to be aware of the two critical questions to be asked in any situation: What exactly is the general information a child requires to understand the learning task? What is the specific information he requires as feedback for the hypotheses he will be generating?

LEARNING THROUGH THINKING   Everyone solves problems in his mind. We imagine how to get downtown before the stores close; we consider such difficulties as where we might park; we hypothesize such alternative solutions as driving through busy streets, taking the subway or walking; and we compare likely outcomes to find out which solution would get us downtown sooner. In effect, the entire learning process is accomplished within the cognitive structure of the individual. He organizes his own general information, generates the hypotheses he will test and also organizes the specific information that will provide the basis for confirming or negating his hypotheses.

Many problems faced by a child is school can in fact be solved in the head: "What is the most appropriate way to write this paper?" "How might I get the answer to this question?" "What will happen if I dissolve this powder into that liquid at a particular temperature?" But many other problems of learning tasks cannot be tackled in the child's head; his direct interaction with the environment is required. Often of course both experience within the head and outside are required.

Since learning in the head is in effect vicarious, or interiorized, behaviour, a child should not be expected to accomplish something in his head that he would not be able to accomplish in the real world. A child who has not compared the relative capacity of two differently shaped jugs by trying to pour the contents of one jug into the other should not be required to make intellectual decisions about which jug contains the most. Furthermore, children must sometimes be persuaded that generating and testing hypotheses in their heads is a feasible and worthwhile undertaking at school. Or, rather, they should not learn that trying to imagine solutions to problems does not pay off—either because adults place a premium on observable learning activity, or because attempts to learn covertly tend to be too costly.

Children and instructors

My two original assumptions, or prerequisites for learning, are that a child arrives at school willing and able to learn, and that he expects the school environment to make sense. In short, a child expects that all the noise he meets at school will be translatable into meaningfulness under the attack of his basic learning process. The primary obligation of instructors therefore would seem to be to make the environment, and the learning tasks, meaningful to children.

The fact that children might try to make sense out of what is going on at school is liable to be overlooked. Teachers are sometimes surprised, for example, if children make errors in reading that indicate that they are trying to make sense out of what is written rather than to read nonsense. A good deal of effort in reading and in other subjects is expended in trying to get children to say things aloud that they do not understand. The thought behind such drills, if there is any, seems to be that if a child repeats something that is meaningless to him often enough, it will become meaningful. An alternative possibility of course is that his native learning capacity will tell him that the business of schools is to deal in nonsense.

In the long run what a child learns in school may be less important than the fact that he learns, and wants to keep on learning. A child's experience in learning at school will determine his perception of the pursuit of understanding and knowledge generally. By trying to force a child to learn what is not meaningful to him, we may in fact succeed in making the process of learning meaningless.

Within our general context many specific topics related to instruction in classrooms could be discussed. I shall look at just three: reinforcement, anxiety and feedback. The chapter will conclude with a brief look at some issues more directly related to teachers as individuals, and to their own attitudes and motivation.

REINFORCEMENT   Reinforcement for meaningful learning seems basically to reside in success in learning. A child trying to make sense of noise is reinforced if in fact he makes sense of it. Achievement of a skill is adequate reinforcement for learning the skill. If reinforcement of some other kind is required, then it should be concluded that whatever the child is expected to do does not make sense to him. Alternatively, reinforcement might be regarded as a form of specific information, a signal to a child that he has done something correctly.

Some psychologists would distinguish the reinforcement of learning, which they might well accept could be success or relevant information, from reinforcement for getting into a learning situation. How can a child be expected to learn, they will ask, if you cannot even get him to sit in his seat and look and attend to the teacher? Behavioural modification procedures may then be proposed to reinforce the child for attending to the teacher.

Once again, to my mind, everything depends on the relevance of the entire situation to the child. If special programs or techniques of reinforcement are required to get him to attend to the teacher, then something has already gone wrong that may not be rectified by the reinforcement program. If a child will not attend to his teacher, then what the teacher is doing is not of interest to him. No one has discovered a way to *stop* a child from paying attention to something that interests him—hence the unfair competition to teachers from airplanes, lawn mowers or fire engines that pass the window. If what the teacher is doing *is* of interest to a child, then attending to the teacher must itself be reinforcing.

It might be objected that something must be done when a child's interest cannot be held by the teacher; but it is not clear what is gained by implying or asserting that the fault lies in the child. A child's attention can be demanded and even purchased for a while; but his interest cannot. The responsibility of the teacher is to find a child's interest and to hold it. This might seem to be an inordinately difficult task, and even one that should not lie wholly within the purview of a teacher. Shouldn't the child contribute something? But a child can contribute nothing unless his interest is aroused. Without interest, there is no possibility of his learning or even paying attention.

However, the degree of interest that a child will manifest in a learning situation is not determined solely, nor even in large measure, by the child. In fact it can be asserted that all children who have not been spoilt for learning can be interested in anything, provided two conditions are met. The first condition is that the learning situation make sense, and the second is that it contain novelty. Interest, in other words, is not a special condition that the child is responsible for generating, or that the teacher is responsible for stimulating. Rather, interest is the natural condition of a child who is in a situation that is new but not entirely noisy to him, so that he can relate the novelty to at least something that he knows already. Children constantly pursue experiences that involve learning; this is the reason teachers who have nothing new or intelligible to offer a child have such difficulty in holding his attention.

Individuals develop their idiosyncratic interests for a variety of reasons, including the activities and persons they have been exposed to in the past and the success or pleasure that particular undertakings have yielded. Interests are incremental; they build upon themselves. It is difficult to establish an interest in an area—whether keeping a room tidy or learning to read—where no interest has been displayed before. Something must be found to ensure that the new activity makes sense. The new area must be related to something the child knows and values already.

If a child believes that a task is irrelevant or uninteresting or beneath his dignity, he is very unlikely to learn much. This is not a simple matter of ill will on the part of the child. If his manner of perceiving the task does not justify his addressing attention and applying basic learning strategies to it, then he will find learning that much more *difficult*. And a child can no more tell himself to ignore his feelings and get on with the job than a teacher can demand the child's full attention and enthusiasm. Attitudes are changed by information, not remonstration. Much though the teacher may resent the fact, it may be necessary to convince a child that a learning task is worthwhile.

Even the best of teachers has difficulty working with children who basically reject school and everything associated with it. Even good teachers tend to become bad teachers when confronted by children who seem wilfully to reject everything, even the hand of friendship, that may be offered at school, simply because it *is* offered at school. These children raise problems of enormous complexity; and it would be irresponsible to suggest that there might be easy answers.

A child displays consistent patterns and thought not only about people and events around him; he has a *self-concept*. He can learn that he is good, or he can learn that he is bad. He can trust himself, or he can distrust himself. He may regard himself as likable or unlikable, strong or weak, respected or despised, competent or inadequate, sure to succeed or destined to fail. A child acquires his perceptions of himself through the same reasoning and by the same processes that he develops perceptions of everyone and everything else around him. He tries to make sense of his world. If a prediction of failure or inadequacy or ridicule is more likely to be successful than anything positive, then the negative expectation will become part of the child's self-concept. If there is one thing a child can tolerate less than being told he is wrong, it is proving himself wrong to himself. Children do not resist learning; they resist situations in which they expect to fail to learn.

ANXIETY The experimental evidence indicates that a "moderate degree of anxiety", aroused perhaps by the threat of good or bad grades on the student's record, will facilitate rote learning[5]. Tasks that are meaningful to the learner, on the other hand, are self-monitoring; and anxiety may upset the delicate balance of cognitive activity involved. Anxiety raises the activity level of an individual; it arouses him. You are not likely to fall asleep if you are mildly anxious about the task confronting you. Some tonic state of arousal is required for learning to take place; and to a moderate degree this arousal can be provided by anxiety as well as by a more pleasant emotional state.

Frequently, however, the effect of anxiety on learning is far from facilitatory. Negative emotional states are distracting. They may force you to concentrate, but rarely on the task at hand. They tend to make impossible the shifts of attention and tests of a variety of hypotheses that many learning situations demand. Another disadvantage even of moderate anxiety is that it raises the amount of information required to make a decision. The more we are afraid of being wrong, the more information the brain must process at any one time. The human brain does not function efficiently when the individual is reluctant to risk making a mistake. Yet this is precisely the condition of a person who is anxious.

Anxiety is usually accompanied by rejection of, or even hostility towards, any person or thing perceived as a possible cause of the feeling. If a child perceives a teacher, or a school as responsible for his miserable emotional state, he will most probably not want to identify or collaborate in any mutual undertaking such as learning.

Anxiety is not easy for a teacher to handle. It cannot be reduced by exhortation, as we all know when we are about to keep an appointment with the dentist or the examiners. Anxiety is founded on our beliefs and expectations, on our theory of what the world is like. For anxiety to be reduced, some new and persuasive evidence must be forthcoming. The best evidence for a child that anxiety is not necessary in a learning situation is evidence that learning can succeed without too high a price being demanded. A child cannot be conned into believing this; he must experience it for himself. And the experience can only be achieved in a situation he can handle, not in a situation fraught with difficulty. More can be obtained by demanding less. And if the terms I have used offend you because of possible connotations of featherbedding, remember that in the present context a task that is "difficult" is one that is "meaningless", while one that "demands less" is one that makes sense.

FEEDBACK   The notion that immediate knowledge of results is a critical part of learning has been derived largely from studies of nonsense learning. Students striving to learn lists of nonsense syllables perform better when they know how well they are doing, especially if this can be related fairly favorably to some standard or norm.

But a slogan like "provide knowledge of results immediately" is of little practical value in education, and can even be misleading, if in fact the teacher does not know what the feedback is supposed to accomplish. Imagine a child reading aloud from a book. He has read five words of a sentence correctly, but now misreads the sixth. Instead of reading "Johnny dropped the ball and ran" he reads "Johnny dropped the ball and bat". At this point in many classes there would be no need for the teacher to correct the child, and little likelihood that the child would be permitted to correct himself. Half the class would shout the right word (having learned from adults that literal accuracy is highly prized). Certainly the reader would receive feedback; but would that feedback be of any use to him? As we have seen, feedback is useful to the extent that it answers the specific question a child asks in his hypothesis testing. If the hypothesis of the child in our reading example is that *r-a-n* spells *bat*, then the immediate feedback is relevant and presumably useful. But there are other possibilities.

Suppose that the child was not mechanically reading one word after another, as if they had nothing to do with each other, but was trying to make sense of the entire sentence. In that case, for as far as he had got, *bat* was just as likely to be in context as *ran*, and he had made a good prediction. And if a competent reader must always rely on such predictions, or more precisely on information derived from context, then the child who made the error was doing well. The feedback he would receive, however, would not be relevant to the question, "What does this sentence mean?" but to the question "What is the next word?" If the child was reading for meaning—which seems likely, since *bat* is a reasonable possibility for as far as he had read—then he would probably have discovered his error a few words later and been able to correct it himself. One notable characteristic of good readers is that they correct their own errors when such errors make nonsense of what they are reading. In other words, the feedback such a child requires can only come when he has read a few words more and found that his prediction about meaning is not supported. But such feedback is denied to him if he gets the "immediate" but totally inappropriate feedback that he has read a word wrong. Such feedback may direct the child into poor reading, forcing him to worry more about words than about meaning.[6]

A teacher may even interfere by being helpful. Imagine that our illustrative reader had paused after reading the first five words of his sentence correctly: "Johnny dropped the ball and . . .". At this point a well-meaning teacher might provide the next word, or tell the child to sound it out. But the child might not have been having trouble with the next word. Since he must identify any word before he says it, the fact that he does not say a word does not mean that he has not identified it. He might very well have known the word, and hesitated because he was trying to figure out what it was doing there. He might have been trying to make sense of the five words he had already read, and not have been ready to move on. Once again the teacher's intervention could discourage him from worrying about sense. Such a consequence could indeed serve a beginning reader badly.

The previous examples underline two important points of pedagogy. The first is that reading, like many other potentially meaningful school activities, can provide its own feedback. It is not necessary for the teacher or the rest of the class to say "You are wrong" when a child is reading for meaning; it is not even necessary for a child to read aloud for meaning to get feedback. Reading itself will supply feedback. To emphasize the point, activities that are meaningful provide their own feedback; it may not be necessary for the teacher to intervene at all.

The second point is that feedback may come too soon: Immediate knowledge of results can be irrelevant. If a teacher is not sure of what a child is doing it might be better to leave him alone. Reinforcement that is irrelevant and feedback that comes too soon may have the same untoward effect. They may both help persuade a child that school is indeed not a rational place, but one where events and their consequences occur in basically unpredictable and meaningless ways. It may be better for a child to be occasionally ignored—which at least he can understand—than to have his learning distorted into meaninglessness.

Some problems with teachers

Teachers are human and therefore learn, or shut their eyes to learning, in the same way as children. The psychology of teachers is a topic as
broad as the psychology of children, and as relevant to our concerns in
classrooms. I have little space here to elaborate upon how teachers develop
and change as a consequence of their experience in school—though I am
not sure it might not be as useful to write a book for children on the
psychology of teachers as to write a book for teachers on the psychology
of children. In place of a lengthy discussion, I shall make one general statement and look briefly at two illustrative topics.

The general statement is that teachers cannot exclude themselves
from the analysis of this book about the way individuals perceive and interpret their world and modify their cognitive structure as a consequence
of their experience. And a significant part of the world of teachers is of
course made up of the children whom they attempt to teach. What goes
on in the classroom supplies general and specific information to teachers,
just as much as to children. A worthwhile exercise would be to consider
the kinds of general and specific information a teacher requires about a
child in order to teach that child effectively, or to provide that child with
the information he requires, and the extent to which this general and specific information about the child is available to the teacher. What kinds
of information can be supplied by tests, by observation and by the child's
own demands or questions? The analysis might be made with respect to
a specific subject matter, and even to a particular learning situation.

The question might also be broadened to consider the kinds of general
and specific information available to a teacher not only from his pupils
but also from his colleagues, from administrators, from parents and from
the many other sources of influence and pressure in his world—ranging
from his training in teachers' college to the daily press.

Out of many possibilities, the two areas I have selected to examine
involve some attitudes of teachers towards children and the receptivity of
teachers to new ideas.

LEARNING AND WORK   The popular perception of a teacher's role, which
is often shared by teachers themselves, is not far removed from that of
the conductor of a potentially unruly orchestra of inadequately trained
and poorly motivated musicians, each barely able to read music and unsure of how to handle his instrument. In a classroom the instrument that
children are required to play, but are scarcely credited with knowing how
to use, is the brain. In such a situation the manifestation of harmonious
music, or of learning, is not expected to occur without a major effect on
the part of all concerned. The teacher, to drop the analogy, is held re-

sponsible for whether or not children learn; and the question of whether children do in fact learn is felt to depend on just one factor—work.

It is quite remarkable how frequently the term *work* arises in an educational context. It is the teacher's responsibility to keep students working. Children have their schoolwork and their homework. The child who works hardest is the best student. And hard work guarantees success. But there is no evidence that work or effort or the expenditure of energy will infallibly produce learning. On the contrary, most learning takes place in an atmosphere of quiet confidence and relaxation. A student who works hard and long on a topic may very well be experiencing difficulty with that topic, and his learning is likely to be minimal and insufficient.

The notion that work is essential for learning is probably due to a confusion of effort with *application*. There is no doubt that any child, or adult, needs to apply himself to a task in order to learn. But application in this sense means only attention; and attention does not demand effort, only interest—a by-product of meaningfulness.

The equation of learning with work can lead to markedly puritanical attitudes towards children on the part of teachers. "Good children" are the ones who work hard, and do not seem to be particularly concerned with enjoying themselves. A child who is relaxed and self-assured may not be "pulling his weight", or otherwise exerting sufficient effort. In any case, he is not exercising his full capacity; without a struggle there is no chance that he will attain his "potential". A classroom of children quietly reading material of their choice cannot be working; nor probably is their teacher, according to this viewpoint.

It is also widely believed that children will not learn unless they are "challenged". Anything a student does that is easy or enjoyable is suspected of having no learning value. But it is not difficult to demonstrate that little learning of any value will occur unless the task is easy and enjoyable. Children who are unable to read Shakespeare, and who would not understand his plays if someone read to them, are expected to learn Shakespeare and to improve their reading at the same time. The fact that nothing will be read with comprehension if the reading task is beyond the child, and that reading cannot be improved with incomprehensible material, may escape attention.

It is also extensively believed that children left to their own devices will not "extend themselves" and engage in any activity that promotes learning. Underlying this view is a belief that children are naturally lazy, malevolent and unwilling to learn; that their preferred state is slothful ignorance. An example of this attitude can again be found in reading, where it is frequently held that if a child is not constantly forced to read literature beyond his actual level of competence and interest, he will automatically regress to the level of nursery rhymes and comic books. However, a child is unlikely to want to read anything unless he can read it with relative ease; and even if he does conscientiously strive to read beyond his capacity he will have the utmost difficulty comprehending or memorizing. The fear that a child will never progress if he is permitted to stay with material that he finds easy neglects the fact that a nonlearning situation is boring, and boredom is aversive. An easy task is not incompatible with learning. A child may reread a favorite book a dozen times; and though he may be able to recite many passages by heart, he will still learn more about how to read fluently.

An overriding educational concern with work and application rather than with spontaneity and enjoyment leads almost inevitably to problems of planning and control. The focus of a teacher's attention is diverted from the process of learning to its product, to performance and behaviour. A large part of conventional guidance for teachers is directed to the matter of *discipline*, that is, ensuring that predetermined paths are followed and that digressions do not occur.

Once again I do not propose to become involved in the practical issue of whether it is realistic to expect large groups of children to progress at an equal rate towards identical goals, abstaining from restlessness and resentment in the process. I intend only to observe that such an expectation is clearly incompatible with the descriptions of children and of learning outlined in this book. Besides the idiosyncratic ways in which children learn, there are other constraints on teachers; these include the expectations of parents and principals, and the exigencies of syllabi and curricula. Instead of entering an argument outside the range of educational psychology, I shall reiterate one elementary but fundamental point: control is a problem only to the extent that the activity in which a child is required to engage is meaningless to him. In effect, teachers are confronted by two simple alternatives—to engage the attention of children through activities that make sense to them, and from which they can learn; or to engage their attention through discipline and control. Regrettably the two alternatives are largely incompatible with each other; regrettably also teachers often do not have a free choice between them.

An atmosphere in which behaviour must be determined by discipline and control is one in which anxiety and frustration tend to be high not only for the individuals subject to manipulation (namely, children) but also for the person attempting to maintain the manipulation (namely, the teacher). One consequence of high anxiety is a drop in learning efficiency on the part of students and teachers alike. And two almost inevitable consequences of frustration are resentment and hostility, again on the part of teachers as well as students. All these consequences are clearly incompatible with learning; and there is little need to elaborate on the undesirability of interfering with the learning of children. But the probability that teachers themselves may become resistant to learning is less often examined, although it is not an uncommon phenomenon.

THE ADAPTABILITY OF TEACHERS   The conceptualization of children offered in this book—and also the constantly changing state of the art in all areas of education and educational psychology—would seem to demand that teachers be always alert for new information and receptive to change. Yet an open mind and a readiness to adapt are not widely recognized characteristics of teachers. For reasons which are not altogether clear, but which we can think about, teachers often tend to be inflexible in their thinking and conservative in their attitudes—at least in the context of their work.[7]

The consequence of such rigidity is largely negative. Teachers may find it difficult to examine new ideas objectively, and to employ fresh perspectives when confronted with stale situations. Everyone has a deep investment in his own cognitive structure; we are reluctant to modify any theory that has stood us in relatively good stead and that we feel comfortable with. One might think that teachers' environments would make learning a central part of their existence; but their vocation seems often to have the opposite effect. One of the greatest concerns of educational innovators, and even of authors of educational texts, is how to loosen up teachers so that they will consider new ideas, not to mention implement them. This concern is not always external to teachers; many teachers acknowledge it themselves.

One explanation for the resistance of some teachers to new ideas is that teachers are in fact trained not to think; that their experience in teachers college is directly opposed to the kind of education this book would recommend for anyone. According to this view, teachers in training are not always presented with meaningful information which they can relate to what they know already. Rather they are bombarded with "facts" or prescriptions to be summarily digested. The subsequent utility of ideas in the classroom is less a consideration than the passing of examinations. The term *teacher training* itself implies an emphasis on the kinds of behaviours teachers should exhibit rather than on the rationale of alternative educational or psychological points of view. It is rare for a teacher to ask "What should I know in order to make a decision in a particular situation?" Instead the most common question is "What do you suggest I should do?"

On the other hand, practising teachers frequently object that the rigid organizational structure of school itself tends to make innovation difficult and open-mindedness suspect. Hierarchical chains of responsibility result in everyone having a "superior", who serves as a fount of higher information and a source of critical supervision. Thus individual initiative is dampened. Other members of the teaching staff too concerned with cruising in an unrockable boat can easily discourage or isolate a young enthusiast.

As a result of such inertia in schools, teachers may feel that change would be more easily initiated from outside the school than from within. Many teachers, for example, do not believe that they can do anything about age grading, teaching to tests, competitiveness, discrimination between faster and slower learners, sexual discrimination, overemphasis on academic subjects and excessive concern with socialization or neatness. I have no comment to make on any of these problems except to agree that they all tend to make school less meaningful and more difficult for both children and teachers. The fact that the solutions are often obvious does not in any way simplify their application. Instead I want to look at one or two other determinants of resistance to learning and to change—determinants that again apply to children and teachers alike.

The first determinant is anxiety, or insecurity. Teachers are responsible for a good deal that goes on in school; and the community tends to hold them responsible for everything that goes on there—and also for everything the community believes goes on there. These days, for example, a key word is *accountability*; a teacher must demonstrate that he achieves, just as a child must demonstrate that he works. All this stress tends to encourage teachers to limit their objectives, to teach to the tests they know must be given at the end of term, and in case of failure to put the blame on the children. The insecurity of a teacher may become particularly chronic when he is unsure of what community expectations are—if indeed the community itself knows—and when he is uncertain even about his own goals. Few teachers are really aware of what they can reasonably be expected to achieve with children at school.

A common consequence of anxiety is conservatism, the tendency to pull in our horns. If we are insecure, the unknown is frightening and change is threatening. We may not like the status quo much; but who knows how bad things could become—especially if we are to be held responsible both for the change and for its consequences? If we are anxious, we tend to cling to those around us, and to act like them; hence inertia is frequently attributed to the entire staff of a school. Anyone who is anxious, as we have seen, requires much more information before he will make a decision. Anyone who is afraid of the cost of an error will either remain indecisive or react erratically.

Emotional factors also affect learning. Much of the commerce at school between children and teachers, and among children and teachers, is at an emotional level, especially when pressure is high. People who have a deep emotional involvement in an issue do not usually look for rational explanations; indeed they may prefer not to reason at all. Many teachers have been observed to be intolerant of complexity; they do not want to become immersed in theoretical arguments, or to examine underlying assumptions. And teaching—as I have perhaps demonstrated all too well—is a complex enough matter in the first place. Books like the present one are not easily digestible for teachers harassed by classroom responsibilities. The consequence of such antipathy to open-ended thinking is a tendency to reduce complex problems to simplistic terms and to look only for simple solutions, which do not usually exist.

Transition

The final chapter should not be the end of a book. A manuscript when its author is done with it is nothing, dead words in a paper tomb. The only hope of life and purpose for a book lies in the difference it might make to a reader, in the sense that the reader is able to make of it.

My purpose in writing this book is by no means fulfilled with its completion. Whether the reader will be better able to understand children, or be less confused by the literature of educational psychology, now passes out of my hands. My success will not even depend on the extent to which a reader has agreed or disagreed with the book, but on whether he is able to fit it into a far broader scheme of things.

At this transitional stage then I see no value in a reiteration of "major points" or in an attempt to bring arguments to a neat conclusion. Instead, I shall take my leave with just a very rough sketch-map of where we started and of the ground I have tried to cover. It is now for the reader to decide the point we have reached, and how to proceed from there.

I began with a discussion of theories and of their role in any endeavor involving the pursuit of knowledge and understanding. A theory is an attempt to make sense of what would otherwise be a meaningless collection of "raw data", of random facts and pointless experiences. A theory fulfills three functions—to summarize the past, make sense of the present and predict the future—through a constant endeavor to relate the unknown to the known. Theories should not be evaluated in terms of whether they are true or false, but whether they are useful. To what extent do they succeed in organizing past experience in order to interpret the present and predict the future?

The present book is itself a theory, an attempt to conceptualize a child's interaction with his environment in terms that are congruent with scientific research and experimental data, but that at the same time make sense to a teacher. The aim of the theory that is this book is to assist teachers in summarizing coherently evidence about children from their own and other people's observations, in making sense of their current experiences with children and also of the information and arguments about children in the educational literature and, finally, in planning their interactions with children. The test for the theory of this book is the extent to which a teacher finds it useful.

Part of the theory of the book is that there is a private theory in the head of all of us, a theory of what the world is like and of how it is organized. This theory, which I have called cognitive structure, is every individual's attempt to summarize what he knows of the world. Without such a theory our past would be incoherent, our present incomprehensible and our future a barrage of surprises.

Everything we cannot relate to cognitive structure remains noise—a signal that carries no information, that makes no sense. The phrase "makes sense", which I have used extensively, means that new information can be related to what we already know. In fact if you have made sense of the present paragraph so far, it must have been because your cognitive structure has already been sufficiently influenced by this book so that you can interpret its rather specialized terminology.

Cognitive structure is often inadequate. We make mistakes, become confused, and our prophesies fail. When cognitive structure proves inadequate as a theory of the world, we modify it. Learning is our modification of cognitive structure in order to make more sense of experience.

Children attempt to make sense of their environment from the moment they are born. There is no reason to try to account for a child's ability to learn, because a child *is* a learning device, the most efficient there is. A child who cannot learn is not a child, he is not human. Our tidy world of people and objects, of time and space, causes and consequences, is not immediately apparent to an infant; he has to learn. And the only way he can learn is by trying to make sense of things. From the time of his birth, a child tries to make sense of his world.

There is no reason to try to account for a child's motivation to learn. Anything a child cannot understand, cannot make sense of or cannot predict is stimulus enough for him to learn. What children cannot tolerate is a situation in which there is nothing to learn, the state of boredom. So motivated is an infant to learn that he will seek out uncertainty, and ignore the familiar. The powerful characteristic that we call curiosity is a rejection of everything a child knows already in favor of the unexplored.

Finally, there is no reason to try to account for the reinforcement of a child's learning. Learning is its own reward. A child does not need to be bribed to learn, only to stay in a situation where learning is impossible. For an organism that feeds on information, information is reward enough. A child will not stop learning until he learns that trying to learn may not succeed, until learning causes him pain or guilt. A learning device can learn to shut itself off.

The learning process—and the fact that it can be wholly initiated and directed from within the child—has been one of the two major threads of this book. The other thread has been language. We began by looking at language as an example of learning, laying bare the complexity of language the more to wonder at the ability of a child to grasp its secret and reinvent its structure for himself. Spoken language was our paradigm for examining the potent intellectual drive, self-initiated and self-directed, that spurs a child to make sense of his world. He needs no reinforcement to learn spoken language—only exposure to situations he cannot make sense of, and the possibility of experimenting in such situations until he has become their master.

A child does much more than make sense of language, he uses it. As soon as he learns any part of language, that part becomes a tool for his learning more about language and more about everything else. Language is more than a medium by which information is fed to a child, it is the principal means by which he goes out and gets the information he has decided he wants. Provided it can be used, language becomes an indispensable tool for human learning.

But language is neither the end nor the beginning of learning. Everything that we see or hear or feel is as much determined by what we know already, by cognitive structure, as by the particular events in our environment. There are, however, limits to how much new information the brain can handle, and to how much new information it can retain.

We took into account that children should not be considered to be all the same, even though they all begin life equipped with the same basic learning mechanism. Children have different abilities, interests and attitudes, all of which are part of their preferred way of interacting with the world. Children have feelings. Their responses to the world are not purely intellectual, but are influenced by perceptions that are cognitively determined. Fears and anxiety are never irrational to the individual who has them. No aspect of an individual's interaction with the world—whether of the way he acts upon his environment or of the manner in which his environment affects him—can be regarded as independent of the theory of the world in his head.

Given then that cognitive structure can be conceptualized as the core of all a child's learning, we moved at last into school. We looked at instruction not as a process by which a teacher funnels knowledge into a child, but as the manipulation of a child's environment to facilitate his learning in particular ways. We examined the advantages and disadvantages any medium of instruction might have in terms of the kinds of information a child would require in order to learn. We even looked briefly at some typical learning problems of teachers, and attempted to emphasize that the teacher and his students have much in common.

The Teacher's Dilemma

Teachers are often confronted by a dilemma. On the one hand, they are frequently criticized for a number of inadequacies, and led to believe that they could improve their performance if only they would master up-to-date techniques and take advantage of modern materials and technology. Their entire education—from teachers college through a daily barrage of advice, opinion and commercial and editorial importuning—has led them to believe that by following precepts laid down by someone else they should become better teachers. They have been led to believe that somewhere a magic method for teaching every subject exists—if only they could discover who guards the secret.

The belief in a holy grail of instruction is also reflected in the attitudes of many parents, principals, trustees, publishers, instructional developers, education departments and governments. The mammoth "Right to Read" program in the United States, for example, like the earlier program for putting a man on the moon, was premised on the notion that if sufficient resources are poured into a project, and the problem is attacked systematically, then a workable technology will be found to achieve the ultimate objective.

But the other side of the teacher's dilemma is this: infallible methodologies for instruction do not exist, and probably never will. There is only one reliable way to improve instruction, and that is to assist the instructor in understanding children and in avoiding excessive demands and restrictive practices that can cripple children's comprehension and learning. Teaching a child to read is nothing like putting a man on the moon. For a start, it does not require a whole new technology. Children have been learning to read ever since mankind invented reading. No one method of reading will teach every child, though every method of instruction ever devised seems to have been able to teach at least some children. But this diversity merely demonstrates the amazing flexibility of children. Almost all the millions of children who have learned to read throughout history, including ourselves, have probably learned with (or in spite of) instructional methods, classroom environments and badly printed sanctimonious materials which today we would stigmatize as inadequate, inappropriate and out-of-date.

Before educational researchers can draw any conclusions about the relative merits of instructional methods, they must "control" or subsequently remove the two major sources of variance in any educational study. The first of these two sources of variance, or unpredictability, is the individual child. The researcher must exclude from consideration the fact that one child is not identical with the next, and that different children respond differently to the same materials or methods. The second prime source of variance is the teacher. Not only do teachers "muddy the data" because they do not all teach in the same stereotyped way, they also contribute "unreliability" because they are "eclectic". Few teachers are likely to rely on one method uniquely or blindly. Instead they use their past experience and their insight into individual children to interfere with the cafeteria-style service that the "scientific" presentation of instructional materials requires. Sometimes the intelligence of teachers is regarded as an impediment to an instructional program, with the result that some materials are being promoted today as being "teacher proof"; they cannot be tampered with.

I am not being anti-scientific. I am not suggesting a return to ignorance in education. Far from it, I think that absence of knowledge is probably a fair description of the state that much of education is in today. It is not the case that the majority of teachers are ignorant and that technology is scientific. On the contrary, many teachers have great insights into instruction, but are painfully unaware of the theoretical justification for their intuitions, while many of the prepackaged programs to which they are expected to adhere are inflexible, oversimplified and theoretically naive.

Instructional developers may devise "systematic" programs that skilfully take a child through a sequence of steps with a minimum of error and a guarantee of a specified terminal level of success. But the objectives may be constrained by the limitations of the instruction itself; and success is related to what the program can achieve, not to the more general, flexible, skills that we expect children to develop at school. Where are the materials that take into account that there are limits to how much and how fast anyone can put information into short-term and long-term memory, that learning necessarily involves the risk of error, that reading requires a minimal use of visual information, that guessing is an essential part of listening and learning and that memorization will interfere with comprehension? What piece of instructional technology recognizes that children first make sense of the world without any adult assistance, that they have superb intellectual capacities, that they learn independently of adult motivation, and that their undirected learning behaviour is neither random nor unsystematic?

To repeat, I do not hold that it is scientific to trust technology and reject the teacher. On the contrary, I believe that an understanding of how children—and all other individuals—must strive to comprehend and to learn will show that much faith in technology and teacher-independent instruction is not only ill founded but unnecessary. Nor do I intend to imply that there is no role for teachers in the classroom, that children learn best when left entirely alone. The teacher makes the critical decisions about what, when and how a child should learn. Having made these decisions, the teacher must now function to facilitate the child's learning. The teacher's dilemma is resolved when we recognize that his contribution to a child's learning depends primarily on the strength of the teacher's own understanding of the child, not on his blind faith in instructional methodology.

Children know how to learn—that is the theme of this book. And it is the responsibility and privilege of teachers to make learning possible by ensuring that what is to be learned is comprehensible. Anything that a child can comprehend will serve as a springboard for learning, while nonsense precludes any kind of intellectual leap. The teacher's role is to help a child to make sense of school and of the world.[1]

Notes

Chapter 1 On Making Sense

[1] No particular significance should be attached to my use of the words "mind" and "brain". I try to follow the dictates of everyday language, generally using "mind" when mental states are the primary concern and "brain" when the topic is more clearly physiological. It is an act of faith among hard-nosed experimental psychologists that mental states are direct reflections of underlying physical states or processes in the brain. But no one has yet verified chemically or microscopically how our awareness that Paris is the capital of France might be laid down in the cells of the cerebral cortex. There is nothing scientific about substituting the word "brain" in contexts where "mind" seems linguistically more appropriate. Or at least, I shall hold that opinion until something causes me to change my brain.

[2] The term "cognitive structure" is employed in somewhat overlapping ways by a number of psychological theorists. Jean Piaget, for example, asserts that there are two "invariant functions" of intelligence in all living organisms; *adaptation* to the environment and *organization* of information that the environment provides. This organization of information accumulated through experience is Piaget's concept of cognitive structure. He distinguishes two aspects of adaptation in *assimilation*, or the manner in which the individual interprets the environment by relating experience to cognitive structure, and *accommodation*, the modification of cognitive structure in the light of experience. There will be a number of references to Piaget and to other conceptualizations of cognitive structure throughout these Notes. Some specific references will be given in due course.

[3] For a brief and general discussion of the need to impose order on the world, see Walker Gibson, *The Limits of Language*, New York: Hill & Wang, 1962.

[4] The notion that categorical distinctions might be made perceptually on the basis of distinctive features was first developed in the context of the sounds of language (see

Roman Jakobson and Morris Halle, *Fundamentals of Language,* The Hague: Mouton, 1956), then later adapted for the identification of the letters of written language (see Eleanor J. Gibson, *Principles of Perceptual Learning and Development,* New York: Appleton, 1969, Ch. 5), and for visual pattern perception generally. For a clear description of the "feature analytic" model of pattern perception see a book that will be cited a number of times as a basic reference for many of my topics, Peter Lindsay and Donald A. Norman, *Human Information Processing: An Introduction to Psychology,* New York: Academic Press, 1973.

[5] P. Dunn-Rankin, The similarity of lower-case letters of the English alphabet, *Journal of Verbal Learning and Verbal Behavior,* 1968, 7, 990–995.

[6] Roger Brown, How shall a thing be called? *Psychological Review,* 1958, 65, 1, 14–21; David R. Olson, Language and thought: Aspects of a cognitive theory of semantics, *Psychological Review,* 1970, 77, 257–273.

[7] Lindsay and Norman, *op.cit.*; also Hebb's notions of the establishment of "reverberating circuits" and "cell assemblies" in the brain, Donald O. Hebb, *Organization of Behavior,* New York: Wiley 1949.

[8] Allan M. Collins and M. Ross Quillian, Retrieval time from semantic memory, *Journal of Verbal Learning and Verbal Behavior,* 1969, 8, 240–247.

[9] Brown, *op. cit.*

[10] I owe the term "isa" to Lindsay and Norman, *op. cit.*, and their collaborator Peter E. Rumelhart, whom they cite. Much of the discussion and illustration of cognitive networks in this chapter is generally based on the material developed or cited.

[11] Collins and Quillian, *op. cit.* For a general paper by these authors and other discussions of structures of knowledge, see Endel Tulving and Wayne Donaldson (eds.), *Organization of Memory,* New York: Wiley, 1972; and John R. Anderson and Gordon H. Bower, *Human Associative Memory,* Washington, D.C.: Winston, 1973, Chs. 5 and 9.

[12] See Ch. 3 of this book.

[13] For a recent elaboration see Fred Attneave, How do you know? *American Psychologist,* 1974, 29, 7, 493–499.

[14] Most introductory psychology tests provide a general outline of the physiology of the brain. A more specific and detailed but very readable introductory book is R. L. Gregory, *Eye and Brain: The Psychology of Seeing,* New York: McGraw-Hill, 1966. See also R. W. Sperry, Neurology and the mind-brain problem, *American Scientist,* 1952, 40, 219–232. See also Note 24 below.

[15] See Jerome S. Bruner, On perceptual readiness, *Psychological Review,* 1957, 64, 123–152. This paper and other important contributions by the same author are collected in Jerome S. Bruner, *Beyond the Information Given,* New York: Norton, 1973. An excellent introduction to the "information processing" approach to cognitive psychology reflected in the present book is Ulric Neisser, *Cognitive Psychology,* New York: Appleton, 1967. For an experimental perspective, see Wendell R. Garner, To perceive is to know, *American Psychologist,* 1966, 2, 1, 11–19; for a theoretical critique, Earl Hunt, What kind of a computer is man? *Cognitive Psychology,* 1971, 2, 57–98.

[16] Piaget terms this phenomenon of attention-fixation *centration.* Piaget is not easy to read, at least for readers without a good deal of free time on their hands and a moderate prior exposure to his ideas. His rather abstruse French is not always translated into limpid English. Moreover he has written prolifically and his ideas are to be found scattered and changing through a score of books. However, a number of summaries or reviews of his work have appeared in English; three that can be particularly recommended are: John H. Flavell, *The Developmental Psychology of Jean Piaget,* New

York: Van Nostrand, 1963; Hans G. Firth, *Piaget and Knowledge*, Englewood Cliffs, N.J.: Prentice-Hall, 1969; and Herbert Ginsburg and Sylvia Opper, *Piaget's Theory of Intellectual Development: An Introduction*, Englewood Cliffs, N.J.: Prentice-Hall, 1969. For those who wish to plunge more directly into Piaget any of the following would be relevant: Jean Piaget, *Structuralism*, New York: Basic Books, 1970; ———, *The Science of Education and the Psychology of the Child*, New York: Viking, 1971 ——— and Barbel Inhelder, *The Psychology of the Child*, New York: Basic Books, 1969.

[17] There is no easy introduction to Information Theory for readers unsettled by mathematical symbolism and arguments. Some fairly brief and fairly plain-language attempts to discuss the main concepts are provided in George A. Miller, What is information measurement? *American Psychologist*, 1953, 8, 3–11 (reprinted in George A. Miller (ed.) *Mathematics and Psychology*, New York: Wiley, 1964); in the chapter by John Brown in Brian M. Foss (ed.), *New Horizons in Psychology*, Hammondsworth: Pelican, 1966; and in Chapter 2 of Frank Smith, *Understanding Reading*, New York: Holt, Rinehart and Winston, 1971.

[18] For a vigorous critique of the tendency to nominalize in psychology, see Gilbert Ryle, *The Concept of Mind*, London: Hutchinson, 1949. More recently and briefly: Robert E. Ebel, And still the dryads linger, *American Psychologist*, 1974, 29, 7, 485–492.

[19] This is of course far from an original idea. For Piaget, for example, thought is "interiorized action" (see Note 16 above).

[20] The classic reference is Frederick C. Bartlett, *Remembering*, Cambridge: University Press, 1932. See also Neisser, *op. cit.*

[21] The term "plans" is taken from an eminently readable classic on the information-processing decision-making characteristics of the mind: George A. Miller, Eugene Galanter and Karl H. Pribram, *Plans and the Structure of Behavior*, New York: Holt, Rinehart and Winston, 1960.

[22] Ryle, *op. cit.* Also, David R. Olson, What is worth knowing and what can be taught, *School Review*, 1973, 82, 1, 27–43.

[23] Michael Polanyi, *The Tacit Dimension*, Garden City, N.Y.: Doubleday, 1966. Collins and Quillian, in their chapter in Tulving and Donaldson (*op. cit.*), use the term "implicit knowledge" in the rather different sense of specific facts that can be recovered indirectly from our more general knowledge of the world without having specifically been learned, for example, that canaries have blood.

[24] A more rigorous formulation is that consciousness is a component of attention involving a mechanism for integrating information from different sensory modalities. See Michael J. Posner and Stephen J. Boies, Components of attention, *Psychological Review*, 1971, 78, 5, 391–408. Two other interesting references in this difficult area are Tim Shallice, Dual functions of consciousness, *Psychological Review*, 1972, 79, 5, 383–393; R. W. Sperry, A modified concept of consciousness, *Psychological Review*, 1969, 76, 6, 532–536.

[25] This is the classical *conservation* problem of Piaget, see Note 16 above.

Chapter 2   Limits to Comprehension

[1] Frank Smith and Peter Carey, Temporal factors in visual information processing, *Canadian Journal of Psychology*, 1966, 20, 337–342. More generally, see Ulric Neisser, *Cognitive Psychology*, New York: Appleton, 1967. Also for a general coverage of many topics in this chapter: Steven W. Keele, *Attention and Human Performance*, Pacific Palisades, Calif.: Goodyear, 1973.

[2] James McKeen Cattell, Ueber die Zeit der Erkennung und Benennung von Schriftzeichen, Bildern und Farben, *Philosophische Studien*, 1885, *2*, 635–650, translated and reprinted in *James McKeen Cattell, Man of Science, 1860-1944* (Vol. 1), Lancaster, Pa., Science Press, 1947.

[3] Frank Smith, The use of featural dependencies across letters in the visual identification of words, *Journal of Verbal Learning and Verbal Behavior*, 1969, *8*, 215–218.

[4] For discussions of distinctive features of letters see Eleanor J. Gibson, *Principles of Perceptual Learning and Development*, New York: Appleton, 1969 (Ch. 5); and Frank Smith, *Understanding Reading*, New York: Holt, Rinehart and Winston, 1971. (Ch. 9).

[5] In brief, N distinctive features will permit selection among 2^N alternatives (provided the alternatives are all equally probable and that each feature halves the number of alternatives). See the references cited in Note 17, Chapter 1.

[6] Claude E. Shannon, Prediction and entropy of printed English, *Bell Systems Technical Journal*, 1950, *30*, 50–64.

[7] George A. Miller, *Language and Communication*, New York: McGraw-Hill, 1951.

[8] *Ibid.*

[9] *Ibid.*

[10] While not wishing to divulge professional secrets of the speed reading business I can reveal the key to reading fast. It is this: *read fast*. Speed reading courses have two basic objectives: the first is to force students to read faster, and the second is to persuade them that they will not lose comprehension by doing so. The present chapter and the next should demonstrate that slowing down is not an efficient way to read if you are having difficulty comprehending. If you cannot comprehend what I have been saying, let alone remember it, you should try to read through again faster, before worrying about the detail, in order to get the feeling of what entire passages are about.

[11] Norman H. Mackworth, Visual noise causes tunnel vision, *Psychonomic Science*, 1965, *3*, 67–68.

[12] Rose-Marie Weber, The study of oral reading errors: A survey of the literature, *Reading Research Quarterly*, 1968, *4*, 96–119.

[13] Roman Jakobson and Morris Halle, *Fundamentals of Language*, The Hague: Mouton, 1956.

[14] George A. Miller and Patricia E. Nicely, An analysis of perceptual confusions among some English consonants, *Journal of the Acoustical Society of America*, 1955, *27*, 338–353.

[15] George A. Miller, G. A. Heise and W. Lichten, The intelligibility of speech as a function of the context of the test materials, *Journal of Experimental Psychology*, 1951, *41*, 329–335.

[16] John A. Swets, W. P. Tanner, Jr. and T. G. Birdsall, Decision processes in perception, *Psychological Review*, 1961, *68*, 301–320; and more recently John A. Swets, The receiver operating characteristic in psychology, *Science*, 1973, *182*, 990–1000. Also Eugene Galanter, Contemporary psychophysics, in *New Dimensions in Psychology* (Vol. 1), New York: Holt, Rinehart and Winston, 1962.

[17] Karl S. Lashley, In search of the engram, *Symposium of the Society of Experimental Biology*, 1950, *4*, 454–482.

[18] Frederick C. Bartlett, *Remembering*, Cambridge: University Press, 1932; Neisser, *op. cit.*, Charles N. Cofer, Constructive processes in memory, *American Scientist*, 1973, *61*, 5, 537–543.

[19] See Neisser, *op. cit.*; Richard C. Atkinson and Richard M. Shiffrin, The control of short-term memory, *Scientific American*, 1971, *225*, 2, 82–90; and Donald A. Norman

(ed.), *Memory and Attention: An Introduction to Human Information Processing*, New York: Wiley, 1969. A rather different perspective is offered in Fergus I. M. Craik and Robert S. Lockhart, Levels of processing: A framework for memory research, *Journal of Verbal Learning and Verbal Behavior*, 1972, *11*, 671–684.

[20] George Sperling, The information available in brief visual presentations, *Psychological Monographs*, 1960, *74*, 11, Whole No. 498.

[21] George A. Miller, The magical number seven, plus or minus two: some limits on our capacity for processing information, *Psychological Review*, 1956, *63*, 81–97.

[22] Herbert A. Simon, *The Sciences of the Artificial*, Cambridge, Mass.: M.I.T. Press, 1969.

[23] Frank Smith and Deborah Lott Holmes, The independence of letter, word and meaning identification in reading, *Reading Research Quarterly*, 1971, *6*, 3, 394–415.

[24] Herbert A. Simon, How big is a chunk?, *Science*, 1974, *183*, 482–488. This topic is discussed further in Chapter 5.

[25] George Mandler, Organization and memory, in Kenneth W. Spence and Janet T. Spence (eds.), *The Psychology of Learning and Motivation*, New York: Academic Press, 1967. See also three articles by James J. Jenkins and three of his students (Thomas S. Hyde, David A. Walsh and Robert Till) in a single issue of the *Journal of Verbal Learning and Verbal Behavior*, 1973, *12*, 5.

[26] See Note 16, Ch. 1. Bruner (Note 15, Ch. 1) has an analogous formulation that our first memory structures are *enactive*, they are representations of physical movements and their consequences.

[27] Ralph N. Haber, Eidetic images, *Scientific American*, 1969, *220*, 36–44.

[28] A. R. Luria, *The Mind of a Mnemonist*, New York: Basic Books, 1968.

[29] Allan Paivio, *Imagery and Verbal Processes*, New York, Holt, Rinehart and Winston, 1971. Also William D. Rohwer, Jr., Images and pictures in children's learning; Research results and educational implications, *Psychological Review*, 1970, *73*, 393–403.

[30] John D. Bransford and Jeffrey J. Franks, The abstraction of linguistic ideas, *Cognitive Psychology*, 1971, 2, 331–350. See also Jacqueline S. Sachs, Memory in reading and listening to discourse, *Memory and Cognition*, 1974, *2*, 1A, 95–100.

[31] Sylvia Farnham-Diggory (ed.), *Information-Processing in Children*, New York: Academic Press, 1972.

[32] Gary M. Olson, Memory development and language acquisition, in Timothy E. Moore (ed.), *Cognitive Development and the Acquisition of Language*. New York: Academic Press, 1973.

[33] Olson, *op. cit.*

[34] Farnham-Diggory, *op. cit.*

Chapter 3   Two Faces of Language

[1] Psycholinguistics is a relatively young interdisciplinary area of study at an intersection between psychology and linguistics. Psychologists are primarily concerned with human behaviour, of which language as a *process* is one part, rather than with the *products* of human behaviour, such as cars, cakes, paintings, words or sentences. Linguists, on the other hand, are usually concerned with the comparative and historical description of language as a *product*, or with analyses of words, sentences, sounds and spellings. They also engage in semantic speculation concerning the relationship of language sounds or written symbols to objects or events in the environment, a relationship frequently

loosely characterized as "meaning". Psycholinguists stand with a foot in each camp and are primarily concerned with how individuals learn, comprehend and use language. The present book reflects the broad psycholinguistic view that thought cannot be ignored in any discussion of language and that the study of language is central to any attempt to understand human comprehension and learning.

A number of introductory psycholinguistics texts are available, including Peter Herriot, *An Introduction to the Psychology of Language*, London: Methuen, 1970; James Deese, *Psycholinguistics*, Boston: Allyn and Bacon, 1970; Roger Brown, *Psycholinguistics: Selected Papers*, New York: Free Press, 1970; Dan I. Slobin, *Psycholinguistics*, Glenview, Ill: Scott, Foresman, 1971. More up-to-date in terms of current controversy over semantic issues, though restricted largely as its title indicates to children's language, is the first chapter of Roger W. Brown, *A First Language: The Early Stages*, Cambridge, Mass.: Harvard University Press, 1973.

Introductory linguistics texts include John Lyons, *Introduction of Theoretical Linguistics*, Cambridge, University Press, 1968; Henry A. Gleason, Jr., *Linguistics and English Grammar*, New York: Holt, Rinehart and Winston, 1965. An interesting collection of summary papers is John Lyons (ed.), *New Horizons in Linguistics*, Harmondsworth: Penguin, 1970.

[2] Some of these issues are discussed later in the chapter.

[3] George A. Miller, Decision units in the perception of speech, *I.R.E. Transactions on Information Theory*, 1962, *8*, 81–83; Philip Lieberman, On the acoustic basis of the perception of intonations by linguists, *Word*, 1965, *21*, (1), 40–54.

[4] George K. Zipf, *The Psycho-Biology of Language: An Introduction to Dynamic Philology*, Cambridge, Mass.: M. I. T. Press, 1965. For an educational perspective, see E. Brooks Smith, Kenneth S. Goodman and Robert Meredith, *Language and Thinking in the Elementary School*, New York: Holt, Rinehart and Winston, 1970.

[5] Charles C. Fries, *The Structure of English: An Introduction to the Construction of English Sentences*, New York: Harcourt Brace Jovanovich, 1952.

[6] George A. Miller, Some preliminaries to psycholinguistics, *American Psychologist*, 1965, *20*, 15–20.

[7] Endel Tulving and Cecille Gold, Stimulus information and contextual information as determinants of tachistoscopic recognition of words, *Journal of Experimental Psychology*, 1963, *66* (4), 319–327; John Morton, Interaction of information in word recognition, *Psychological Review*, 1969, *76* (2), 165–178.

[8] In fact I adapted it from the theorizing of Noam Chomsky, who almost single-handedly inspired psychology to pay attention to linguistics in the late 1950s, and who is still the linguist whom anyone concerned with language production and comprehension must follow or refute. Chomsky is not easy to read, at least when he writes on psycholinguistics, but an excellent introduction is available in Judith Greene, *Psycholinguistics: Chomsky and Psychology*, Harmondsworth: Penguin, 1972. My miniature grammar, incidentally, would usually be written with rather different symbols, for example $S \rightarrow NP + VP$, where S is short for "sentence", NP for "noun phrase" and VP for "verb phrase". I avoid these specific labels to preclude any implication that the grammar depends on the prior determination of parts of speech. The grammar determines syntactic function, and the actual labels or symbols used are irrelevant.

[9] This discussion is still Chomsky-based; see the preceding note, and also Roderick A. Jacobs and Peter S. Rosenbaum, *English Transformational Grammar*, Waltham, Mass.: Blaisdell, 1968.

[10] John Macnamara, Cognitive basis of language learning in infants, *Psychological Review*, 1972, *79* (1), 1–13.

[11] Alvin M. Liberman, The grammars of speech and language, *Cognitive Psychology,* 1970, *1* (4), 301–323.

[12] Colin Cherry, *On Human Communication,* New York: Wiley, 1961. More specifically, see Anne N. Triesman, Strategies and models of selective attention, *Psychological Review,* 1969, *76* (3), 282–299.

[13] Noam Chomsky and Morris Halle, *The Sound Pattern of English,* New York: Harper & Row, 1968.

[14] Generative semantics is a wide, complicated and rapidly developing field. For an overview, see chaps. 5 and 7 in John R. Anderson and Gordon H. Bower, *Human Associative Memory,* Washington, D.C.: Winston, 1973. Another introductory source that I have already mentioned is the first chapter of Brown, *op. cit.,* 1973. More technically, see the collection of papers in Charles J. Fillmore and D. Terrance Langendoen (eds.), *Studies in Linguistic Semantics,* New York: Holt, Rinehart and Winston, 1971. A volume that I have leaned on particularly is Wallace L. Chafe, *Meaning and the Structure of Language,* Chicago: University of Chicago Press, 1970. See also Herbert H. Clark, Semantics and comprehension, in T. A. Sebeok (ed.), *Current Trends in Linguistics, Vol. 12, Linguistics and Adjacent Arts and Sciences,* The Hague: Mouton, 1973.

[15] The example and argument are taken from Allan M. Collins and M. Ross Quillian, How to make a language user, in Endel Tulving and Wayne Donaldson (ed.), *Organization of Memory,* New York: Academic Press, 1972.

[16] J. E. Martin, A study of the determinants of preferred adjective order in English, unpublished doctoral dissertation, University of Illinois, 1968; cited by Thomas G. Bever (see note 21 below).

[17] Chafe, *op. cit.;* Michael A. K. Halliday, Relevant models of language, *Educational Review,* 1969, *22* (1), 26–37; see also Halliday's, *Explorations in the Functions of Language,* London: Edward Arnold, 1973.

[18] B. F. Skinner, *Science and Human Behavior,* New York: Macmillan, 1953; *Verbal Behavior,* New York: Appleton, 1957.

[19] Lev S. Vygotsky, *Thought and Language* (trans. by Eugenia Haufmann and Gertrude Vaker), Cambridge, Mass.: M. I. T. Press, 1962; A. R. Luria, The functional organization of the brain, *Scientific American,* 1970, *222* (3), 66–78.

[20] Noam Chomsky, *Syntactic Structures,* The Hague: Mouton, 1957.

[21] I owe this analogy to an important article by Thomas G. Bever, The cognitive basis for linguistic structures, in John R. Hayes (ed.), *Cognition and the Development of Language,* New York: Wiley, 1970—another volume of papers most relevant to this and later chapters.

[22] Eve Clark, What's in a word? On the child's acquisition of semantics in his first language, in Timothy E. Moore (ed.), *Cognitive Development and the Acquisition of Language,* New York: Academic Press, 1973, another important volume.

[23] David R. Olson, Language and thought: Aspects of a cognitive theory of semantics, *Psychological Review,* 1970, *77* (4), 257–273; Roger Brown, How shall a thing be called? *Psychological Review,* 1958, *65* (1), 14–21.

[24] Luria, *op. cit.*

[25] Benjamin Lee Whorf, *Language, Thought and Reality: Selected Writings of Benjamin Lee Whorf* (ed. by John B. Carroll), New York: Wiley, 1956.

[26] Roger W. Brown and Eric H. Lenneberg, A study in language and cognition, *Journal of Abnormal and Social Psychology,* 1954, *49,* 454–462.

[27] This is a brief section for a large topic. There will be later discussions of relevant topics in more detail; language learning in Chapter 6, language differences in Chapter 7 and the use of language for instruction in Chapter 8.

[28] See Eve Clark, *op. cit.* Much of the rest of Moore, *op. cit.*, is also relevant. Another important volume of collected papers is John B. Carroll and Roy O. Freedle (eds.), *Language Comprehension and the Acquisition of Knowledge*, Washington, D.C.: Winston, 1972.

[29] A few specific forms seem to be lacking until after five, for example, the passive. See Carol Chomsky, *The Acquisition of Syntax in Children from Five to Ten*, Cambridge, Mass.: M. I. T. Press, 1969; also Melissa Bowerman, Structural relationships in children's utterances: Syntactic or Semantic? in Moore, *op. cit.*

Chapter 4   Learning

[1] See notes 2 and 16, Chapter 1. Very approximately, the arrow labelled *perception/comprehension* might be regarded as synonymous with what Piaget calls "assimilation," while the *learning* arrow represents Piaget's "accommodation". Piaget asserts that neither assimilation nor accommodation can take place independently of the other, and I would not want to dispute his view.

[2] Karl R. Popper, *Objective Knowledge: An Evolutionary Approach*, Oxford: Clarendon Press, 1973. Popper is generally relevant; his view of the scientific method is almost completely analogous to the model of learning developed in this chapter. But he is not always easy to read; I highly recommend a most readable summary of his views; Bryan Magee, *Popper*, London: Fontana, 1973.

[3] Peter Lindsay and Donald A. Norman, *Human Information Processing: An Introduction to Psychology*, New York: Academic Press, 1973, chap. 13. See also Walter Kintsch, *Learning, Memory and Conceptual Processes*, New York: Wiley, 1970.

[4] Arthur W. Melton, Implications of short-term memory for a general theory of memory, *Journal of Verbal Learning and Verbal Behavior*, 1963, 2, 1–21. (This particular journal issue is devoted to memory and is an important reference on the topic.) An alternative view is presented in Endel Tulving and Donald M. Thomson, Encoding specificity and retrieval processes in episodic memory, *Psychological Review*, 1973, *80*, (5), 352–373.

[5] Eve Clark, What's in a word? On the child's acquisition of semantics in his first language, in Timothy E. Moore (ed.), *Cognitive Development and the Acquisition of Language*, New York: Academic Press, 1973.

[6] *Ibid.*

[7] John Holt, *How Children Fail*, New York: Pitman, 1964.

[8] Thomas G. R. Bower, The object in the world of the infant, *Scientific American*, 1971, 225 (4), 30–38.

[9] Jean Piaget, *The Construction of Reality in the Child* (transl. by Margaret Cook), New York: Basic Books, 1954.

[10] Robert L. Fantz, Visual experience in infants: Decreased attention to familiar patterns relative to novel ones, *Science*, 1964, *146*, 668–670; Elizabeth K. Bond, Perception of form by the human infant, *Psychological Bulletin*, 1972, 77 (4), 225–245; Jerome Kagan, The determinants of attention in the infant, *American Scientist*, 1970, *58*, 298–306.

[11] See the preceding note and also note 16, Chapter 1.

[12] Bower, *op. cit.*

[13] W. Schiff, The perception of impending collision: A study of visually directed avoidant behavior, *Psychological Monographs*, 1965, 79, Whole No. 604.

[14] Herbert Clark, Space, time, semantics, and the child, in Moore, *op. cit.*

[15] Bower, *op. cit.*

[16] Eleanor J. Gibson, *Principles of Perceptual Learning and Development*, New York: Appleton, 1969.

Chapter 5   Meaningfulness and Memorization

[1] See John H. Flavell, Stage-related properties of cognitive development, *Cognitive Psychology*, 1971, 2 (4), 421–453.

[2] See any general introductory psychology text.

[3] See, for example, Eli Saltz, *The Cognitive Bases of Human Learning*, Homewood, Ill.: Dorsey, 1971; Jerome S. Bruner, Jacqueline J. Goodenow and George A. Austin, *A Study of Thinking*, New York: Wiley, 1956; Irving E. Sigal, The attainment of concepts, in M. L. Hoffman and Lois W. Hoffman (eds.), *Review of Child Development Research*, New York: Russell Sage, 1964.

[4] Katherine Nelson, Some evidence for the cognitive primacy of categorization and its functional basis, *Merrill-Palmer Quarterly*, 1973, 19, 21–39; S. I. Offenbach, R. Baecher and M. White, Stability of first-grade children's dimensional preferences, *Child Development*, 1972, 43, 689–692; John Macnamara, Cognitive basis of language learning in infants, *Psychological Review*, 1972, 79 (1), 1–13; Janellen Huttenlocher, The origins of language comprehension, in Robert L. Solso (ed.), *Theories in Cognitive Psychology*, New York: Halstead Press, 1974.

[5] This discussion is primarily based on Bruner, Goodenow and Austin, *op. cit.* Also relevant is the discussion of cognitive styles in Chapter 8.

[6] Tracy S. Kendler and Howard H. Kendler, Reversal and non-reversal shifts in kindergarten children, *Journal of Experimental Psychology*, 1959, 58, 56–60; Howard H. Kendler and Tracy S. Kendler, Effects of verbalization on reversal shifts in children, *Science*, 1961, 134, 1619–1620.

[7] See Jerome S. Bruner, The course of cognitive growth, *American Psychologist*, 1964, 19, 1–15. Bruner refers to this type of memory representation as *iconic*, placing it between the "enactive" and "symbolic" forms of representation in development. Like Piaget, Bruner does not assert that the earlier forms of representation are replaced by the later-developing forms; instead the forms supplement each other.

[8] For an important and provocative discussion of this theme which stresses educational implications, see W. J. McKeachie, The decline and fall of the laws of learning, *Educational Researcher*, 1974, 3 (3), 7–11.

[9] The German philosopher Herman Ebbinghaus is usually credited with developing the first nonsense syllables about eighty years ago. For a literate summary of Ebbinghaus's career and that of other pioneering experimental psychologists, see Edwin G. Boring, *A History of Experimental Psychology*, New York: Appleton, 1950. For some obscure reason, learning lists of nonsense syllables has become known as "verbal learning", and has an extensive literature. Reviews are available in Charles N. Cofer and Barbara F. Musgrave (eds.), *Verbal Behavior and Learning*, New York; McGraw-Hill, 1963; George Mandler, Verbal learning, in (ed.), *New Directions in Psychology* (vol. 3), New York: Holt, Rinehart and Winston, 1967.

[10] See James Deese and S. M. Hulse, *The Psychology of Learning*, New York: McGraw-Hill, 1967.

[11] See Peter H. Lindsay and Donald G. Norman, *Human Information Processing: An Introduction to Psychology*, New York: Academic Press, 1972, chap. 9.

[12] Richard M. Shiffrin, Forgetting: Trace erosion or retrieval failure? *Science*, 1970, *168*, 1601–1603. In some psychological quarters learning has been regarded not altogether facetiously as a matter of interfering with interference. For recent summaries of the vast experimental literature on learning and forgetting, see Leo Postman and Geoffrey Keppel (eds.), *Verbal Learning and Memory*, Harmondsworth: Penguin, 1969; and Carl P. Duncan, Lee Sechrest and Arthur W. Melton (eds.), *Human Memory: Festschrift for Benton T. Underwood*, New York: Appleton-Century-Crofts, 1972.

[13] This is known as the Skaggs-Robinson hypothesis; for an original source, see E. S. Robinson, The "similarity" factor in retroaction, *American Journal of Psychology*, 1927, *39*, 297–312.

[14] For example, see David Ausubel, *Educational Psychology: A Cognitive View*, New York: Holt, Rinehart and Winston, 1968.

[15] Clyde E. Noble, An analysis of meaning, *Psychological Review*, 1952, 52 (6), 421–430; Meaningfulness and familiarity, in Cofer and Musgrave, *op. cit.*

[16] General review volumes include W. E. Vinacke, *The Psychology of Thinking*, New York: McGraw-Hill, 1952; Michael Wertheimer, *Productive Thinking*, New York: Harper and Row, 1959. More recent studies tend to involve computer simulation and sophisticated mathematics; for example, see Herbert A. Simon and Allen Newell, *Human Problem Solving*, Englewood Cliffs, N.J.: Prentice-Hall, 1971; and the same authors' Human problem solving: The state of the theory in 1970, *American Psychologist*, 1971, *26* (2), 145–159. On the "logical" nature of thought, see John Ceraso and Angela Provitera, Sources of error in syllogistic reasoning, *Cognitive Psychology*, 1971, *2*, 400–410; Peter Wason and Philip N. Johnson-Laird, *Psychology of Reasoning, Structure and Content*, Cambridge, Mass.: Harvard University Press, 1972.

[17] The formulation is attributed to the French mathematician Poincaré, who introspected upon the processes of his own inspiration. His insight is discussed briefly in many introductory psychology texts, for example, William N. Dember and James J. Jenkins, *General Psychology: Modelling Behavior and Experience*, Englewood Cliffs, N.J.: Prentice-Hall, 1970, p. 497.

[18] Cited in George A. Miller, Eugene Galanter and Karl H. Pribram, *Plans and the Structure of Behavior*, Hinsdale, Ill.: Dryden Press, 1960. For a fascinating and scholarly history of techniques for memorizing, see Frances A. Yates, *The Art of Memory*, London: Routledge & Kegan Paul, 1966.

[19] John Ross and Kerry Ann Lawrence, Some observations on memory artifice, *Psychonomic Science*, 1968, *13* (2), 107–108.

[20] See Herbert A. Simon, How big is a chunk? *Science*, 1974, *183*, 482–488. Simon presents evidence that short-term memory holds a fixed number of chunks, that learning time is proportionate to the number of chunks to be learned, and that children's memory span appears shorter because they chunk less efficiently.

[21] Karl S. Lashley, The problem of serial order in behavior, in L. A. Jeffress (ed.), *Cerebral Mechanisms in Behavior: The Hixon Symposium*, New York: Wiley, 1951; H. Quastler, Human channel capacity, in H. Quastler (ed.), *Three Survey Papers*, Urbana, Ill.: Control Systems Laboratory, University of Illinois, 1956, 13–33. For this topic, and many others in this chapter, see Steven W. Keele, *Attention and Human Per-*

formance, Pacific Palisades, Calif.: Goodyear, 1973; and Michael Posner and Steven W. Keele, Skill learning, in Robert M. W. Travers (ed.), *Second Handbook of Research on Teaching*, Skokie, Ill.: Rand McNally, 1973.

[22] Lashley, *op. cit.*

Chapter 6   Learning To Speak and To Read

[1] My descriptions of children's language acquisition are derived from the work of a number of psycholinguists, some of whose studies are outlined in Frank Smith and George A. Miller, *The Genesis of Language*, Cambridge, Mass.: M. I. T. Press, 1966. More recent and detailed discussions of the work of these investigators are included in their own books: Roger Brown, *Psycholinguistics: Selected Papers*, New York: Free Press, 1970; David McNeill, *The Acquisition of Language: The Study of Developmental Psycholinguistics*, New York: Harper & Row, 1970; Dan I. Slobin (ed.), *The Ontogenesis of Grammar*, New York: Academic Press, 1972; Lois Bloom, *Language Development: Form and Function in Emerging Grammars*, Cambridge, Mass.: M. I. T. Press, 1970; Paula Menyuk, *The Acquisition and Development of Language*, Englewood Cliffs, N.J.: Prentice-Hall, 1971. See also note 1, Chapter 3.

[2] Lois Bloom, Lois Hood and Patsy Lightbown, Imitation in language development, *Cognitive Psychology*, 1974, 6 (3), 380–420.

[3] Note particularly Roger Brown, *A First Language: The Early Stages*, Cambridge, Mass.: Harvard University Press, 1973; and Timothy E. Moore (ed.), *Cognitive Development and the Acquisition of Language*, New York: Academic Press, 1973. At a more elementary level, Philip S. Dale, *Language Development: Structure and Function*, Hinsdale, Ill.: Dryden Press, 1972; James Britten, *Language and Learning*, Coral Gables, Fla.: University of Miami Press, 1970.

[4] See especially Eve Clark, What's in a word? On the child's acquisition of semantics in his first language time, Herbert Clark, Space, semantics and the child; and Melissa Bowerman, Structural relation in children's utterances: Syntactic or semantic?; all in Moore, *op. cit.*; Jeremy M. Anglin, *The Growth of Word Meaning*, Cambridge, Mass.: M. I. T. Press, 1970. See also John MacNamara, Cognitive basis of language learning in infants, *Psychological Review*, 1972, 79 (1), 1–13; and Nancy Katz, Erica Baker and John MacNamara, What's in a name? A study of how children learn common and proper names, *Child Development*, in press.

[5] Brown, *op. cit.*, 1973, presents a critique of the pivot–open class grammar distinction; he notes particularly that the youngest children's grammar is richer than these simple formulations suggest. For example, a single two-word pivot–open class surface structure might be employed to represent various deep structures, indicating the existence of a variety of underlying rules.

[6] David McNeill, Developmental psycholinguistics, in Smith and Miller, *op. cit.*

[7] MacNamara, *op. cit.*; Brown, *op. cit.*, 1973; Herbert Clark, *op. cit.*

[8] See Chapter 3.

[9] Brown, *op. cit.*, 1973.

[10] Bowerman, *op. cit.*

[11] Carol Chomsky, *The Acquisition of Syntax in Children from Five to Ten*, Cambridge, Mass.: M. I. T. Press, 1969; David S. Palermo and Dennis I. Molfese, Language acquisition from age five onward, *Psychological Bulletin*, 1972, 78 (6), 409–428.

[12] Brown, *op. cit.*, 1973.

[13] *Ibid.*

[14] MacNamara, *op. cit.*

[15] At a more general level the argument that grammatical markers such as those for tense, number and specificity are largely redundant in everyday spoken language situations is elaborated by Wallace L. Chafe, *Meaning and the Structure of Language*, Chicago: University of Chicago Press, 1970. See also Chapter 3.

[16] Courtney Cazden, Environmental assistance to the child's acquisition of grammar, unpublished doctoral dissertation, School of Education, Harvard University, 1965; *Child Language and Education*, New York: Holt, Rinehart and Winston, 1972.

[17] Frank Smith, *Understanding Reading*, New York: Holt, Rinehart and Winston, 1971; *Psycholinguistics and Reading*, New York: Holt, Rinehart and Winston, 1973. For alternative points of view, see Eleanor J. Gibson and Harry Levin, *The Psychology of Reading*, in press.

[18] The examples are drawn from Noam Chomsky and Morris Halle, *The Sound Pattern of English*, New York: Harper & Row, 1968. A less technical summary of the relevant argument is provided in Carol Chomsky, Reading, writing and phonology, *Harvard Educational Review*, 1970, *40* (2), 287–309.

[19] For example, bilingual readers may read words in a passage of mixed English and French with the right meaning but in the wrong language. See Paul A. Kolers, Three models of reading, in Harry Levin and Joanna P. Williams (eds.), *Basic Studies on Reading*, New York: Basic Books, 1970.

[20] See Chapter 3.

[21] Betty Berdianski, Bruce Cronnell and J. Koehler, Jr., *Spelling-Sound Relations and Primary Form–Class Descriptions for Speech-Comprehension Vocabularies of 6–9 Year Olds*, Los Alamitos, Calif.: Southwest Regional Laboratory (Technical Report No. 15), 1969. The complexity of their rules has not inhibited such researchers from trying to teach some of them to children; for example, see Bruce Cronnell, Designing a reading program based on research findings in orthography, *Elementary English*, 1973, 27–34.

[22] Kenneth S. Goodman, Analysis of oral reading miscues: Applied psycholinguistics, *Reading Research Quarterly*, 1969, 5 (1), 9–30.

[23] Andrew Biemiller, personal communication. See also Jeanne Chall, *Learning to Read: The Great Debate*, New York: McGraw-Hill, 1967.

[24] Smith, *op. cit.*, 1973, chap. 10.

[25] Karl S. Lashley, The problem of serial order in behavior, in L. A. Jeffress (ed.), *Cerebral Mechanisms in Behavior: The Hixon Symposium*, New York: Wiley, 1951.

[26] H. D. Brown, Categories of spelling difficulty in speakers of English as a first and second language, *Journal of Verbal Learning and Verbal Behavior*, 1970, 9, 232–236.

Chapter 7   Differences

[1] There are no convenient general sources of discussion on *cognitive style*, a term becoming widely and quite loosely used in educational psychology. Many recent introductory psychology texts mention the topic. A more thorough discussion of a number of aspects of cognitive style will be found in Leona E. Tyler, *The Psychology of Human Differences*, New York: Appleton-Century-Crofts, 1965, chap. 9. See also David P. Ausubel and Edmund V. Sullivan, *Theory and Problems of Child Development*, New York: Grune & Stratton, 1970; R. D. Hess and V. C. Shipman, Early experience and the socialization of cognitive modes in children, *Child Development*, 1965, *36*, 869–886; Nathan Kogan, Educational implication of cognitive styles, in Gerald S. Lesser (ed.), *Psychology and Educational Practice*, Glenview, Ill.: Scott, Foresman,

1971; George Shouksmith, *Intelligence, Creativity and Cognitive Style*, New York: Wiley, 1970.

[2] H. A. Witkin, R. B. Dyk, H. F. Faterson, D. R. Goodenough and S. A. Karp, *Psychological Differentiation*, New York: Wiley, 1962.

[3] *Ibid.*

[4] David P. Ausubel, *Educational Psychology: A Cognitive View*, New York: Holt, Rinehart and Winston, 1968, pp. 170–174.

[5] Jerome Kagan, Impulsive and reflective children: Significance of conceptual tempo, in J. D. Krumboltz (ed.), *Learning and the Educational Process*, Skokie, Ill.: Rand McNally, 1965.

[6] Nathan Kogan and Michael A. Wallach, *Risk Taking: A Study in Cognition and Personality*, New York: Holt, Rinehart and Winston, 1964.

[7] John Holt, *How Children Fail*, New York: Pitman, 1964.

[8] James G. Greeno, On the acquisition of a simple cognitive structure, in Endel Tulving and Wayne Donaldson (eds.), *Organization of Memory*, New York: Academic Press, 1972. See also David E. Hunt and Edmund V. Sullivan, *Between Psychology and Education*, Hinsdale, Ill.: Dryden Press, 1974.

[9] H. A. Witkin, Cognitive style and the teaching-learning process, address to the American Educational Research Association, Chicago, 1974.

[10] See note 17, Chapter 1.

[11] Most introductory psychology and educational psychology texts provide an outline history of IQ tests. A more specific reference is W. B. Dockrell, *On Intelligence*, Toronto: Ontario Institute for Studies in Education, 1970. Piaget's view, permeating much of his writing, is that intelligence does not *cause* intelligent behaviour, but *is* adaptive, functional behaviour. See Jean Piaget, *The Origins of Intelligence in Children* (transl. by Margaret Cook), New York: International Universities, 1952. See also William Rohwer, Paul Ammon and Phebe Cramer, *Understanding Intellectual Development: Three Approaches to Theory and Practice*, New York: Holt, Rinehart and Winston, 1974.

[12] Much of the controversy has been transatlantic, with British psychologists tending to a single underlying, or "general", factor view of intelligence derived from Galton, Burt and Vernon. See Cyril Burt, *The Factors of the Mind*, London: University of London Press, 1940; Philip E. Vernon, *The Structure of Human Abilities*, London: Methuen, 1961. The American tradition of Spearman, Thurstone and Guilford supports a multiplicity of factors; see Louis L. Thurstone, *The Vectors of Mind*, Chicago: University of Chicago Press, 1935.

[13] J. P. Guilford, *The Nature of Human Intelligence*, New York: McGraw-Hill, 1971.

[14] Jerome S. Bruner, *The Process of Education*, Cambridge, Mass.: Harvard University Press, 1960.

[15] John B. Carroll, A model of school learning, *Teachers College Record*, 1963, *64*, 723–733.

[16] Benjamin S. Bloom, *Individual Differences in School Achievement: A Vanishing Point?* Bloomington, Ind.: Phi Delta Kappa, 1971.

[17] The reference is to the followers of Piaget; see note 16, Chapter 1.

[18] See John H. Flavell, Stage-related properties of cognitive development, *Cognitive Psychology*, 1971, *2*, 421–453. A number of relevant issues are touched upon in Jerome S. Bruner, Rose S. Olver and Patricia M. Greenfield (eds.), *Studies in Cognitive Growth*, New York: Wiley, 1966.

[19] Eleanor J. Gibson, *Principles of Perceptual Learning and Development*, New York: Appleton, 1969, especially chap. 20.

[20] Eric H. Lenneberg, *Biological Foundations of Language*, New York: Wiley, 1967.

[21] W. L. Bryan and N. Harter, Studies in the telegraphic language: Acquisition of a hierarchy of habits, *Psychological Review*, 1899, 6 (4), 346–376.

[22] General references for this range of topics include Herbert Ginsburg, *The Myth of the Deprived Child: Poor Children's Intellect and Education*, Englewood Cliffs, N.J.: Prentice-Hall, 1972; Frederick Williams (ed.), *Language and Poverty*, Chicago: Markham Press, 1970; Frederick Williams, Jack L. Whitehead and Leslie M. Miller, Relations between language attitudes and teacher expectancy, *American Educational Research Journal*, 1972, 9 (2), 263–278; Michael Cole and Jerome S. Bruner, Preliminaries to a theory of cultural differences, in Ira J. Gordon (ed.), *Early Childhood Education*, Chicago: National Society for the Study of Education (71st Yearbook), 1972; 161–179.

[23] William Labov, *The Study of Nonstandard English*, Champaign, Ill.: National Council of Teachers of English, 1970; Roger W. Shuy (ed.), *Social Dialects and Language Learning*, Champaign, Ill.: National Council of Teachers of English, 1965; Johanna S. DeStefano (ed.), *Language, Society and Education: A Profile of Black English*, Worthington, Ohio: Charles A. Jones, 1973.

[24] Basil Bernstein, *Class, Codes and Control*, London: Routledge & Kegan Paul, 1969; Social class and linguistic development, in A. H. Halsey, J. Floud and C. A. Anderson (eds.), *Education, Economy and Society*, New York: Free Press, 1961, 288–314, also the chapters by Bernstein, Sociolinguistic approach to socialization, in Williams, *op. cit.* Underlying many of Bernstein's insights and formulations are those of another important British linguist whose work is also widely dispersed: Michael A. K. Halliday, Language function and language structure, in John Lyons (ed.), *New Horizons in Linguistics*, Harmondsworth: Penguin, 1970.

Chapter 8   Instruction and Instructors

[1] I am indebted for many of the underlying ideas in this section—and indeed throughout this chapter—to David R. Olson, although he would not necessarily agree with the interpretation. In particular I have drawn upon the introduction by Olson, and Olson and Jerome S. Bruner, Learning through experience and learning through instruction, in a volume that breaks new ground in educational theory: David R. Olson (ed.), *Media and Symbols: The Forms of Expression, Communication and Education*, Chicago: National Society for the Study of Education (73rd Yearbook, part 1), 1974.

[2] Karl R. Popper, *Objective Knowledge: An Evolutionary Approach*, Oxford: Clarendon Press, 1973; Bryan Magee, *Popper*, London: Fontana, 1973.

[3] David R. Olson, Language and thought: Aspects of a cognitive theory of semantics, *Psychological Review*, 1970, 77 (4), 257–273.

[4] An expansive literature asserts the success of computer-assisted instruction, usually in achieving limited and arbitrarily selected aims. For the sober reflections of a rather disenchanted early enthusiast, see Anthony G. Oettinger, *Run Computer Run: The Mythology of Educational Innovation*, Cambridge, Mass.: Harvard University Press, 1969.

[5] Janet A. Taylor and Kenneth W. Spence, The relationship of anxiety level to performance in serial learning, *Journal of Experimental Psychology*, 1952, 44, 61–64.

[6] Kenneth S. Goodman, Analysis of oral reading miscues: Applied psycholinguistics, *Reading Research Quarterly*, 1969, 5 (1), 9–30.

[7] Edward J. Nussel and Mildred Johnson, Who obstructs innovation? *Journal of Sec-*

ondary Education, 1969, *44* (1), 3–11. General books on the topics of teachers and teaching are Philip W. Jackson, *Life in Classrooms,* New York: Holt, Rinehart and Winston, 1968; and Jere E. Brophy and Thomas L. Good, *Teacher-Student Relationship: Causes and Consequences,* New York: Holt, Rinehart and Winston, 1974. An excellent survey article on student and teacher attitudes is S. B. Khan and Joel Weiss, The teaching of affective responses, in Robert M. W. Travers (ed.), *Second Handbook of Research on Teaching,* Skokie, Ill.: Rand McNally, 1973.

Transition

[1] I have reserved the last word for the friends who have helped and encouraged me during the lengthy preparation of this book. At my publishers, David Boynton and Richard Owen have been a constant source of sympathetic and literate support, and Elyce Misher a skilled and sensitive editor. Among my colleagues, David Olson will recognize in these pages reflections of innumerable lunchtime discussions and disagreements. Many others at the Ontario Institute for Studies in Education provided ideas and stimulating criticism; to label them "students" or "research staff" would be misleading and inappropriate, for I have learned from them all. At home, four individuals suffered, strove and celebrated with me, and to them this book is affectionately dedicated: Mary-Theresa, Laurel, Melissa and Nicholas.

Toronto, 1975.

Name Index

Ammon, Paul, 260
Anderson, C. A., 261
Anderson, John R., 249, 254
Anglin, Jeremy M., 258
Atkinson, Richard C., 251
Attneave, Fred, 249
Austin, George A., 256
Ausubel, David, 257, 259, 260

Baecher, R., 256
Baker, Erica, 258
Bartlett, Frederick C., 250, 251
Berdianski, Betty, 259
Bernstein, Basil, 261
Bever, Thomas G., 254
Biemiller, Andrew, 259
Birdsall, T. G., 251
Bloom, Benjamin S., 260
Bloom, Lois, 258
Boies, Stephen J., 250
Bond, Elizabeth K., 255
Boring, Edwin G., 256
Bower, Gordon H., 249, 254
Bower, Thomas G. R., 255, 256
Bowerman, Melissa, 255, 258
Bransford, John D., 252
Britten, James, 258
Brophy, Jere E., 262
Brown, H. D., 259
Brown, John, 250
Brown, Roger W., 249, 253, 254, 258
Bruner, Jerome S., 249, 252, 256, 260, 261
Bryan, W. L., 261
Burt, Cyril, 260

Carey, Peter, 250
Carroll, John B., 255, 260
Cattell, James McKeen, 251
Cazden, Courtney, 259
Ceraso, John, 257
Chafe, Wallace L., 254, 259
Cherry, Colin, 254
Chomsky, Carol, 255, 258, 259
Chomsky, Noam, 253, 254, 259
Clark, Eve, 254, 255, 258
Clark, Herbert H., 254, 256, 258

Cofer, Charles N., 251, 256
Cole, Michael, 261
Collins, Allan M., 249, 250, 254
Craik, Fergus I. M., 252
Cramer, Phebe, 260
Cronnell, Bruce, 259

Dale, Philip S., 258
Deese, James, 253, 257
Dember, William N., 257
DeStefano, Johanna S., 261
Dockrell, W. B., 260
Donaldson, Wayne, 249, 254, 260
Duncan, Carl P., 257
Dunn-Rankin, P., 249
Dyk, R. B., 260

Ebbinghaus, Herman, 256
Ebel, Robert E., 250

Fantz, Robert L., 255
Farnham-Diggory, Sylvia, 252
Faterson, H. F., 260
Fillmore, Charles J., 254
Firth, Hans G., 250
Flavell, John H., 250, 256, 260
Floud, J., 261
Foss, Brian M., 250
Franks, Jeffrey J., 252
Freedle, Roy O., 255
Fries, Charles C., 253

Galanter, Eugene, 250, 251, 257
Garner, Wendell R., 249
Gibson, Eleanor J., 249, 251, 256, 259, 261
Gibson, Walker, 248
Ginsburg, Herbert, 250, 261
Gleason, Henry A., Jr., 253
Gold, Cecille, 253
Good, Thomas L., 262
Goodenough, D. R., 260
Goodenow, Jacqueline J., 256
Goodman, Kenneth S., 253, 259, 261
Gordan, Ira J., 261
Greene, Judith, 253
Greenfield, Patricia M., 260

Subject Index

Accuracy, feasibility in reading, 59–60
overimportance in instruction, 59–61
signal detection theory, 62–63
student's dilemma, 63–64
Acoustic information (*see* Hearing)
Alternatives (*see* Uncertainty)
Alphabet, 181–182, 188–190
Ambiguity, 85
of sentences, 85, 89–90, 99
of words, 88–90, 181
Analysis by synthesis, 100
Animal experiments, 141
Anxiety, 64, 81, 233–234
See also Risk
Attention, 27–30, 133–135

Babies (*see* Infants)
Behavior modification, 231–233
Boredom, 81, 134, 243
Brain, 25–26, 49–59, 89, 131, 166–167

Case relations, 103
Category interrelations, 16–22
learning, 123–124
Categorization, and language, 111–112
and learning, 125–127
and memorization, 71
Category systems, 14–15
categories as concepts, 15
Children, age differences, 206–208
attitude to learning, 81
categorization, 147–148
and cognitive styles, 198–199
expectations at school, 226–228
and instructors, 230
intelligence, 206
language, 93, 116–117, 169
and learning, 124–129
learning to read, 186–188
learning speech, 169–178, 213–214
learning strategies, 151
memory, 77–82
and reversal shifts, 152
vision, 131–136
Chinese writing, 182
Chunking, 71, 164–165

Class inclusion relations, 17–21
Cocktail party problem, 100
Cognitive interrelations (*see* Category interrelations)
Cognitive questions, 28
See also Attention; Uncertainty
Cognitive structure, 9–48
and consciousness, 43–44
dynamics, 37–42
and language learning, 122–130, 162
and motor skills, 165–167
organization, 13–25
summarized, 243–245
theory of the world, 10
See also Categorization; Category interrelations
Cognitive styles, 195–199
Composition, 191–194
Comprehension, 9–48
definition, 9, 32–35
development, 175–178
and dialect, 212
and language, 83, 91
and learning, 118–130
limits, 49–82
making sense of the world, 10
and meaning, 107
and prediction, 92–94
and reading, 180–186
relativeness, 36, 46–47
tests, 47
Concept learning, 143–152
Concepts, 15
Conditions of learning, 157
Consciousness, 44
Creativity, 37, 161
Criterion, 62–64

Deafness (*see* Hearing limitations)
Decoding (*see* Phonics)
Deep structure, and children's speech, 174
See also Language
Dialect, differences, 93, 208–214
and thought, 210–212
Discovery learning, 159

Uncertainty, 29–34
  of English letters and words, 54–58
Understanding (*see* Comprehension)

Verbal descriptions, by children, 79
  compared with pictures, 75–77, 223–224
Vicarious experience, 36
Vision, 49–59, 141–142, 166–167
  by infants, 131–136
  learning to see, 131–136
Visual image, 67
Visual information, 50–61
  and reading, 179
  trade-off with nonvisual information, 50–51

Whorfian hypothesis, 114–116
Word identification, rate, 52–58
Words, difficulty of defining, 87
  informativeness in reading, 182–183
  multiplicity of meanings, 88–90
  pivot and open class, 174
  and referents, 32
  segmentation in speech, 87–88, 100
  See also Spelling
Written and spoken language, comparison of, 180–182
  See also Reading
Writing, 188–193
  compared with reading, 188–190
  composition, 191–193
  word representation, 190–191

About the Author

Frank Smith was born and grew up in England. After a period in the Royal Navy he spent ten years travelling widely in Europe and Asia, as a newspaper reporter and magazine editor, before his concern with language and learning took him to undergraduate studies at the University of Western Australia. His graduate work was done at the Center for Cognitive Studies at Harvard University, where he received his Ph.D. in psycholinguistics in 1967, and he has been involved in psychological and educational research ever since.

His first publications were short stories and a novel called *Brothers' Keepers* (1964), followed by *The Genesis of Language* (1967, edited with George A. Miller), *Understanding Reading* (1971) and *Psycholinguistics and Reading* (1973).

Frank Smith is Professor of Education at the Ontario Institute for Studies in Education, where for seven years he has worked with scores of teachers and hundreds of school children. His wife teaches and practises art; they have three children and live in Toronto with a horse, a dog and a sailing dinghy.

Photograph courtesy of Mary Marshall